Also by Nick Cave

*And the Ass Saw the Angel*
*The Death of Bunny Munro*
*The Sick Bag Song*
*Stranger Than Kindness*

# FAITH, HOPE AND CARNAGE

# NICK CAVE   SEÁN O'HAGAN

CANONGATE

First published in Great Britain in 2022
by Canongate Books Ltd, 14 High Street, Edinburgh EH1 1TE

canongate.co.uk

2

*British Library Cataloguing-in-Publication Data*
A catalogue record for this book is available on
request from the British Library

ISBN 978 1 83885 766 0

Typeset in Bembo by
Palimpsest Book Production Ltd, Falkirk, Stirlingshire

Printed and bound in Great Britain by
Clays Ltd, Elcograf S.p.A.

For my family
N.C.

For Kieran
S.O'H.

A little child shall lead them.

*Isaiah 11:6*

# Contents

~

# A Beautiful Kind of Freedom

~

Seán O'Hagan: *I'm surprised you agreed to do this given that you haven't done any interviews for a long time.*

Nick Cave: Well, who wants to do an interview? Interviews, in general, suck. Really. They eat you up. I hate them. The whole premise is so demeaning: you have a new album out, or new film to promote, or a book to sell. After a while, you just get worn away by your own story. I guess, at some point, I just realised that doing that kind of interview was of no real benefit to me. It only ever took something away. I always had to recover a bit afterwards. It was like I had to go looking for myself again. So five or so years ago I just gave them up.

*So how do you feel about this undertaking?*

I don't know. I do like having a conversation. I like to talk, to engage with people. And we've always had our big, sprawling conversations, so when you suggested it, I was kind of intrigued to see where it would go. Let's see, shall we?

*When I spoke to you back in March (2020), your world tour had just been cancelled because of the pandemic. I have to say, you sounded remarkably philosophical about it.*

It was a strange moment, that's for sure. When Covid hit and my manager, Brian, told me that we wouldn't be going on tour, I felt this kind of emptying out, like the whole world had dropped out from under me. We'd all put an enormous amount of thought and effort into how we were going to present *Ghosteen* live – we'd been rehearsing with ten backing singers and created a whole visual structure for the show that felt completely unique and very exciting. A lot of work, mental energy and expense. So when I heard it definitely wasn't going to happen, I was initially horrified. It struck at the very core of my being because I was this thing that toured. It's what I was.

Now, I say this with great caution because I know how disappointed the fans were, but, to be honest, that feeling of existential collapse, well, it lasted about half an hour. Then I remember standing in my manager's office and thinking somewhat guiltily, 'Fuck! I'm not going on tour. And perhaps for an entire year.' Suddenly, there was an extraordinary sense of relief, a sort of wave washing through me, a kind of euphoria, but also something more than that – a crazy energy.

*A sense of potential, maybe?*

Yes, but true potential. Potential as powerlessness, ironically. Not the potential to do something, but the potential not to do something. It suddenly struck me that I could just be at home with Susie, my wife, and that was amazing in itself because we'd always measured our relationship in terms of my leaving and my returning. Suddenly, I could see my kids, or just sit in a chair on my balcony and read books. It was like I had been given the license to just *be*, and not do.

*And as it went on, there was the sense that time was out of joint, the days just drifting into each other. Did you feel that?*

Yes, time seemed altered. It seems almost wrong to be saying this, but on one level, I really loved the strange freedom it gave me. I loved getting up in the morning and having another day where I could just exist and not have to do anything. The phone stopped ringing constantly and very quickly my days became beautifully repetitious. It was oddly like being a junkie again, the ritual, the routine, the habit.

Now, I'm saying all this even though the previous tour, when we played the *Skeleton Tree* album live, was one of the defining periods of my professional life, just being on that stage every night with that fierce energy coming off the audience. It is difficult to exaggerate the extraordinary feeling of connection. It was life-changing. No, actually life-saving! But it was also seriously punishing, physically and mentally. So when the recent tour was cancelled, the initial disappointment was replaced by a feeling of relief and, yes, a strange and wayward potential. I feel guilty even saying this, because I know how devastating the pandemic has been for many people.

*From the chats we had back then, it was clear that you sensed early on that the lockdown would be a time for reflection.*

I instinctively felt that. I remember feeling that it really didn't seem right to try and do a performance online from my kitchen, or from my bathtub, or in my pyjamas, or whatever else it was that some artists were doing back then, all those artless and conspicuous displays of fellow feeling. It felt to me like it was a moment to sit inside history and just think. I felt chastened by the world. I had a weird, reflective time throughout that Covid summer. I'll never forget it, sitting on my balcony, reading a lot, writing loads of new stuff, responding to questions on The Red Hand Files. It was an interesting time, despite the constant background hum of anxiety and dread.

*I remember that we were talking on the phone right at the start of the pandemic, and you said, 'This is the big one.'*

Yes, I think I'd just read something that really brought home to me the sheer immense power of the virus, and how extraordinarily vulnerable we all were, and how completely unprepared as a society. You and I were both pretty spooked by this invisible thing that was outside the door. Everyone was. It really did feel like the end times had arrived, and the world had been caught sleeping. It felt as though, whatever we assumed was the story of our lives, this invisible hand had reached down and torn a great big hole in it.

*That makes me think of the idea of the disrupted narrative I have heard you talk about in relation to your songwriting: how both the subject matter and meaning of your more recent songs have become less straightforward and more elusive.*

Well, exactly. My songs have definitely become more abstracted, for want of a better word, and, yes, less dominated by a traditional narrative. At some point, I just grew tired of writing third-person songs that told a structured story that began at the beginning and moved obediently towards their conclusion. I just became suspicious of the form. It felt unfair to inflict these stories on people all the time. It felt like a kind of tyranny. It was almost as if I was hiding behind these neat, manicured narratives because I was afraid of the stuff that was boiling away inside me. I wanted to start writing songs that were truer somehow, that were authentic to my experience.

*Specifically to your more recent experience?*

Yes. Which was one of rupture, I would say, same as most people's. But purely from a personal point of view, living my life within a neat narrative didn't make much sense any more. Arthur died and everything changed. That sense of disruption, of a disrupted life, infused everything.

In terms of what you and I are doing here, it is difficult for me to go back there, but it is also important to talk about it at some point, because the loss of my son defines me.

*I totally understand. So telling a straightforward story in a song, however dramatic, became altogether less important to you?*

Yes, but I didn't step away from highly visual songs; it's more that the storylines became more twisted, entangled, mutilated – the form itself became more traumatic. My music began to reflect life as I saw it.

That said, the songs on my last few albums are still narrative songs, but the narratives have been pushed through the meat grinder. *Ghosteen*, for instance, is still telling a story. In fact, it's telling a vast, epic tale of loss and longing, but it's all busted up and blown apart.

*It's certainly a very different kind of narrative, much more ambitious, even conceptual.*

Yes. Radically different. There's nothing linear about those songs. They shift direction, or rupture, or, worse, atomise before your eyes. The songs exist on their own freakish terms, really.

*I sense that some fans have not been altogether happy with where your music has gone.*

Yeah, there are definitely a number of disgruntled older fans who wish I'd go back to writing so-called 'proper' songs, but I can't see that happening any time soon. There is a deep nostalgia for the old songs and it follows our band around like a dozy old dog. I guess the Bad Seeds have been around for so long, and undergone so many iterations, that some people feel very attached to the past or, more precisely, to their own pasts, to the so-called better days. So the idea that we would make a different kind of music seems to them like a kind of betrayal almost. And I understand that in a way, but you can't allow the nostalgic or sentimental impulses of certain long-time fans to hold back the natural forward motion of the band. Thankfully, there are so many people who are eager to journey with us, to experience the lovely discomfort and danger that comes from attempting something new.

*For me,* Push The Sky Away*, which you released in 2013, seems with hindsight to signal what was to come, with certain songs like 'Higgs Boson Blues' and 'Jubilee Street' sounding somehow looser and less linear. Would you agree?*

Well, it's certainly important because that's when Warren and I started writing the music together. Creatively, that was a seismic change for me and not something I ever expected to happen – to have an actual songwriting collaborator with whom I have a deep synchronicity. That was a radical change that came out of my frustration with the traditional way of doing things, which was to write a song and present it to the band.

*Could we talk about how* Ghosteen *was made, particularly the creative dynamic between you and Warren?*

I suppose the big change was that, by the time we wrote *Ghosteen*, Warren and I were purely improvising. I would play the piano and sing, and Warren would play electronics, loops, violin and synth, with neither of us really understanding what we were doing or where we were going. We were just falling into this sound, following our hearts and our understanding of each other as collaborators, towards this newness. We spent days playing more or less non-stop. Then there were more days of sifting through it all and collecting the bits that sounded interesting. And, in some instances, that was maybe just a minute of music or a single line. After that, it was really about constructing songs from these lovely, disparate parts. Our editing process was initially akin to collage or a kind of musical assemblage. Then we'd work at building songs on top of that.

*It sounds, dare I say it, like there was an element of winging it involved.*

No, that's really not the case. We weren't just two guys who don't know what they're doing. There's a deep intuitive understanding between the two of us, and, of course, twenty-five years of us working together. It's an informed improvisation, a mindful improvisation.

*By 'mindful', do you mean meditative? Or considered?*

I mean that it's intuitive, but also considered, if that makes sense. In terms of the lyrics, I'm never improvising from scratch. That's important to stress. Having done a tremendous amount of thinking about the project, I come to the studio with loads of ideas and an enormous number of written words, most of which, by the way, are discarded. Nevertheless, there is always what you might call a lyrical context, and there are also certain dominant or overarching themes that have preoccupied me in the weeks or months leading up to the sessions. It's a very liberating way to work.

*So to be clear, you are not improvising in the way that jazz musicians improvise on a melody or a theme?*

No, it's more that we are trying to arrive at a formal song through the perilous process of improvisation, to stumble upon form through musical adventuring. I think that might be key, that we are actually using a kind of mutual unknowing in an attempt to catch songs.

*I imagine that process could go horribly awry in the wrong hands.*

Well, it does much of the time. But you only need ten songs, ten beautiful and breath-taking accidents to make up a record. You have to be patient and alert to the little miracles nestled in the ordinary. One of Warren's singular talents is to be able to hear the potential in something that is unformed and in its infancy. He is amazing in that regard. He hears things in a wholly unique way.

7

One of the reasons we work well together is because I have the ability to see words weaving themselves around a piece of unformed music, tying it together, making sense of it. It's a visual thing, to see the song, to give it a rich narrative intent.

*So when you're working in this way, do you also spend hours in the studio meticulously editing the lyrics?*

No, never. When I'm working on the songs at home, they take a long time to write, a lot of thought and a real care and dedication to the form. But when we're in the studio, I'm a butcher who is happy to cut the legs off a treasured lyric in a heartbeat. In a way, the lyrics lose their concrete value and become things to play with, dismember and reorganise. I'm actually very happy to have arrived at a place where I now have an utterly ruthless relationship to my words.

*I have to say, it sounds like quite a brave, even reckless, way for a songwriter to work.*

Well, improvisation is essentially an act of acute vulnerability. But it is also a path to creative freedom, to wild adventure, in which the things of true value can often emerge through musical misunderstandings. Our improvisation is rarely harmonious. It's often a struggle for dominance, but then suddenly it just falls together for a moment or two – a bit like warring lovers!

*Temperamentally, the two of you are quite different, I guess.*

Yes, but we're usually in tune with each other, even though we are coming at things from very different directions. A little thing can nag at me and put me off the whole song, whereas Warren's always looking at the bigger picture. He's much more instinctive than me. He can see the beauty of things earlier than I can. It's a great gift.

But you also have to understand that Warren doesn't really care about lyrics in the way I do. He's much more interested in emotion and sound and music. From early on, he'll be saying, 'This is fucking amazing!' whereas I am really uncertain right up to the wire. It just takes me a lot longer to arrive at a song. Somehow that difference sets up the right kind of dynamic.

*Given that you have such an investment in getting the words right, is it accurate to say that this process of discarding and dismantling, while liberating, may not work for certain types of songs — ballads, say?*

Well, you couldn't do it with a Hal David lyric.

*Or, indeed, some of your own songs?*

No. That is true, but I've made over twenty albums and I can't just keep doing the same thing over and over. You have to operate, at least some of the time, in the world of mystery, beneath that great and terrifying cloud of artistic unknowing. The creative impulse, to me, is a form of bafflement, and often feels dissonant and unsettling. It chips away at your own cherished truths about things, pushes against your own sense of what is acceptable. It's the guiding force that leads you to where it wants to go. It's not the other way around. You're not leading it.

*I really sensed that when I first heard* Ghosteen. *I'm not sure what I was expecting, but it really took me by surprise it was such a conceptual leap.*

Well, I'm glad to hear that. We were locked into such an intense, often mystifying way of working when we made it. The atmosphere in the studio was extremely, I don't know, *concentrated*. Unsettling and strange. I don't know if I can even really articulate it fully, but I do think the great beauty of *Ghosteen* ultimately lies in the tenuous grip both Warren and I had, not only on the songs themselves, but on our own sanity.

*It does sound like that, but in a good way.*

Well, Warren was in a strange place at the time, plagued by his own problems, and I was trying to, well, I don't know, contact the dead,

I guess. It was a strange, haunted time – never leaving the studio, working, trying to sleep, working, trying to sleep – and out of that confusion came this weird, beautiful, holy music.

*That spiritual intensity is palpable. There is such a heightened, almost exalted feel to the music on that record.*

There were spirits in the air, that's for sure. I knew we were making something that was powerful and moving and original. I was sure of it. Whereas *Skeleton Tree* made little sense to me, even when we listened to it all the way through for the final time in the studio. It was too close to the time of my son's death for me to feel anything or to reason clearly.

*That's understandable.*

Yes, and it's interesting that I can still listen to *Ghosteen* in, well, a kind of awe.

*Given how radically different* Ghosteen *was to what came before, did you initially have any trepidation about how it would be received?*

You never can predict how people will react, but I guess I did expect it to be divisive to some degree. I was on tour when we did a kind of preview on YouTube with some beautiful accompanying graphics. I remember I started reading the early online comments. I don't know what I was thinking, but they were so bad! I mean truly awful – 'This is shit!' and 'Nick Cave R.I.P.' and vomit emojis, stuff like that. So I thought the record was just going to fall into a fucking black hole. It was very painful. Then the reviews came in and the tide shifted. It was as if people were changing their mind the more they listened and connected to it. And it pretty much stayed like that. Critically, it was very well received.

*It's quite difficult to describe the atmosphere of that record without resorting to words like 'wonder' and 'joy', which paradoxically diminish it somehow.*

What was really exciting lyrically was that I was able to find lines through improvising in the studio that I could never have found by writing songs in my office, alone at my desk. It was quite beautiful.

*Okay, so give me an example of a line that could only have been arrived at in that way?*

Well, an obvious example would be when I speak-sing 'And I love you' over and over on 'Spinning Song', and then follow it with 'Peace will come'. I could never have actually written something like that down on a piece of paper, yet it is perhaps my favourite moment on that record. Before, those lines would never have made it into an actual song. Not in a million years. There wouldn't have been a place for them and, even if there had been, I don't think I would have had the nerve or the confidence to sing them. Those lines are so sudden and raw.

*Yes, and also sound spiritually ecstatic.*

Well, initially, I had a strong lyrical idea for the record that was very much based on a series of ecstatic images. I saw the record as a series of highly visual, connecting images. I *actually* saw it.

*Do you mean that it all came to you in a vision?*

I had a persistent mental image of a man standing on a beach surrounded by panicking animals; the hills were on fire, there were screaming animals racing back and forward, sea creatures leaping out of the ocean, and a spiral of spirit children that climbed up to the sun. It was a wild recurring hallucination, part horror, part bliss, that somehow embedded itself in my imagination. I'd lie in bed at night and see these images, filing by, one after the other.

*Was this before you started writing the songs?*

I may have written a few rough lyrics, but it was certainly long before I started making the record. In fact, I actually wrote a long, wildly descriptive letter about it to my brother, Tim, who is not someone I normally have the opportunity to discuss creative ideas with. But I was excited! I told him that I had *seen* the record, and that it would be centred around a hallucinatory image of wild animals on fire, running up and down a beach, and a dark force, part leviathan, part child, beneath the sea, and children ascending into the sun. He thought it was kind of funny, you know, the mad ambition of it all.

*So in the studio, did you essentially set out to describe or evoke those visionary images?*

Yes. For me, the images were really the starting point for the whole thing and they remained central to the meaning of the record.

*It's intriguing to me that you began from images rather than words, from the visual rather than the written.*

Yes, it does seem to be the case that of late the single radiant image has become more compelling than the narrative itself, the extremely vivid solitary image at the heart of a song or, indeed, several songs.

*And by allowing that central image to occur in more than one song, are you somehow foregrounding your lyrical preoccupations for the listener?*

Now that you mention it, yes! For me, the repetition of an image, or a series of images that follow the songs around and change meaning depending on the context, is a big part of the reason that the record has that strange, uncanny feeling. It's an inbuilt feeling of *déjà vu* almost, and a sort of building of intention. The songs feel as if they are in conversation with each other. Really, what I was aiming for on *Ghosteen*, though, was the creation of a single moment that was being looked at from various different points of view. I didn't quite get there, though.

*What was that single moment?*

I'm not even sure. Maybe it's more that there seemed to be a single impulse at work, and the songs looked at that impulse from different points of view. I think of *Ghosteen* as essentially an epic story created from a contained moment that is very difficult for me to describe. It's an ecstatic, spiritual declaration emerging out of an ordinary moment.

*Okay, so an ordinary moment rather than an epiphany of some kind?*

Yes. And perhaps the central image is a static one – the line in 'Spinning Song' that goes, 'You sitting at the kitchen table listening to the radio.' This line is, of course, unremarkable as an image. But to me it is anything but ordinary, because it is the last memory I have of Susie before the phone rang with news that our son had died. It is a commonplace image, but for me it's transcendent because it's the last unbroken memory of my wife. Essentially, *Ghosteen* rises out of that moment of peace, of calm, of simplicity, before everything shattered. It's quite hard to explain but I think that comes close to it.

*There are lines on* Ghosteen *where the imagery seems so vivid and dreamlike that it's as if you are channelling your unconscious thoughts or dreams. Or maybe accessing another part of your consciousness?*

I'm glad we are talking about this, because they're mysterious to me also, but they are at the very heart of what I do now, as a songwriter. As I said, I had these wildly vivid images in my mind long before I made *Ghosteen*. Then, when I started writing at home, other more solid images presented themselves: a guy driving his car through a fire; a feather spinning upwards; a remembered time in a hotel in New Orleans where Susie and I conceived our children;

Jesus in the arms of his mother; the leviathan moving beneath the water. These were the images that kept emerging, echoing each other, as I was writing. If you look at my notebooks, these explicit imaginings recur over and over again – roadkill rising from its own blood, the three bears, a mother washing her child's clothes. They became the framework that the record was hung upon. They recur throughout the record, alongside the idea of the migratory spirit, the Ghosteen that passes from image to image, and from song to song, threading them together. For me, the record became an imagined world where Arthur could be.

*Where you could evoke his spirit, perhaps?*

Well, I think *Ghosteen*, the music and the lyrics, is an invented place where the spirit of Arthur can find some kind of haven or rest.

Seán, this idea is as fragile and as open to question as an idea can be, but for me, personally, I think his spirit inhabits this work. And I don't even mean that in a metaphorical way, I mean that quite literally. This isn't an idea I have articulated before, but I feel him roaming around the songs.

*So not as an imaginative projection? Much more than that.*

No, not imaginative. *Literal*. But this is a whispered intuition and as an idea easily dismantled. I don't know, it's kind of hard to talk about.

*I can understand that. For me, songs like 'Sun Forest' and 'Hollywood' seem close to dream songs.*

Yes, I can see that, but I don't think they are in any way surrealistic, which is what the term 'dream song' immediately suggests. There is a precise meaning behind even the most fractured images that ended up in the finished songs. And, as a whole, they are a collection of images, tightly knitted together to form a sort of 'impossible realm'. So it's absolutely important to me that I find the meaning behind the appearance of a particular image.

*So a line or an entire song can reveal its meaning afterwards?*

Yes. It isn't always a case of 'meaning first, image second'. In fact, these days it's often the other way around. There have been moments when I'm singing a line I've written and suddenly I am over-whelmed by its intent. It's like, 'Okay! That's what it's about.' But that doesn't mean I have attached an arbitrary meaning to it. The meaning was always there embedded in the song and waiting to reveal itself.

*You're often trusting a line to reveal its meaning at some point?*

Yes. Exactly.

*More so than when you write a finished song down on paper and record it?*

Yes, much more so. And it has taken me a long time to get there and have the confidence to do that. It requires a certain conviction to trust in a line that is essentially an image, a vision – a leap of faith into the imagined realm. I'm hoping that the image will lead me somewhere else that will be more revealing or truthful than a more literal line would be. It's a matter of faith. What's interesting, too, is that often, when I write a line that is essentially an image, it does something to me physically to write that line down, to articulate that image. I have a physical reaction to it that signifies its importance in the scheme of things.

*It affects you on a physical level?*

Yes. I know it's a valuable line when my body reacts accordingly. An almost erotic enchantment – a sort of sunburst! At the same time, I may not even be sure what it means, so it is really a kind of intuition. Eventually, the image tracks down its meaning, even if it is just emotional. It is important that the line behaves in this way – that it seeks out its intent – because it is very hard to sing something, night after night, that has no emotional value. A dishonest line tends to deteriorate somehow after repeated singing; a truthful line collects meaning.

*So, essentially, you have to understand the deeper meaning of a line or a song before you let it out into the world.*

Yes, otherwise the false line, the meaningless line, will always ambush you when singing it live. Every time I'm on stage singing that particular song, I'm thinking, 'Here comes that fucking line!' It's the same feeling you have when you steal a line, which we all do from time to time. Or maybe you write down someone else's line in your notebook because you think it's cool and it finds its way into a song. You think, 'I'll change it later,' but you don't. Now, every time you sing that song, you can see that line coming towards you, like a saboteur! It's extraordinarily distracting. There aren't that many of them, but there are a few and they do hang around like a curse.

*Can you give me one example of a song that has a line like that?*

Let me think. On *Ghosteen*, the song 'Fireflies' has the line, 'the sky is full of momentary light'. Now, I originally wrote, 'the sky is full of exit wounds of light'. I fucking loved that line, but there was something about it that was troubling me, and then I realised I'd taken it from *Night Sky with Exit Wounds* by the wonderful Vietnamese poet Ocean Vuong. I did think for a moment, 'It's a fucking great line and I can probably get away with it,' but it made me anxious, distressed, even. So at the very last moment I changed it. Songwriters constantly take things from other places, consciously and unconsciously, but you really need to be vigilant. If you let something like that pass, it can ultimately affect your own relationship with the song. It forever harbours a falsehood.

*I guess when you improvise, you're creating a space for myriad possibilities, even beautifully accidental ones.*

Yes. It seems to me that my best ideas are accidents within a controlled context. You could call them informed accidents. It's about having a deep understanding of what you're doing but, at the same time, being free enough to let the chips fall where they may. It's about preparation, but it's also about letting things happen.

*In all this, is it difficult at times to hold on to the original impulse or vision?*

Well, it's not like you have any real control over the creative process when you start improvising in a studio. In fact, it's almost the opposite: you have to surrender in a way and really just let yourself be led by the secret demands of the song. In a sense, it's the not-knowing and not being totally in control that is so invigorating. For me, that's the really beautiful thing about it. It seems that just by being open, you become a conduit for something else, something magical, something energising. Now, that said, for that magical thing to happen, there has to be certain things in place. It can't just be a couple of guys who don't know what they're doing, sitting around bashing shit out. Warren and I are two people who are in tune with each other, have developed a kind of expertise around accidental music, and who trust our process.

*It seems that because the songs are not telling a straightforward story and relying more on imagery, even allegory, they can't help but be more elusive in terms of meaning.*

Yes, but it's never a conscious move on my part to make a song seem in any way difficult or challenging. *Ghosteen* is a complex record, but I don't think it's a lyrically difficult one. The images are clear and precise.

I was reading Stevie Smith yet again last night, a poet I love more than most, and keep coming back to over the years. On one level, she wrote very simple poems that are almost child-like, but often I don't know what she is really getting at. Yet there is something about that mystery that makes her work so compelling and moving to read. Shocking, really, with their threads of rage. You're held one step before meaning. Actually, you're held one step before knowing. That might be a better way of putting it.

*'Before knowing' is good.*

Yes, 'before knowing', I like that, too. You know, I hope people might listen to these songs and come upon a line or a verse that somehow resonates with them, both spiritually and inexplicably. I feel that instinctive, mysterious connection can have a deeper impact on the psyche of the listener. It feels as if it connects to the listener in a different way, as if we have stumbled upon the song and its implicit meaning together. There is a sense of discovery, shared and binding, that creates that sublime and baffling moment between the artist and the listener. I hope this is the case.

## 2

# The Utility of Belief

~

*Could we jump in and talk about things of the spirit, generally?*

Where would you like to start?

*Well, once when I described your later songs as 'spiritual', in terms of both their form and subject matter, you immediately countered that with the word, 'religious'. I thought that was revealing.*

The word 'spirituality' is a little amorphous for my taste. It can mean almost anything, whereas the word 'religious' is just more specific, perhaps even conservative, has a little more to do with tradition.

*Because religion requires a deeper commitment and makes specific demands on the believer?*

Religion is spirituality with rigour, I guess, and, yes, it makes demands on us. For me, it involves some wrestling with the idea of faith – that seam of doubt that runs through most credible religions. It's that struggle with the notion of the divine that is at the heart of my creativity.

*Maybe we can explore that later. But are you saying, in terms of your faith and beliefs generally, you are essentially a conservative?*

Yes, that's always been the case, and not just in terms of my faith. I think temperamentally I'm conservative.

*That's quite a loaded word.*

Well, it's loaded for you, maybe.

*Definitely. But do you mean you're a traditionalist?*

Okay, traditionalist, if you prefer that word. I'm not really that interested in the more esoteric ideas of spirituality. I'm drawn to what many people would see as traditional Christian ideas. I'm particularly fascinated with the Bible and in particular the life of Christ. It has been a powerful influence on my work one way or another from the start.

*And yet it is little discussed when critics write about your work. Do you think journalists tend to shy away from the subject?*

Oh God, yes! For sure. I remember an interview with some music paper from about thirty years ago, where the journalist sat down and said, 'Before we even begin, I've been told by my editor, "Don't get him started on God"'!

*Does this interest in the more traditional aspects of religion date back to your childhood?*

There's certainly an element of nostalgia to it, I admit, and that probably goes back to the time when I first heard those Bible stories. I attended church a couple of times a week when I was young, because I was in the cathedral choir. And I learned a lot by going to church. I became familiar with, and really loved, the stories of the Bible. I was just drawn to the whole thing. I remember buying a little wooden cross from the cathedral gift shop, with a silver Jesus on it, you know, to wear around my neck. I was around eleven years old. There was a piece of paper attached that said, 'Made from the wood of the True Cross.' I thought, 'Wow, the *True Cross.*'

*Ah, they were lying to you, even then!*

Ha! Yes. And I asked my mother, 'Mum, is this made of the actual cross that Jesus died on?' And she said, 'Maybe, darling,' in such a way that I knew it wasn't, but it still somehow retained its mystery.

The point being, I always had a predisposition towards these sorts of things. And, later, when I became interested in art, it was often certain religious works that I turned to, above all. I felt that they possessed a kind of supplemental power, beyond the art itself. That was a doorway, too.

*So, back in your younger, wilder days, when you drew on biblical imagery as a source for your songwriting, was that also a reflection of a deeper interest in the divine?*

Well, I was surrounded by people who displayed zero interest in spiritual or religious matters, or if they did, it was because they were fiercely anti-religious. I was operating in a Godless world, to say the least, so there was no real nurturing of these ideas. But I was always struggling with the notion of God and simultaneously feeling a need to believe in something.

*I have to say that was not always immediately apparent.*

No, I guess not! But I think people just saw what they wanted to see. I mean, those early Birthday Party shows were religious in their way, with all that rolling around on stage and purging of demons and speaking in tongues. It was old time, God-bothering religion! Or at the very least, preoccupied with religious matters. But, of course, I also had a huge appetite for mayhem. My life was extremely chaotic, and my music was, too, of course, but I was always trying to find some kind of spiritual home. Perhaps the chaos was one of the reasons for my underlying yearning for some deeper, more substantial meaning, but I don't know for sure. The idea that there was no God or no such thing as the divine – no spiritual mysteries to speak of, nothing beyond what the rational world could offer us – was just too difficult for me to accept.

*So did you see religion as a way to give your life a degree of order?*

No, I don't think that's right. I had a major taste for havoc – but I had other things going on, too, genuine preoccupations. I might wake in my hotel room surrounded by the detritus of a heavy night on the road – empty bottles, drug paraphernalia, maybe a stranger in my bed, all that kind of shit, but also an opened copy of the Gideon's Bible with passages underlined. It was forever that way.

*Back then, I assumed the Bible was simply a source of inspiration for your songs in much the same way that you were drawn to writers like William Faulkner, Flannery O'Connor and the whole Southern Gothic tradition.*

Well, a big part of the attraction of those writers was that they were also wrestling with religious ideas. And the Bible is an incredible source of imagery and bold, instructive human drama. Just the language itself is extraordinary. I think there was always a yearning within me for something else, something beyond myself, from which I felt excluded. Even in the most chaotic times, when I was struggling with addiction, I always felt desirous of those who had a religious dimension to their lives. I had a kind of spiritual envy, a longing for belief in the face of the impossibility of belief that addressed a fundamental emptiness inside me. There was always a yearning.

*I sense that you are actively attending to that yearning now.*

Well, yes, mainly because as I've gotten older, I have also come to see that maybe the search *is* the religious experience – the desire to believe and the longing for meaning, the moving towards the ineffable. Maybe that is what is essentially important, despite the absurdity of it. Or, indeed, because of the absurdity of it.

When it comes down to it, maybe faith is just a decision like any other. And perhaps God is the search itself.

*But doubt is still a part of your belief system, if I can call it that?*

Doubt is an energy, for sure, and perhaps I'll never be the person who completely surrenders to the idea of God, but increasingly I think maybe I could be, or rather that I was that person all along.

*It's intrinsically human to doubt, though, don't you think?*

Yes, I do. And the rigid and self-righteous certainty of some religious people – and some atheists, for that matter – is something I find disagreeable. The hubris of it. The sanctimoniousness. It leaves me cold. The more overtly unshakeable someone's beliefs are, the more diminished they seem to become, because they have stopped questioning, and the not-questioning can sometimes be accompanied by an attitude of moral superiority. The belligerent dogmatism of the current cultural moment is a case in point. A bit of humility wouldn't go astray.

*So, just to make sure I've got this right: you would like to get past your doubt and just believe wholeheartedly in God, but your rational self is telling you otherwise.*

Well, my rational self seems less assured these days, less confident. Things happen in your life, terrible things, great obliterating events, where the need for spiritual consolation can be immense, and your sense of what is rational is less coherent and can suddenly find itself on very shaky ground. We are supposed to put our faith in the rational world, yet when the world stops making sense, perhaps your need for some greater meaning can override reason. And, in fact, it can suddenly seem the least interesting, most predictable and least rewarding aspect of your self. That is my experience, anyway. I think of late I've grown increasingly impatient with my own scepticism; it feels obtuse and counter-productive, something that's simply standing in the way of a better-lived life. I feel it would be good for me to get beyond it. I think I would be happier if I stopped window-shopping and just stepped through the door.

*I'd say, be careful what you wish for; certitude is seldom good for creativity.*

I guess not, but who says creativity is the be all and end all? Who says that our accomplishments are the only true measure of what is important in our lives? Perhaps there are other lives worth living, other ways of being in the world.

*Have you considered the idea of doing something other than writing songs and performing?*

Well, I think it is more that you arrive at a point where the reason for making art, making music, changes. You find that it can serve another purpose, entirely. You come to understand that this wayward energy you've always had, directed in the right way, can actually help people. That music can draw people out of their suffering, even if it is just temporary respite.

*So you don't see music as simply an escape?*

No, it's more than that. I think music has the ability to penetrate all the fucked-up ways we have learned to cope with this world – all the prejudices and affiliations and agendas and defences that basically amount to a kind of layered suffering – and get at the thing that lies below and is essential to us all, that is pure, that is good. The sacred essence. I think music, out of all that we can do, at least artistically, is the great indicator that something else is going on, something unexplained, because it allows us to experience genuine moments of transcendence.

But to answer your original question: right now, I feel very attached to the work I'm doing, so I'm not considering doing something else. There is a real feeling of joy around the things I'm involved in. I feel a true connection with people and also a feeling of duty towards the fans who have invested so much in the band. I feel compelled to keep going, because I love what I do and value my relationship with my audience. But what I was trying to say is that we may ultimately find that, to our surprise, our creative endeavours are not the defining element of our lives. They are perhaps a means to an end.

*In your case, have you considered what that end might be?*

That's what I'm trying to find out.

*And the people you surround yourself with creatively, do any of them share your deep interest in God and religion?*

It's hard to say, but I think probably not.

*Have any of them ever expressed reservations about the religious element in your songs?*

No. Not that I've heard. No one has ever said, 'Oh no, not another Jesus song.' Not to me, anyway. They may well be thinking that, but they've never said it.

*Not even Blixa [Bargeld], who is known for his strong opinions?*

No, not even Blixa! Blixa was not a believer, as far as I know, but he liked to discuss religion. He's curious about life and he knows his stuff, more than most. He had inflexible and shockingly extreme views on certain things, but he was interested in ideas too. That was my experience, although he may have changed. I wouldn't know.

Mick Harvey had no time for organised religion. His father was a vicar, so Mick had seen religion from the inside and as a consequence was fiercely anti-religious. I'm not sure if his views have tempered with time, though. I doubt it.

*A lot of people who have endured a religious upbringing and are now particularly resistant to it – I include myself, to a degree.*

Yes, sadly, organised religion can be atheism's greatest gift.

*What about Warren? Where does he stand on all this?*

Warren is very spiritual in his own way. He arrives there through his music, but I am not sure he spends a lot of time wrestling with the idea of God. Not that I've ever spoken to him about it, mind. He's certainly very open to the world and I sense that he feels close in his own way to spiritual matters.

*He certainly looks the part.*

Yes. John the Baptist! His head looks like it belongs on a platter.

*Could you talk a bit more about the tension between doubt and faith that you alluded to earlier? I know it's something you have grappled with for a while.*

There is something about that dynamic that interests me, not least because I have to accept that part of the fire and energy of my life comes from the fact that I devote a significant portion of my time to thinking about and agonising over something that may well not exist! So, in a way, it may actually be the doubt, the uncertainty and the mystery that animates the whole thing.

*It certainly seems to me, from some of the conversations we had before we embarked on this book, that you may actually be shedding what's left of your scepticism and edging closer to God.*

Maybe. You know, it's good for me to talk about these things, because, as I say, I don't really tend to do that. Sometimes you need to say out loud what you think or talk to someone else about the ideas you hold, just in order to see if they are valid. It helps clarify things for me to be challenged on my beliefs. This is the essential value of conversation, that it can serve as a kind of corrective.

I think, more recently, particularly within the pandemic, I've had the opportunity, and felt the desire, to apply myself to the practice of belief and to spiritual acceptance. By doing that, I feel I could get to a place where my relationship with God was a little less fraught, shall we say. And to me the benefits are self-evident. I'd certainly be happier for it.

*But that would require a leap of faith — a leap beyond the rational.*

Perhaps, but rational truth may not be the only game in town. I am more inclined to accept the idea of poetic truth, or the idea that something can be 'true enough'. To me that's such a beautiful, humane expression.

*It is, but to me the idea of the existence of God being 'true enough' sounds like a way of hedging your bets.*

Well, the idea of poetic truth, or metaphorical truth, as I've heard it called — the idea of things being 'true enough' — can be of real practical benefit. Metaphorical truth, as far as I can make out, works on the premise that even though something may not be literally or empirically true, it may be beneficial to us, personally and in evolutionary terms, to believe it.

*In what way might it be beneficial to believe in something that is literally or empirically untrue?*

If you attend Narcotics Anonymous, for instance, which is something I know about because when I first got clean I used to go to meetings, you come up against the 'true enough' idea all the time. Essentially, you have a group of apparently hopeless drug addicts, many of whom may not have a spiritual bone in their body, who are being asked to hand their lives over to a higher power in order to get clean. Initially, many of them are reluctant to even consider doing that, which is a perfectly rational response. I mean, why should you surrender your life to something that you think doesn't exist? But they are told to just 'walk the walk' and many are desperate enough to follow the instructions — it's a life-or-death choice, after all — and so they hand their will and their lives over to something that may very well not exist. And, in a great many instances, they get better, they get clean, their lives greatly improve. Not only that, but what often happens is that many of them end up handing their lives over to a higher power as a matter of course. They find that believing in something that is 'true enough' works throughout all aspects of their life. I guess what I am saying is that the believing itself has a certain utility – a spiritual and healing benefit, regardless of the actual existence of God.

*And it's more or less understood that this higher power is God.*

Well, they say it can be what you want it to be, as long as it's something more powerful than yourself. It could be the group itself, for instance, but I think it's generally understood by most as some kind of divine power. Essentially, you are being asked to surrender and have faith, and, if you are prepared to do that, you find that it works.

So, for me personally, having a religious dimension in my life is highly beneficial. It makes me happier, it makes my relationships with people more agreeable, and it makes me a better writer – in my opinion.

*So do you believe in redemption in the Christian sense?*

Well, I think we're all suffering, Seán, and more often than not this suffering is a hell of our own making, it is a state of being for which we are responsible, and I have personally needed to find some kind of deliverance from that. One way I do that is to try to lead a life that has moral and religious value, and to try to look at other people, all people, as if they are valuable. I feel that when I have done something to hurt an individual, say, that the wrong-doing also affects the world at large, or even the cosmic order. I believe that what I have done is an offence to God and should be put right in some way. I also believe our positive individual actions, our small acts of kindness, reverberate through the world in ways we will never know. I guess what I am saying is – we *mean* something. Our actions *mean* something. We are of *value*.

I think there is more going on than we can see or understand, and we need to find a way to lean into the mystery of things – the impossibility of things – and recognise the evident value in doing that, and summon the courage it requires to not always shrink back into the known mind.

*This ties in to your recent music, which, as we've already talked about, is often reaching beyond the earthly and towards some notion of transcendence.*

For me, writing and playing music – especially playing music – is a kind of firming up of this religious condition. I think the sense of elevation you heard in those songs comes from our attempts to do just that, to reach towards some greater mystery. I think that's why *Ghosteen* has had such a deep impact on many people – a spiritual impact.

I think of *Ghosteen* as a religious record, because it is concerned with the human struggle and the need to, in some way, transcend our suffering. Actually, it is not just concerned with that struggle; it is, *in itself*, evidence of that struggle.

*Also a vivid articulation of that struggle.*

I do think *Ghosteen* has a particular power, in the manner of certain religious music. Listening to it can be spiritually healing. I know that sounds overblown, but there are letters that come into The Red Hand Files that attest to that. Many letters. I think this is because of the way it was recorded – what Warren and I were going through at the time.

*You've alluded to that before. So Warren was also going through a difficult time during the recording of the album?*

Yes, I think there were things going on in Warren's personal life that he was finding extremely difficult. *Ghosteen* is sort of imprinted with our souls' yearning. There are spirits trapped inside it. You can feel them on the record.

*Indeed you can, but do you think you created that music in the presence of something or someone divine?*

That's a big question, Seán. What I will say is that, from where I'm standing, an explicit rejection of the divine has to be bad for the business of songwriting. Atheism has to be bad for the business of making music. It has to put you at a distinct disadvantage because it's a kind of narrowing of options and a denial of the fundamentally sacred dimension of music. It's just very limiting, in my experience. Many people will, of course, disagree, although I tend to think most musicians have more time for these spiritual considerations, because when they make music, when they lose themselves in music, fall deep inside it, they encounter such strong intimations of the divine. Of all things, music can lift us closer to the sacred.

*And yet there are many great songs and pieces of music that don't reach into the divine. You've written some of them.*

Well, I don't know what those songs are. A song doesn't have to be explicitly religious to have transcendent qualities.

*Did this notion of transcendence apply when you were writing your older, less obviously religious songs?*

Yes, I think so.

*A song like 'Breathless', for instance, seems to me to exalt the luminous beauty of the everyday. Is that not a wondrous subject in and of itself?*

Yes, and the luminous and shocking beauty of the everyday is something I try to remain alert to, if only as an antidote to the chronic cynicism and disenchantment that seems to surround everything, these days. It tells me that, despite how debased or corrupt we are told humanity is and how degraded the world has become, it just keeps on being beautiful. It can't help it.

But 'Breathless' is, in fact, an explicitly religious song. A love song to God.

*No! It was one of the songs we played at our wedding. I never took it for a God song.*

Well, that's what's known as Jesus smuggling! And it worked. But, to be honest, it's not about a God that is separate from nature, or apart from the world; rather, it's about a God that is in attendance and animating all things.

*That's fine, but I think I'll stick with my earthly, romantic version, if you don't mind.*

Feel absolutely free.

*Are you saying that all your great songs in some way have that transcendent – or religious – element? Or that they at least reach for it?*

I mean that all my songs are written from a place of spiritual yearning, because that is the place that I permanently inhabit. To me, personally, this place feels charged, creative and full of potential.

There are also an increasing number of songs I have written that seem mysterious to me, that I can listen to with a kind of reverence because I feel personally removed from them, as if they have come from some other place. *Ghosteen* certainly is a record that feels as if it came from a place beyond me and is expressing something ineffable. I don't know quite how to explain this, Seán, except that perhaps God is the trauma itself.

*You're going to have to try to explain that one. What do you mean by 'God is the trauma itself'?*

That perhaps grief can be seen as a kind of exalted state where the person who is grieving is the closest they will ever be to the fundamental essence of things. Because, in grief, you become deeply acquainted with the idea of human mortality. You go to a very dark place and experience the extremities of your own pain – you are taken to the very limits of suffering. As far as I can see, there is a transformative aspect to this place of suffering. We are essentially altered or remade by it. Now, this process is terrifying, but in time you return to the world with some kind of knowledge that has something to do with our vulnerability as participants in this human drama. Everything seems so fragile and precious and heightened, and the world and the people in it seem so endangered, and yet so beautiful. To me it feels that, in this dark place, the idea of a God feels more present or maybe more essential. It actually feels like grief and God are somehow intertwined. It feels that, in grief, you draw closer to the veil that separates this world from the next. I allow myself to believe such things, because it is good for me to do so.

*So, the 'true enough' idea applies in this instance, too?*

Very much so – the utility of belief.

*Has your thinking on belief and, indeed, beauty been deepened by your experience of lockdown, by simply having the time to reflect?*

I think so. There is something about slowing down that is just quietly powerful, don't you think? I mean, I've been thinking about this stuff for years, but this moment has made it more necessary somehow. My love of the world and for people feels stronger, I mean that quite genuinely, and I don't think I'm alone in feeling that. I think this is what happens when we experience collective traumas such as this. We become connected by our mutual vulnerability. You know, I have no time for cynicism. It feels hugely misplaced at this time.

*I totally agree. Am I to take it your particular understanding of this moment of collective trauma is very much rooted in your personal experience?*

Yes, of course. Everyone finds their own way through grief, but my experience of it has been, in the end, a spiritual and life-changing process. And it was Arthur who brought me to this place. And brought Susie there, too. It's an ongoing thing. It ebbs and flows. But the collective grief of the pandemic does have familiar echoes. Grief can have a chastening effect. It makes demands of us. It asks us to be empathetic, to be understanding, to be forgiving, despite our suffering. Or to ask ourselves, what is it all for? What is the purpose of any of it?

*Do you think this precarious moment we are living through could be collectively transformative in any lasting way?*

Yes. I remain cautiously optimistic. I think if we can move beyond the anxiety and dread and despair, there is a promise of something shifting not just culturally, but spiritually, too. I feel that potential in the air, or maybe a sort of subterranean undertow of concern and connectivity, a radical and collective move towards a more empathetic and enhanced existence. I may be completely off the mark here, but it does seem possible – even against the criminal incompetence of our governments, the planet's ailing health, the divisiveness that exists everywhere, the shocking lack of mercy and forgiveness, where so many people seem to harbour such an irreparable animosity towards the world and each other – even still, I have hope. Collective grief can bring extraordinary change, a kind of conversion of the spirit, and with it a great opportunity. We can seize this opportunity, or we can squander it and let it pass us by. I hope it is the former. I feel there is a readiness for that, despite what we are led to believe. I have a hope that, in time, we can come together, even though, right now, we could not be further apart.

# 3

# The Impossible Realm

~

*I was just listening to* Skeleton Tree *again, and remembering when I first heard it. Back then, I had assumed that most of the songs had been written after Arthur's death.*

No, the opposite in fact, but I can see why you might think that. I found that aspect of *Skeleton Tree* quite perplexing myself, to tell you the truth. I was disturbed by it, especially at the time. But when I think about it, it's always been the way. I've always suspected that songwriting had a kind of secret dimension, without getting too mystical about it.

*You actually touched on that idea back in 1998, in your lecture 'The Secret Life of the Love Song', that songs could be prescient in some way.*

Yes, that's right! If I remember correctly, I wrote about how my songs seemed to have a better handle on what was going on in my life than I did, but back then, it was more of a playful observation, comical, even.

*Do you take the idea more seriously now?*

Yes, I think so.

*So, just to be clear, this is not what we talked about earlier – the idea that a song can reveal its true meaning some time afterwards?*

No. It's different, but connected. For me, the prescient element of songwriting is stranger, more unsettling.

*In the lecture, you used 'Far From Me' off* The Boatman's Call *as one example.*

Yes. Over its three verses, that song describes the trajectory of a particular relationship I was in at the time. And then, in the final verse, it describes in detail the unhappy demise of that relationship. Now, in that instance, the song had written its final verse long before the relationship actually fell apart, so it was as if it had some secret knowledge or ability to look into the future. In the essay, I wrote about it in a light-hearted, whimsical way, but, as I say, I'm not sure I feel that way any more.

*'The song had written its final verse' is an intriguing way of putting it. Do you believe the song somehow wrote itself?*

Well, that's what it feels like with some songs. The more I've written, the harder it is to disregard the fact that so many songs seem to be some steps ahead of actual events. Now, I'm sure there are neuro-logical explanations for that in the same way that there are for a phenomenon like *déjà vu*, say, but it has become increasingly unnerving – the uncanny foresight of the song. And despite how it may appear from what I'm saying here, I'm really not a super-stitious person. But the predictive aspect of the songs became too frequent, too insistent and too accurate to ignore. I don't really want to make too much out of it except to say that I think songs have a way of talking into the future.

I tend to think my records are built out of an unconscious yearning for something. Whether that is a yearning for disruption, or a yearning for peace, very much depends on what I was going through at the time, but my music does often seem to be one step ahead of what is actually going on in my life.

*I guess a song, like any work of art, is always going to unconsciously reveal something of the person who created it. If you write a truly honest song, it cannot help but be emotionally and psychologically revealing.*

Yes, that's true. Songs have the capacity to be revealing, acutely so. There is much they can teach us about ourselves. They are little dangerous bombs of truth.

*Can you elaborate on the idea that songs often possess a latent meaning that is only revealed much later? It's fascinating territory.*

I guess I believe that there exists a genuine mystery at the heart of songwriting. Certain lines can appear at the time to be almost incomprehensible, but they nevertheless feel very true, very true indeed. And not just true, but necessary, and humming with a kind of unrevealed meaning. Through writing, you can enter a space of deep yearning that drags its past along with it and whispers into the future, that has an acute understanding of the way of things. You write a line that requires the future to reveal its meaning.

*This imaginative space you're describing sounds pretty intense. When you described it as unsettling a while back, were you specifically referring to* Skeleton Tree?

*Skeleton Tree* certainly disturbed me, because there was so much in that record that suggested what went on to happen. It explicitly forecast the future, so much so that it was hard for many people to believe I had written almost all of the songs before Arthur died. The way that it spoke into the events that surrounded Arthur's death was, at the time, very distressing. Now, I'm not really somebody who gets too engaged in this sort of thing. In fact, in the past, if someone started talking to me in this way, I would have dismissed him or her entirely. I think you and I are similar in that regard, yet at the same time, we are open to certain ambiguities in life. We cautiously acknowledge that there are, I don't know, *mysteries*.

*Yes, I never quite know what to do with those kinds of experiences, whether to accept them or try to find a rational explanation for them – which is always somehow unsatisfying.*

That's very true. But after Arthur died, things intensified for me in that regard. I felt both unsettled and reassured by a preternatural energy around certain things. The predictive nature of the songs was a small part of that. In fact, Susie became totally spooked by my songs. She has always seen the world in signs and symbols, but even more so since Arthur died. For me, her openness and layered understanding of things is one of her most deeply attractive qualities.

*Do you feel able to talk some more about the nature of that 'preternatural energy' you felt? Was it akin to a heightened state of awareness?*

Well, after Arthur died, the world seemed to vibrate with a peculiar, spiritual energy, as we've talked about. I was genuinely surprised by how susceptible I became to a kind of magical thinking. How readily I dispensed with that wholly rational part of my mind and how comforting it was to do so. Now, that may well be a strategy for survival and, as such, a part of the ordinary mechanics of grief, but it is something that persists to this day. Perhaps it is a kind of delusion, I don't know, but if it is, it is a necessary and benevolent one.

*If so, that kind of magical thinking is a strategy for survival that a lot of people use. Some sceptics might say it is the very basis of religious belief.*

Yes. Some see it as the lie at the heart of religion, but I tend to think it is the much-needed utility of religion. And the lie – if the existence of God is, in fact, a falsehood – is, in some way, irrelevant. In fact, sometimes it feels to me as if the existence of God is a detail, or a technicality, so unbelievably rich are the benefits of a devotional life. Stepping into a church, listening to religious thinkers, reading scripture, sitting in silence, meditating, praying – all these religious activities eased the way back into the world for me. Those who discount them as falsities or superstitious nonsense, or worse, a collective mental feebleness are made of sterner stuff than me. I grabbed at anything I could get my hands on and, since doing so, I've never let them go.

*That's completely understandable. But even in the most ordinary times, all those things you mention – sitting in silence in a church, meditating, praying – can be helpful or enriching even to a sceptic. Do you know what I mean? It's as if the scepticism somehow makes those moments of reflection even more quietly wondrous.*

Yes, there is a kind of gentle scepticism that makes belief stronger rather than weaker. In fact, it can be the forge on which a more robust belief can be hammered out.

*When you came to perform* Skeleton Tree*, was that also unsettling for you?*

Well, it became suddenly very difficult to sing those songs. I mean, without stating the obvious, the very first line of the first song on that record, 'Jesus Alone', begins with the lines: 'You fell from the sky and landed in a field near the River Adur.' It was hard to hear *and* to sing – and hard to fathom how I had come to write a line like that given the events that followed. And the record is full of instances like that.

I'm aware I might be flailing around a bit here, but what I'm basically trying to say is that maybe we have deeper intuitions than we realise. Maybe the songs themselves are channels through which some kind of greater or deeper understanding is released into the world.

*Could it even be that the heightened imaginative space you enter when you write a song is by its very nature self-revelatory? Poets like William Blake and W. B. Yeats certainly believed that. I doubt they would have had any problem with the prophetic or revelatory nature of songwriting.*

No, I don't think they would. And that ties in to what we've spoken about before, that there is another place that can be summoned through practice that is not the imagination, but more a secondary positioning of your mind with regard to spiritual matters. It's complex, and I'm not sure I can really articulate it. The priest and religious writer Cynthia Bourgeault talks about 'the imaginal realm', which seems to be another place you can inhabit briefly that separates itself from the rational world and is independent of the imagination. It is a kind of liminal state of awareness, before dreaming, before imagining, that is connected to the spirit itself. It is an 'impossible realm' where glimpses of the preternatural essence of things find their voice. Arthur lives there. Inside that space, it feels a relief to trust in certain glimpses of something else, something other, something beyond. Does that make sense?

*I think so, but I think I'd probably find it difficult to inhabit that space or give it the kind of deeper meaning that you do.*

Well, you've talked to me in the past about going into a church and lighting a candle for someone. That, for me, is like putting a kind of tentative toe into this particular space.

*For me, lighting a candle for someone may be more an act of hope than faith. And I tend to think of it as one of the few residual traces of my Catholic upbringing.*

Perhaps, but to go into a church and light a candle is quite a consequential thing to do, when you think about it. It is an act of yearning.

*I guess so. And yet I struggle with what it means exactly. It may be that it just makes me feel better about myself.*

I think at its very least it is a private gesture that signals a willingness to hand a part of oneself over to the mysterious, in the same way that prayer is, or, indeed, the making of music. Prayer to me is about making a space within oneself where we listen to the deeper, more mysterious aspects of our nature. I'm not sure that is such a bad thing to do, right?

*No, not bad, but not rational, either. Then again, it may be that the most meaningful things are the most difficult to explain.*

Yes, I think so. And I do think the rational aspect of our selves is a beautiful and necessary thing, of course, but often its inflexible nature can render these small gestures of hope merely fanciful. It closes down the deeply healing aspect of divine possibility.

*I have to say that I am slightly in awe of other people's devotion. When I go into an empty church, it always feels meaningful somehow – and vulnerable – to just linger there for a moment or so. Do you know Larkin's poem, 'Church Going', which touches on that very thing?*

Yes! 'A serious house on serious earth it is.' And yes, there's something about being open and vulnerable that is conversely very powerful, maybe even transformative.

For me, vulnerability is essential to spiritual and creative growth, whereas being invulnerable means being shut down, rigid, small. My experience of creating music and writing songs is finding enormous strength through vulnerability. You're being open to whatever happens, including failure and shame. There's certainly a vulnerability to that, and an incredible freedom.

*The two are connected, maybe – vulnerability and freedom.*

I think to be truly vulnerable is to exist adjacent to collapse or obliteration. In that place we can feel extraordinarily alive and receptive to all sorts of things, creatively and spiritually. It can be perversely a point of advantage, not disadvantage as one might think. It is a nuanced place that feels both dangerous and teeming with potential. It is the place where the big shifts can happen. The more time you spend there, the less worried you become of how you will be perceived or judged, and that is ultimately where the freedom is.

*We've talked a lot about the shift in your songwriting style, but it's surely a reflection of a much bigger and more profound shift of consciousness.*

Yes, one that came out of a whole lot of things, but I guess it is essentially rooted in catastrophe.

*Was there ever a point after Arthur's death when you thought you might not be able to continue as a songwriter?*

I don't know if I thought about it in that way, but it just felt like everything had altered. When it happened, it just seemed like I had entered a place of acute disorder – a chaos that was also a kind of incapacitation. It's not so much that I had to learn how to write a song again; it was more I had to learn how to pick up a pen. It was terrifying in a way. You've experienced sudden loss and grief, too, Seán, so you know what I'm talking about. You are tested to the extremes of your resilience, but it's also almost impossible to describe the terrible intensity of that experience. Words just fall away.

*Yes, and nothing prepares you for it. It's tidal and it can be capsizing.*

That's a good word for it – 'capsizing'. But I also think it is important to say that these feelings I am describing, this point of absolute annihilation, is not exceptional. In fact it is ordinary, in that it happens to all of us at some time or another. We are all, at some point in our lives, obliterated by loss. If you haven't been by now, you will be in time – that's for sure. And, of course, if you have been fortunate enough to have been truly loved, in this world, you will also

41

cause extraordinary pain to others when you leave it. That's the covenant of life and death, and the terrible beauty of grief.

*What I remember most about the period after my younger brother, Kieran, died was a sense of total distractedness that came over me, an inability to concentrate that lasted for months. Did you experience that?*

Yes, distraction was a big part of it, too.

*We talked earlier about the act of lighting a candle, and that for me was the only thing that could still my mind. It was as if peace had descended if only for a few moments.*

Stillness is what you crave in grief. When Arthur died, I was filled with an internal chaos, a roaring physical feeling in my very being as well as a terrible sense of dread and impending doom. I remember I could feel it literally rushing though my body and bursting out the ends of my fingers. When I was alone with my thoughts, there was an almost overwhelming physical feeling coursing through me. I have never felt anything like it. It was mental torment, of course, but also physical, deeply physical, a kind of annihilation of the self – an interior screaming.

*Did you find a way to be still even for a few moments?*

I had been meditating for years, but after the accident, I really thought I could never meditate again, that to sit still and allow that feeling to take hold of me would be some form of torture, impossible to endure. And yet, at one point, I went up to Arthur's room and sat there on his bed, surrounded by his things, and I closed my eyes and meditated. I forced myself to do it. And, for the briefest moment in that meditation, I had this awareness that things could somehow be all right. It was like a small pulse of momentary light and then all the torment came rushing back. It was a sign and a significant shift.

But when you mentioned that sense of constant distractedness, I was thinking about how, after Arthur died, there was a raging conversation going on in my head endlessly. It felt different to normal brain chatter. It was like a conversation with my own dying self – or with death itself.

And, in that period, the idea that we all die just became so fucking palpable that it infected everything. Everyone seemed to be at the point of dying.

*You sensed that death was all around you, just biding its time?*

Exactly. And that feeling was very extreme for Susie. In fact, she kept thinking that everyone was going to die – and soon. It was not just that everyone eventually dies, but that everyone we knew was going to die, like, *tomorrow*. She had these absolute existential free-falls that were to do with everyone's life being in terrible jeopardy. It was heart-breaking.

But, in a way, that sense of death being present, and all those wild, traumatised feelings that went with it, ultimately gave us this weird, urgent energy. Not at first, but in time. It was, I don't know how to explain it, an energy that allowed us to do anything we wanted to do. Ultimately, it opened up all kinds of possibilities and a strange reckless power came out of it. It was as if the worst had happened and nothing could hurt us, and all our ordinary concerns were little more than indulgences. There was a freedom in that. Susie's return to the world was the most moving thing I have ever witnessed.

*In what way?*

Well, it was as if Susie had died before my eyes, but in time returned to the world.

You know, if there is one message I have, really, it concerns the question all grieving people ask: Does it ever get better? Over and over again, the inbox of The Red Hand Files is filled with letters from people wanting an answer to that appalling, solitary question. The answer is yes. We become different. We become better.

*How long did it take before you got to that point?*

I don't know. I'm sorry, but I can't remember. I don't remember much of that time at all. It was incremental, or it *is* incremental. I think it was because I started to write about it and to talk about it, to attempt to articulate what was going on. I made a concerted effort to discover a language around this indescribable but very ordinary state of being.

To be forced to grieve publicly, I had to find a means of articulating what had happened. Finding the language became, for me, the way out. There is a great deficit in the language around grief. It's not something we are practised at as a society, because it is too hard to talk about and, more importantly, it's too hard to listen to. So many grieving people just remain silent, trapped in their own secret thoughts, trapped in their own minds, with their only form of company being the dead themselves.

*Yes, and they close down and become numbed with grief. In your case, I wondered at the time if you were even aware of the depth of people's responses to Arthur's death? The incredible wave of empathy directed towards you.*

Well, as far as the fans were concerned, yes. They saved my life. It was never in any way an imposition. It was truly amazing. And what you remember ultimately are the acts of kindness.

*Yes, the small things that people say or do are often the things that stay with you.*

So true, the small but monumental gesture. There's a vegetarian takeaway place in Brighton called Infinity, where I would eat sometimes. I went there the first time I'd gone out in public after Arthur had died. There was a woman who worked there and I was always friendly with her, just the normal pleasantries, but I liked her. I was standing in the queue and she asked me what I wanted and it felt a little strange, because there was no acknowledgement of anything. She treated me like anyone else, matter-of-factly, profes-sionally. She gave me my food and I gave her the money and – ah, sorry, it's quite hard to talk about this – as she gave me back my change, she squeezed my hand. Purposefully.

It was such a quiet act of kindness. The simplest and most artic-ulate of gestures, but, at the same time, it meant more than all that anybody had tried to tell me – you know, because of the failure of language in the face of catastrophe. She wished the best for me, in that moment. There was something truly moving to me about that simple, wordless act of compassion.

*Such a beautifully instinctive and understated gesture.*

Yes, exactly. I'll never forget that. In difficult times I often go back to that feeling she gave me. Human beings are remarkable, really. Such nuanced, subtle creatures.

*Did writing songs help you work your way through your grief and trauma?*

That came much later. Before that happened, I think taking *Skeleton Tree* on the road was in its way a form of public rehabilitation. And doing the In Conversation tour was extremely helpful. I learned my own way of talking about grief.

*When I heard you were doing the In Conversation events, I wasn't sure how they would play out. Just the act of allowing people to ask you whatever they wanted, however inconsequential or profound, seemed risky. Was it a tightrope walk?*

God, yes. When I look back, it was a really strange time to do something like that, because I was so weakened by the circumstances I found myself in. But it was a deeply intuitive decision to just put myself out there, come what may. You have to understand that there was an element of madness to the whole thing. I was living in this 'impossible realm'. To be honest, I really had no idea what I was doing. I found out how to do it by doing it.

*So you entered the 'impossible realm' each time you walked on stage to take people's questions?*

Very much so, and even before I went on stage. That is where I felt Arthur was really with me. We sat backstage with each other, talked to each other, and when I went on stage I felt a very strong, supporting presence and also an enormous strength – his hand in mine. It actually felt like the hand of the woman who had reached out to me in Infinity – as if her hand was somehow his hand. I felt I'd longed him to life. It was very strong and very powerful.

*I had no idea it was that intense – and transformative.*

It was. I did it every night and, through doing it, found a kind of invincibility through acute vulnerability. I was not in any way wallowing in my situation or exploiting it. I was rather matter-of-factly explaining the place in which I'd found myself. I was attempting to help people, and receiving help, in return.

*Yes, that came across. There was definitely something communally powerful about those In Conversation events.*

Well, they were accepted in good faith. Often people opened up in deeply moving ways. It was like giving them a space to do that. And I found a strength and confidence that I could just do this potentially dangerous thing and who cares if it works or doesn't? I knew it would be risky, because I was giving people permission to ask anything they wanted, but my thinking was, 'What does it really matter what happens?' So that was a big shift in my thinking, for sure: to relinquish concern for the outcome of my artistic decisions and let the chips fall where they may. That idea has reverberated through everything I have done since.

*So it was about being open and vulnerable, but also defiant in the face of catastrophe?*

Yes, and that is a powerful place to be, because there was nothing that anyone could ask that I couldn't handle in some kind of way. Looking back, I think the constant articulation of my own grief and hearing other people's stories was very healing, because those who grieve *know*. They are the ones to tell the story. They have gone to the darkness and returned with the knowledge. They hold the information that other grieving people need to hear. And most astonishing of all, we all go there, in time.

*Was making* Ghosteen *another way to enter even more deeply into that realm where Arthur was present?*

I think so, yes. The *Ghosteen* experience came much later and making that record was as intense as things can get. But beautiful, you know, fiercely beautiful. It was energising in the most profound way. But also more than that.

There was a kind of holiness to *Ghosteen* that spoke into the absence of my son and breathed life into the void. Those days in Malibu making that record were like nothing I have ever experienced before or after, in terms of their wild potency. I can't speak for Warren, but I'm sure he would say something similar.

*Was it in any way difficult to make?*

Not difficult, we were just fixated. It was quite something, really, especially the Malibu sessions, where we just lived in the studio. We slept in a house nearby. The studio itself was one room, with the control desk inside it. We slept little, working until we dropped, never leaving the grounds. Day in, day out.

*How did you end up recording in Malibu?*

It was Chris Martin from Coldplay's studio and he let us use it while he went and recorded down the road somewhere else. It was an amazing gesture.

*So you were cocooned in the Coldplay compound?*

Yes. Although that sounds a lot grander than it was! It was an incredibly concentrated experience, terrifying in its intensity, but not creatively difficult, not at all. The opposite. We were sort of mesmerised by the power of the work.

*When you talk about the intense atmosphere in the studio, was it intense only in a positive way?*

Yes, in the best possible way. And Warren was just amazing. We're both bad sleepers and I'd get up at some hideous hour in the morning after going to bed at some hideous hour in the night, and Warren would just be sitting there, in the yard, in his underwear, with his headphones on, just listening, listening, listening. Warren's commitment to the project, his sheer application, was beyond anything I have ever witnessed.

*Did he understand what you were doing without your having to communicate it to him?*

We didn't talk about these things, as such, but the nature of the songs was so close to the bone, it was clear. When you are making music together, conversation becomes at best an auxiliary form of communication. It becomes unnecessary, even damaging, to explain things.

It seems strange now to say it, but I also had this idea that perhaps I could send a message to Arthur. I felt that if there was a way to do that, this was the way. An attempt to not just articulate the loss but to make contact in some kind of way, maybe in the same way as we pray, really.

*Yes, the whole record has a prayerful aspect.*

It does, and in that respect it had an ulterior motive, a secondary purpose, insofar as it was an attempt to somehow bring whatever spirits there may be towards me through this music. To give them a home.

*And to communicate something to Arthur?*

Yes, to communicate something. To say goodbye.

*I see.*

That's what *Ghosteen* was for me. Arthur was snatched away, he just disappeared, and this felt like some way of making contact again and saying goodbye.

# 4

# Love and a Certain Dissonance

~

*I was listening to* Ghosteen *last night and it struck me that the heightened aura of the songs is very much transmitted not just through the words and the music, but through your voice, which seems altered somehow.*

I know what you mean. When I listen to those songs, I almost feel that someone else, or something else, is performing them, and stranger still, that I am their intended audience. It's weirdly disconcerting.

*As if you are singing to yourself? Or for yourself?*

Yes, maybe. I think there was something about the way Warren and I recorded *Ghosteen* – the unconscious interior quality of it all – that brought certain forces to bear on it. As we said before, there is a prayer-like aspect to the record.

And I think our prayers make demands on us; they require something of us, they turn our attention inward. To me, *Ghosteen* feels unique in that way, like a lot of religious music.

*So you don't think there are other songs of yours that have that kind of religious interiority? 'Into My Arms', for instance?*

For me personally, not in the same way, not with such a radical intimacy. If I listen to, say, 'Into My Arms', it's not that it leaves me unaffected; I understand the mechanics of the song and I understand its value. I can actually remember everything about its conception. I recall, very clearly, sitting on the bed in the dormitory of the rehab facility I was in and writing the words, piecing the song together, totally aware of its intent or purpose.

*I hadn't realised you wrote 'Into My Arms' while you were in rehab.*

Yes. They let you go to church on Sundays if you wanted to. I was actually walking back from church through the fields, and the tune came into my head, and when I got back to the facility I sat down at the cranky old piano and wrote the melody and the chords, then went up to the dormitory, sat on my bed and wrote the lyrics. I remember this junkie, who was fresh in and fucked-up, covered in sores, spraying himself all over with Lynx deodorant – as if that was going to change *anything* – and looking at me, and saying, 'What are you doing?' And I said, 'I'm writing a song.' And he said, 'Why?'

*Not a bad question! But, you had to share a dormitory?*

Oh yeah, this was old-school – before there were luxury, five-star rehab facilities. Anyway, back then, I was fully conscious of the act of songwriting: I understood the intent, I knew I had a tune and a pleasing set of lyrics, I knew I had a good song. And even though I love 'Into My Arms', and it has served me very well, I don't get moved when I play it in the same way that other people seem to when they listen to it. I'm more moved by their reaction to it than by the song itself, because I can sense the emotional impact it's having on other people. It just feels like I created something for them to enjoy and sent it out into the world along with all my other songs.

*Ghosteen* is a different matter entirely. It feels like it has about-faced and turned its attention on me. *Ghosteen* feels like it is moving towards me, with all its secrets and mysteries in tow. It's as if it is trying to tell me something. And perhaps it is! Perhaps it will reveal itself when we finally get to perform it live, but I really don't know.

*You were primed to play* Ghosteen *live when the pandemic hit. It strikes me that we probably would not be having these conversations if you had gone on tour.*

No, probably not, and we would not have become friends, in the same way. For all its great benefits, personally and for the fans, there is also a significant cost to touring. Things are sacrificed, for sure, the greatest being a sense of normality. Friendships, family too – ordinary life, opportunities to do unremarkable things.

Like, I want to go and try to make some ceramics, which is a simple, commonplace activity, but these everyday things are hard to commit to if you are touring all the time.

*You've taken up pottery!*

No, ceramic figurines. My take on traditional Staffordshire figurines, but we can go into that later.

*Okay, I better bone up . . .*

Having said all that, it's heart-breaking that we never got to play *Ghosteen* live. It's like its natural flowering, or coming into being, or whatever you want to call it, was interrupted by the pandemic. It never had the chance to grow up. So it feels like there is much that *Ghosteen* has left to tell us.

*It sounds to me that, when you were creating that record in Malibu, you were essentially a conduit for the songs.*

Yes, it was as if the songs just flowed through us. From somewhere else. I have a very strong relationship to 'Spinning Song', in particular, a very deep connection that feels . . . mysterious. It has a tremendous emotional effect on me. It feels more than the sum of its parts, if you know what I mean?

*Could you talk about how that song came about and maybe also shed some light on why you find it so emotionally resonant?*

Warren and I were improvising on a single, repetitive theme for a couple of hours, at least. Now, when Warren falls into an idea, it takes quite a lot to shift him away from it. When it comes to music, I'm not saying Warren is on the spectrum, but I'm not saying he's not, either! He can sit there in a kind of dissociative state and play essentially the same thing for hours, with minimal shifts, absolutely lost to the moment. It can be both a blessing and a curse, but often it allows me the opportunity to develop a vocal idea. It pushes me beyond the borders of what I might call the 'cherished' idea.

*Which is the idea you carry in your head from the beginning about what the song should be?*

Yes, the exquisite idea — the lyric that I have spent months working on, thinking about, nurturing, mothering, polishing, perfecting, only to find it doesn't fit with the piece of music Warren has fixated upon. So then I'm forced to either abandon the idea, dismantle it or use fragments of it. Once I get to that place, I can end up singing literally anything — sometimes out of boredom, sometimes out of frustration, and often as an attempt to derail or change the course of the song, you know, breach Warren's monomaniacal siege upon the song. And very often it is in the midst of this raw, unfocused, involuntary vocalising that the real treasure is found. It's when you enter this space that other more mysterious influences seem suddenly to be at work.

*Okay, it seems to me there are a couple of things to think about here. Are you saying that the words are now subservient to the music, that the music in fact dictates the words?*

Well, it depends. The words have to have some meaningful relationship to the music, of course, but that does not mean they are subservient. If you take a song like 'I Need You', from *Skeleton Tree*, it is almost entirely based on a misunderstanding between my vocal and the music. I'm unintentionally, or maybe accidentally, singing in a different time signature to the music. Or it could be that the music is playing in a different time signature to the vocals. It depends on who you think is in charge! But the song is wonderful and its disarming tension comes from that misunderstanding. It would be impossible to formally write a song such as that one.

But, to your point, the music can dismantle the structure of a lyric to get at its unconscious or unspoken heart. This is what happened with most of the songs from *Ghosteen* and is one of the reasons why it has such a powerful emotional pull – because the words are coming from the spontaneous unconscious.

*It's fascinating that you arrived at some of these heightened moments out of boredom, which can be an incredibly fertile creative state.*

Well, of course! In my experience, boredom is often close to epiphany, to the great idea. In a way, that is very much the agony of songwriting – because boredom is just boredom until it's not!

But perhaps boredom is the wrong word here. For me, it's more a kind of distraction – a sort of letting go, or a willingness to relinquish control of an idea that you thought was important. I find I can only get to that place through improvisation and, of course, collaboration. The nature of improvisation is the coming together of two people, with love – and a certain dissonance.

*Could you talk some more about the nature of the imaginative space you enter when you are improvising and singing whatever comes into your head?*

I don't know, Seán; I've given it my best shot. It is a semi-conscious place, a twilight place, a distracted place, a place of surrender.

*I wonder if there is an inherent danger in all of this that, as a songwriter, you are abandoning your commitment to the considered lyric, and indeed the well-wrought song, for something altogether more precarious and uncertain?*

Yes. And that is, in fact, what happens. I would say that there are lyrics I have 'written' through these recent sessions that simply do not stand up on the page. Once again, take 'I Need You', which, as a formal lyric, is a disaster, but as a song has an extraordinary emotional power. It's a sacrifice, I guess, but, at this moment in time, one I am prepared to make. I just think the newer songs are more interesting, more emotionally charged and, in their way, more true.

*That said, some of your recent songs are quite elaborately structured. 'Spinning Song' springs immediately to mind in terms of its formal and thematic shifts and turns. Could you talk me through it?*

Okay, so it begins with a kind of folk tale about Elvis Presley that I had written a couple of years ago. As a piece of formal lyric writing, it is what it is: a seven-verse children's poem about the king of rock 'n' roll and his queen. It ends with the image of a spinning feather, or a soul, ascending 'upward and upward' until it eventually finds my wife, Susie, sitting at the kitchen table listening to the radio.

Now, for me, this image of Susie sitting at the kitchen table listening to the radio is crucial, because it became the locus not only of this particular song, but of the album itself. As I think I've told you before, this is the last intact memory I have of my wife before we heard the news of Arthur's death.

At that moment, there is a physical rupture in the song, and the synth begins its upward climb. The way that came about was through us taking a few moments from an extended improvisation, in which I was wearily singing the mantra-like phrase 'And I love you' over and over again, slightly out of tune and slightly out of time. By that point, I had obviously run out of things to sing, but when that part was placed precisely after the lyric about Susie sitting at the kitchen table, it just became extremely moving. To me, at least, it symbolises the breaking apart of our world. It's also the point where the repeated refrain – 'And I love you' – shifts the song from the mythic to the more real and essential. It becomes a broken, exhausted declaration of love.

That's followed in turn by another hard edit of another piece from the original improvisation, where I had started singing in falsetto, which, by the way, was something I'd never done before. And that, too, was probably out of frustration or boredom. Anyway, I sang the lines 'Peace will come in time' and 'A time will come for us'. Now, lyrically, this is all very simplistic stuff and, for that reason, it would be really difficult to write down on a piece of paper and take seriously. And yet it works.

*It's a beautifully affecting moment, for sure, and audacious in its apparent simplicity.*

I have to say that, in my opinion, the three-step movement – from the ruptured child's poem to the broken mantra to the final spiritual proclamation of hope – is possibly the finest piece of songwriting that I have been involved in. Certainly, for me, it is the most poignant. And yet I can't remember doing any of it.

*Really?*

Yes, we definitely had no conscious understanding of its outcome while we were performing it. So, as I've already said, 'Spinning Song' has a profound effect on me as a *listener* because I don't really feel that I was involved in its conception, or that I was consciously aware of the making of it. It really felt that it was made by other hands.

*Your unconscious self? Or some other guiding presence?*

I really don't know.

*Does it matter to you that you don't know?*

It's more that there are some things I'm hesitant to spell out, because they are fragile and mysterious. 'Spinning Song' sets the course for the rest of the record. It provided a space for all manner of forces, imaginative and otherwise, to come out and play.

*When you talk about this, I keep thinking about Yeats's idea of 'the automatic script' — words that emerge trance-like from the unconscious onto the page.*

I don't know about that, but I do think Warren and I were more inclined to let unconscious forces have their influence over the outcome of the songs. I think it is fair to say that we were swept along by whatever spirits or demons took command of us at that time. I say that with a certain amount of caution, because I understand how that sounds. I have made a lot of records in the past, and made them in all kinds of states of mind, and there have been some very strange recording sessions indeed along the way, but none of them come close to *Ghosteen* in terms of its feeling of intense creative possession. I'm sure Warren would say the same.

*Just how strange were some of the past recording sessions?*

Well, for instance, when we were making the *Tender Prey* album, the producer, Tony Cohen, was so fucked-up he took up residence in the studio's air-conditioning vent.

*That's a whole different kind of strangeness! But during the* Ghosteen *sessions was there a feeling of fragility about what you were creating, the sense that the spell could be broken at any moment?*

My good friend Andrew Dominik, the film director, who was at the studio a lot, told me that during the Malibu sessions the music often seemed to hover between something masterful and complete failure, but as the session progressed you could feel the music become infused with a kind of 'saving spirit'.

*What do you think he meant by that? That the music was saved from failure by the spirits in the room? Or that making the music saved you?*

Well, if you were to pin him down, he would probably tell you both. I think Andrew sees music as the purest, or the most holy, of art forms – the closest to God. You just sit in a room with your friends and make music, and connect to this righteous force. He is very envious of that. The simplicity. The directness. As a filmmaker he spends most of his time trying to hang on to the truth of his work, its essence, and not have it contaminated by the industry. This is a perpetual battle for him. Andrew is a tough guy, but you can see the toll it takes.

*Looking back, what do you think informed – or fuelled – that sense of creative possession you just mentioned? Grief? Desperation? Or something more exalted than that?*

Sometimes I try to bring to mind what Arthur has given to me, not just when he was alive but in his absence, too, almost as a way of finding meaning in the hopelessness that descends from time to time. And, well, the truth of it is that Arthur's passing ultimately became a motivating force, so that, over the years, Susie and I have experienced some very beautiful, meaningful things in our lives, *truly* beautiful, meaningful things, and in many ways they lead like a powder trail directly back to Arthur's death. This is the secret, terrible beauty at the heart of loss, of grief. Of course, we would give it all back if we could see him again, but those cosmic deals are not to be made. One of the many things Arthur gave us was *Ghosteen*. Directly, I believe. I hope so, anyway.

*I think, for sure. There is certainly a rare kind of purity or essentialness to some of those songs. 'Ghosteen Speaks', for instance, seems stripped back to its very essence.*

'Ghosteen Speaks' was the last song we recorded for the record. We loved that song but we wondered about it too – how terribly bare it was. I remember when Andrew came into the studio at one point and Warren stuck a pair of headphones on him and said, listen to this. The look on Andrew's face as he listened said it all.

*Did he think it was powerful or too stark?*

I think he felt it had a kind of uplifting but devastating power. Andrew came in a lot. He would drive down from LA, because he needed to be around people, I think. He was also dealing with his own troubles. He was a mess, to tell you the truth, but an honest and very helpful presence. I'd been looking after him at the house I was renting in Hollywood for some weeks before I went into the studio, because he was coming out of the bad end of a long-term relationship, and couldn't really be alone. He was nursing a broken heart and hanging on by a thread.

So the three of us, Warren, Andrew and I were all in this strange, wounded place, I guess. We weren't necessarily discussing these matters, we were inhabiting them. The atmosphere was – I don't know how to describe it – rare. Haunted, even.

*Haunted by absences?*

Ha! Yeah, you could say that.

*You said that Hal Willner dropped by, too. I'm guessing Hal was an interesting guy to have around.*

Yes. Hal sat there in the studio and we played him the record. He didn't say a word throughout. Just sat there with his head in his hands, listening. After it finished, he said, 'I have never heard a record like that in my life.' He was very moved. And then he just left. I think that might have been the last time I saw him. As you know, he recently died from Covid in New York. Poor Hal. It's such a sad and terrible story, so deeply unfair. He was so thoroughly loved by so many. If our lives are somehow measured by the depth of our engagement with the world and the people in it, Hal ought to be fucking canonised, you know. He was a great man.

*Indeed he was. A true original.*

Did I tell you how he brought Lou Reed into the studio when Warren and I were doing the soundtrack for the movie *Lawless*? We had managed to get the bluegrass musician Ralph Stanley to sing an a capella version of 'White Light, White Heat' by The Velvet Underground for the end titles of the movie. It was a complete fucking coup! Amazing. Hal had gone to Virginia or wherever to record him, which was an enormous challenge in itself. Ralph Stanley was, to say the least, highly suspicious of the project. Ralph didn't much like venturing out of his zone, shall we say. God knows what he made of Hal! Anyway, Hal managed to get this extraordinary performance out of Ralph. This was one of Hal's singular talents, to push musicians out of their areas of comfort and to perform across genres with other musicians – these loony ideas that shouldn't have worked, but almost always did!

Warren and I were working in a studio in LA, and Hal comes in with Lou, and Lou sits down and we play him the Ralph Stanley version of 'White Light, White Heat'. And Lou just wept, right there on the sofa.

It was such a beautiful, amazing moment, because we didn't know

Lou that well at that time. I met him a few times afterwards, usually with Hal and our friend, Ratso Sloman. I had dinner with Lou, Hal and Ratso once in New York, which was an enormous pleasure.

*That sounds like quite a dinner!*

Yeah, it was. There was a great love between those guys, but a deep and playful bond too – I think because of their Jewishness. The singer Antony Hegarty was there (Anohni as she is now known). It was a great night. I also played with Lou Reed at an event for Palestine back when I was welcome in those circles! But I did countless projects with Hal. He was such a kind person – lovely to my kids. Ratso, too. Ratso used to take the kids to Coney Island. He introduced them to the magician David Blaine. Such beautiful people. Did you know Hal?

*I only crossed paths with him a few times, usually backstage at one of his events. I met him once maybe twenty years ago. I was staying in Dublin with Gavin Friday and Hal arrived straight from the airport. I opened the front door and he was standing on the step, wearing a rubber O. J. Simpson mask. No explanation. Turned out he'd worn it the whole way into town in the cab.*

There you go. That's Hal.

*God rest his soul.*

Absolutely.

*To go back to Malibu: throughout this period of intense creativity in the studio, there were obviously people coming and going. Did that not break the flow?*

Well, there weren't that many, really. Chris Martin was around, because we were working in his studio. Now, Chris has a whole different energy entirely. He's a sweet guy and a dear friend of mine, which seems to surprise some people.

*I can see why that might be the case. You two are not exactly musical compatriots.*

Obviously, there's a fair amount of daylight between the kinds of music we play, but who fucking cares? I have always been drawn to his generosity of spirit, his engagement with the world. He's a beautiful guy, and we just get on. I had a similar relationship with Michael Hutchence. We just understood each other, and on some fundamental level loved each other, even though musically we were worlds apart.

When we were recording in Chris's studio, he would often appear after he had been working on Coldplay's stuff up the road. He'd just bound into the studio, full of that manic, ecstatic, life-loving spirit of his, and he'd be flying around the studio like a fucking pinball. Him and his girlfriend, Dakota, and her dog, Zeppelin.

*He sounds a bit hyper, which is not what you hear in his music.*

Energetic, definitely. When he calmed down enough, we'd play him the song we had been working on – we were cranking out a new song each day. He would listen, but listen hard, you know, with his deep understanding of the nuts and bolts of songwriting, of pop music and hit-making. Chris is a very funny guy, with a perverse sense of humour, but he's also disarmingly forthright. He tells his truth, as he sees it, as a matter of principle. He's tough and isn't afraid to speak his mind. So he'd listen and then tell Warren and me what he thought. Mostly, he loved the stuff, really loved it, but occasionally he made what were quite challenging suggestions that, if taken on board, would have radically altered the song.

*Did that actually happen? Did you actually change a song on Chris Martin's advice?*

Yes, we did. The third song on the record, 'Waiting For You', is a ballad, but originally we had a very loud, super-aggressive, industrial loop that played completely out of time throughout the song. You can still hear it at the very beginning of the song. Originally, that loop played from start to finish and it absolutely dominated the song. In our minds, we thought it set up a weird, dissonant tension within the song that sounded unnerving and strange. We had never really questioned it, but when we played it to Chris, he turned to us and said, 'I love you guys very much, but is there any chance I could hear the song again without the fucking canning factory?' At which point, Andrew Dominik sprang out of his chair and shouted, 'Thank God someone suggested that!'

*How did you take that?*

At the time, we weren't so pleased, because we liked the brutality of the whole thing, but we complied. We took away the industrial loop, and what was left behind was a very beautiful, vulnerable song shimmering there on its own – a classic, old-school ballad, raw and fragile and unimpeded. So thank God for that!

In a way, it's kind of sad to talk about that time, because the whole place where we lived at the studio burned down in the Malibu fires a couple of weeks after we left.

*That's kind of spooky given the first line of 'Hollywood' is: 'The fires continued through the night.'*

Yes, but the little studio miraculously survived. Everything around it was literally incinerated. I think they've rebuilt it, though. I think it's up and running again.

*To return to 'Ghosteen Speaks', it's incredibly haunting in its spareness.*

Yes, it was reduced to a mantra or a prayer. In fact, the idea of revealing a song's essential self – a place without artifice, decoration or armour, where there was no place to hide – was important throughout the album.

We've talked already about the 'thinness of the mortal veil', right?

Well, 'Ghosteen Speaks' seems to me to be the gateway through which the spirits can enter and play.

*I can see that. So to give this some wider context, how exactly did you used to write and record your songs?*

Back in the early days, with The Birthday Party, if I had a song, I'd just sing the words I'd written to Mick. I didn't really have an instrument to play them on. I played a bit of piano but not much, so really I just had these songs in my mind. Mick was amazing at interpreting and ordering the chaos that was in my head. I'd sing the song, but I'd also sing the guitar part, and so on. Basically, Mick would try and interpret what I meant. It was very primitive, but it worked most of the time, because we just wanted to create something primal and chaotic.

By the time the Bad Seeds were formed, I was writing songs on the piano. I'd just bring in a handful of songs I'd written, and the band would gather round the piano and I would play the songs to them. It was basically, here's a song and it goes like this, and here's another one and it goes like this. And then sometimes there were songs that we'd just put together in the studio. That was pretty much how it worked for years.

*Am I right in thinking that this new improvisatory way of working doesn't lend itself easily to a full band set-up in which everyone has fixed roles?*

Well, it's difficult, because you often find that the rhythm section will impose a shape on a song and take it to a particular place, from which there is no turning back. As soon as Marty, say, comes in on the bass, the song will quickly find its way into a linear form, whereas if you work without a rhythm section, you are freed from that inevitability. Instead of a linear or horizontal song something is created that is more lyrical and, well, vertical! Heaven bound, I guess. I really love the way *Ghosteen* is perpetually ascending.

For all that, I have to say that many of the defining Bad Seeds songs are based on strong linear repetitive bass lines that are very powerful – 'From Her To Eternity', 'Saint Huck', 'Tupelo', 'Stagger Lee', 'Do You Love Me?'. All great songs, really great songs, and Marty was the formidable engine for most of them, but I think Warren and I just tried to move away from that kind of approach for a while.

*Okay, so let's talk about* Skeleton Tree. *I know making that record was a very different kind of experience.*

For me, *Skeleton Tree* was the antithesis of *Ghosteen*. As I've said, *Skeleton Tree* made no real sense to me. When we listened to it all the way through for the final time in the studio in France, even then I didn't understand it. I was a grieving zombie. And to me it just throbbed with pain and darkness and confusion. It made me feel physically ill.

So, essentially, *Skeleton Tree* was a whole different thing. But can we talk about that another time?

*Yes, of course.*

You know, I don't think I have ever actually listened to *Skeleton Tree* all the way through.

*Well, that is not so surprising.*

What's it like, that record? Honestly?

*It's certainly a sombre record, and an intense, slow-burning one. It's a powerful work, hauntingly so, but, yes, very different from Ghosteen.*

Good. I'm glad to hear that.

*Can I just ask – do you and Warren ever lock horns in the studio?*

Not really. We seem to have a clear understanding of each other's roles and where we are going with a song. Warren is bolder about what we do, more prone to hang on to the original stuff. I am more lyric-oriented, which requires a different kind of attentiveness.

So we may disagree from time to time, but it's not the kind of conflict that simmers away. It's not Mick's deep seething rage. It's not Blixa throwing down his guitar and marching around the studio, shouting at everybody.

Those kinds of creative tensions can have their place, mind, but they can also be a massive waste of time and energy.

*Given that you are lead singer and songwriter, have you ever been dictatorial in the studio?*

Ha! Have you done the Enneagram Personality Test?

*Yes, you told me about it and I tried it.*

What number are you? A five?

*Actually, yes.*

I thought so. The Searcher. Well, I'm a classic eight – which means I have, at the pathological end of my personality, a tendency towards the tyrannical. But then so is Mick, I suspect, and, my God, so is Blixa. All classic eight types. The potential for disharmony is enormous! It's like having Hitler, Stalin and fucking Mao Zedong trying to make a record together.

*So that's basically a roundabout way of saying you can be dictatorial.*

I can certainly be assertive when it comes to my fundamental values, perhaps excessively so. I probably have a lot to answer for, but I'm also infinitely malleable about other things. I'd say mostly I'm flexible, though some people might disagree. I think, these days, I'm a listener and a good collaborator. At my most functional, I bring out the good in people, but sadly we don't always behave at our best. I think I wasn't at my best back then, but I'm older and wiser now. I spend more time hanging out at the better end of my character. I hope so. But in those days, there was a fair amount of carnage, a fair amount of blood on the floor. I don't feel so good about that.

*About the way things turned out with Mick and Blixa?*

The person I feel bad about is Mick. I feel that I wasn't as understanding of his position as maybe I could have been. And I'm sorry about that. We had a long, rich, creative collaboration, and in all the animosity that occurred around the time of his leaving, I lost sight of that. I'm very happy that we are friends again. These days, we have a warm and civil relationship, with no small amount of love. I am truly happy about that. We all change, you know. I have, I hope. I don't visit that brutal end of my nature quite so often any more.

*You've definitely mellowed.*

So you keep saying.

*Given how you and Warren work together now, is there a space within that process for songs that may come to you in the more traditional way? Songs that are fully crafted on the page, rehearsed and then recorded?*

I hope so, but right now I honestly don't know. What I will say is that I really cannot imagine ever making an electric guitar-based rock record again. I just wouldn't know what to do.

*The reason I ask is that a song like 'Galleon Ship' sounds quite traditionally structured. If you stripped away the electronica, it would sound almost like a folk ballad. Did it come out of improvisation?*

Yes, it did, but you're right: 'Galleon Ship' sounds like an Irish ballad at its heart. The thing is, when Warren gets a drone going, I often end up singing like an Irishman! I had written 'Galleon Ship' over a period of time. It circles around a bunch of traditional folk tropes, but it has a wonderful heroic nature at its heart – two lover-heroes rising in the morning and standing before the collective sorrow of the world. The vision of thousands of ghost ships. It's kind of corny, too, but affecting. I was happy with that, and the way the music builds into that amazing crescendo. All those layered vocals just launch the song into the stratosphere.

*So you haven't totally abandoned the idea of the well-crafted, traditional narrative song?*

If you mean am I going to return to a more traditional, formal sort of songwriting, something less fractured, less broken, more structured, I don't know. Maybe. I have been thinking about that a lot lately. Listening to Jimmy Webb: 'By The Time I Get To Phoenix', 'Wichita Lineman', 'Where's the Playground, Susie', 'Galveston'. Big, classic, grand themes. God, I love that stuff. Elvis's songs from the seventies: 'Kentucky Rain', 'Always On My Mind'. Kris Kristofferson. Just beautiful.

*Those songs still sound so ambitious – the lyrical sophistication, the melodies, the arrangements. They do seem to belong to another time, another world, though.*

Yes, but the world I inhabit now, at this point in time, does seem very different to when we made *Ghosteen*. It feels more put back together. There is a shape to it. It may not be the same shape as it once was – in fact, it is barely recognisable – but it does, at times, feel like life has returned to a more orderly narrative, rather than something fractured and smashed apart.

I don't take that feeling for granted, Seán. We should never underestimate that sense of being in the groove of life, of moving from one situation to another with the wind at your back, of being purposeful and valuable, of life having some semblance of *order*. It's really something, that feeling, made all the more profound because you know how transitory and easily broken it is. It seems to me, life is mostly spent putting ourselves back together. But hopefully in new and interesting ways. For me that is what the creative process is, *for sure* – it is the act of retelling the story of our lives so that it makes sense. That's why I love those old songs — they gather up the broken pieces of a life and organise them into something that is coherent and meaningful and true. I could listen to them all day.

# 5

# A Kind of Disappearance

~

*Hey, Nick. How are you doing? Are you okay?*

Yes, I'm pretty good.

*I'm really sorry to hear about your mum.*

Thanks, Seán. It's been a strange time. I don't know, it feels like a kind of disappearance.

*It must be tough. And not being able to travel, too . . . I know you were very close. Are you okay to chat about your mum?*

Yes, of course. It's fine.

*I remember when we spoke briefly about her before, you mentioned that she was absolutely supportive of you throughout your life.*

That's right. You know, I would say that her unconditional support enabled me to do whatever it is I have done in life. I really think that my mother's love was the undercarriage of my life. It didn't prevent me from falling, but it probably stopped me from falling all the way.

My mother's love permitted me to experience the world fully, the dark stuff, too – addiction, grief, break-ups, disappointments, all that stuff – without fully falling. My mother was just always there, like a safety net.

*Was she someone you could talk to about difficult subjects? That's not always the case with parents – they can be the last people you turn to when you're in trouble.*

Yes, that's true, but my mum was always there for me. Sometimes when I had a dilemma of some sort, Susie would say, 'I don't know, Nick – ring your mum.' I'd do just that and ask her what to do. She was fair and sensible, mostly. I am going to really miss that, to tell the truth.

*I'm guessing she must have been worried about you at times along the way.*

For sure. When you're young, you just assume your parents are super-resilient, but when I think back, I can see that how she dealt with all that crazy shit was quite extraordinary.

*So how did she deal with all the crazy shit?*

Well, I remember once coming back to Melbourne on a flight from London and it turned out that someone had alerted the police that I would be on the flight and that I would be carrying drugs. I came off the plane and there was Mum waiting for me, and we gave each other the biggest hug, I hadn't seen her in over a year, just as two policeman arrested me and took me and my mother to the police station. There they did a full-scale search of my person and my bags but didn't find anything. They had to let me go, but it was totally clear to everybody that I was completely off my face. It just wasn't their lucky day. Anyway, I remember sitting next to Mum in the car driving home, feeling a bit sheepish. I could tell she was really pissed off, and then she just said, 'Bloody cops.'

What I'm trying to say is that she was unconditionally supportive of me even when I was at my least deserving. That's a mother's love.

*Do you think your more aberrant youthful behaviour, for want of a better term, was in any way a reaction to, or maybe a rejection of, your respectable upbringing?*

No, I don't think it was. My upbringing was in no way oppressive or claustrophobic or morally forthright or whatever, far from it. My parents were essentially free-thinking liberals. If I was rejecting anything, it was the limitations put on me by the culture I lived in – the unspoken idea that you had to be inconspicuous, keep your head down, play by the rules, not make a scene and don't ever get too big for your boots. It's the Australian way. In contrast, my parents were very supportive, even encouraging, of a certain flamboyance of character. But it can't have been easy. I was certainly a cause for concern.

*I can see how that would have been the case.*

Like when my mum came to visit me in London, about a year or so after I had located there. She came on her own. I would go and see her at the little hotel by Hyde Park where she stayed and we'd walk round the park and talk and so on. She wanted to see where I lived but I was reluctant to do that because I lived in a squat in Maida Vale with Anita and Tracy and a bunch of other Australians. All the windows had been smashed out by people in the street who wanted us out, the front door had been set on fire, the toilets had been busted up, and there was no electricity and no water. The place was by any measure a fucking disaster. It was winter and really very grim. Anyway, one day we drove past it in a taxi on the way back to my mum's hotel and I can still remember the look on her face when she saw the state of it – the forlorn and terrible concern.

*God, yes, that sort of thing is hard for a parent.*

But then a couple of days later we were on a train to visit some distant relatives in Dorset. I was reading the *NME* and there was an ad for The Birthday Party playing at some little club in London, and my mother saw it. The look of utter relief, of elation, and, well, pride – you know, that her son's band, The Birthday Party, was in an *English music paper*! That something might come good for her troublesome son. And, Jesus, you don't know what goes on in a parent's heart till you become one yourself.

I remember being on the phone with Anita a couple of years ago and we were talking about the bad old days and I said, 'We were a couple of monsters, you and me.' And she said, 'Well, sure, but you always loved your mother.' I liked that she said that.

*Did she ever show her emotions?*

What? *Anita?* Are you fucking kidding?

*No, your mother!*

Oh, not really. My mum was not one to make a fuss. She was very forbearing, but she went through some very tough stuff in her own life, very tough indeed. I think that was a generational thing, though, that kind of quiet stoicism, and maybe an Australian thing, too. But she was not in any way remote or cold or uncaring. Quite the opposite. It's just that she never spoke of her own feelings, or her own pain, at least until the end, when she finally opened up about it. But I think even that was her way of protecting her children, of keeping them inoculated against life's cruelties.

*That is definitely a generational thing.*

Yes, and in that context I did feel uncomfortable to a degree about the public nature of my life. I always thought my mother must have found it quite confronting given that she was essentially a private person. I was aware that the public nature of my grief, for example, in which I was complicit, might have felt uncomfortable for her and my family. Although, when she saw *One More Time with Feeling*, she rang me up and told me how brave she thought the film was, and how moved she was by it. I was surprised by that, and then she started talking about Dad. I think seeing the film loosened something up in her, or maybe gave her the license to be able to speak about things she hadn't really before, at least to me. She talked very openly about my father's death and certain complicating issues around that, and how it impacted on her. It was very affecting.

*All these years later, she finally talked about it.*

Yes, and it was not that you couldn't or weren't allowed to go there, it was more that she just got on with things and didn't make a fuss. And, of course, I was probably too self-absorbed to have started up a discussion like that.

*I think that's very much what that generation did. And, I have to say, I quite admire that kind of stoicism and forbearance.*

Yes, I really admire it, too. I think we could all learn from it. However, it can also create an environment where things aren't really addressed, and lead to an avoidance of the stuff that ultimately matters, the difficult stuff, the uncomfortable stuff.

Anyway, there is much I regret about my behaviour towards my mother. I wish I had been in a position where I was mature enough to have acknowledged her enormous pain and helped her with it, but for most of my life I was a furious whirlwind of self-absorption, with little time for others. That, too, is a source of deep regret. Children need their parents, but parents need their children, too. Sometimes it's all they have. I have learned that.

*Was your mum religious in any way?*

No. She actually told me she envied those who were religious, but she just couldn't bring herself to fully believe.

*A bit like you, then.*

Oh no, Seán, I believe. Especially today.

*She sounds like a very level-headed person, your mum.*

She was kind and fair and had very definite ideas about common decency and good manners. In a way, she was the embodiment of civility and doing the right thing, but she was not a saint. She possessed a dry, dark, wicked sense of humour, which often took the form of the quiet, acerbic, well-placed remark. She would say something under her breath that was not exactly sarcastic, but made it perfectly clear she was unimpressed by certain pretensions.

*It must have been very difficult for you not to be able to go and see her.*

Yes, not being able to go to Australia was tough. I couldn't visit her in the hospital or go to her funeral. I had to see her from afar on my sister Julie's iPhone, lying there on the bed in the hospital. It was tough, very tough, just to see my darling sister holding it all together, and my mother barely conscious. And then there was the funeral — or Zoomeral, as my son, Earl, bleakly called it. It was a reduced affair, and socially distanced, of course. And yet, despite its obvious shortcomings, it was still a tribute to an extraordinary woman. If there is ever a time to come together, to hug, to be close, it's a funeral, but the stringent protocols around the virus made this impossible. God, this pandemic is full of grim ironies, dying by Zoom being one of them.

*I don't particularly like the word 'closure', but has it been difficult to grieve given all that?*

Well, yes, to be honest. Sometimes I will even literally forget for a moment that my mother has died. I mean, just recently one of the Royal Family wore a Vampire's Wife dress and I was just about to email the picture to my mum, who loved the Queen, being exactly the same age, and I realised suddenly, shockingly, that she was not there to receive it. It was a real jolt.

I mention all this because so many people have written in to

The Red Hand Files having had the same experience. It's a universal phenomenon, a unique consequence of the pandemic that needs to be acknowledged somehow. In many cases the old died alone, more alone than ever, and in Britain, that's saying something.

*When did you last see your mum?*

Well, I haven't been back to Australia since they literally shut the country down and pulled up the drawbridge, so I think the next time will be difficult, too, given that Susie and I would stay with Mum each time we visited. It was just a small unit in Elsternwick, a suburb of Melbourne, and we'd stay there with the kids. Susie always jokes that I've taken her to Australia twenty times but we've never gotten out of Elsternwick. She definitely has a point. And now the house is being sold, which seems odd, too – that it'll be gone. I miss Australia very much – my mother, my family, Melbourne, the physicality of Australia itself, even the bush!

*What did your mother make of your music?*

She went to all my concerts in Melbourne right up till the end. She also went to the In Conversation events. So did my aunt Gwennie, her sister, who is now ninety-five years old and another amazing woman. Gwen and Dawn, two sisters together. Gwennie has a lovely old upright piano in her house in Melbourne, and when I'm on tour in Australia, I go to her house and practise in the mornings and she sits in the other room and listens.

The last time I was in Australia, my mother asked to hear *Ghosteen*. She sat in her wicker chair in the kitchen and listened to it all the way through. She was visibly moved – so visibly that I was concerned about her response and asked her if she was okay. She said, 'This is a very sad record, darling, but a very beautiful one.' Now, the thing was, over the next few weeks, while I was living there with her, I would walk into the kitchen and she would be sitting in her chair listening to it, lost to it, really moved. It was as if it was speaking to her, not just about Arthur, whose death hurt her very deeply, but all the many people a woman of ninety-three has inevitably lost. And, at that age, that's essentially everybody. I was very affected by that. Those were beautiful moments.

*Incredible, really, to have that memory, that connection.*

Yes. Then, as I always did, I left to go back to London, and she stood at the door of her unit, hunched over her walking frame, and waved goodbye, and, as always, there was that unspoken sorrow between us, that this might be the last time we would see each other. And, well, this time it was. I miss her very much.

# 6

# Doubt and Wonder

~

*I know you don't like looking back, but I'm going to throw some of your old quotes at you.*

Really? Must you?

*Don't worry, they're not from interviews. I was re-reading your lecture, 'The Secret Life of the Love Song', from 1998. You wrote, 'the actualising of God through the love song remains my prime motivation as an artist'. Is that still the case?*

Yes, I suppose so. As I've said, the songs I write these days tend to be religious songs in the very broadest sense. They behave as though God exists. They are essentially making a case for belief itself, even though they are at times ambivalent and inconsistent about the existence of God. I guess ultimately what I'm trying to do is to put forward the idea that being alive is of some consequence. That we are of some spiritual value.

I read that interview you sent me, the one with the writer Marilynne Robinson. It's an amazing interview. She's putting forward an idea of religion as essentially reflective and contemplative, that contemplation of the divine is a big part of what it is to be religious. That really chimed with me. Religion is asking the question:

'What if?' And to me, that question is also, in its way, a completely adequate answer. Do you understand what I mean?

*I think so: that it may be enough for us to just contemplate the possibility of God?*

Yes. That is what my songs have asked for some time: 'What if?' A question unencumbered by an answer. Having said that, religion is of little value if it doesn't serve some larger function – the welfare of others.

*Yes, of course. But just to stay with the 'what if' question, does it not in itself leave room for doubt as well as wonder?*

Yes. Doubt and wonder. Well put.

*That's quite a dynamic, though – almost contradictory.*

Well, I think the only way I can fully give myself over to the idea of God is to have the room to question. To me, the great gift of God is that He provides us with the space to doubt. For me at least, doubt becomes the energy of belief.

*That's fair enough, I guess, but it's starting from the premise that God exists and allows us to doubt, which an atheist would argue is essentially flawed logic. What would you say to that?*

Well, Seán, since when has belief in God had anything to do with logic? For me, personally, it is the unreasonableness of the notion, its counterfactual aspect that makes the experience of belief compelling. I find that leaning into these intimations of the divine, that for me do exist, as subtle, softly spoken and momentary as they may be, expands my relationship with the world – especially creatively. Why would I deny myself something that is clearly beneficial because it doesn't make sense? That in itself would be illogical.

*That is certainly an interesting way of looking at things – the rationality of the irrational. Okay, so here's another quote of yours: 'Ultimately the love song exists for me to fill the silence between ourselves and God, to decrease the distance between the temporal and the divine.'*

It's strange to hear these quotes. I don't even know where that essay came from, but I think that is quite aptly put. Songs have a particular power. I don't really know of any other form of expression that has that sense of ascension that can transmit or evoke a sense of rising awe – especially in terms of the collective power of a concert.

*I do wonder how lasting that is, though. Or how transformative it really is. It's kind of hard to measure that.*

Well, perhaps 'transformation' as a word is a little problematic, because transformation essentially means a sudden marked change, and one that has a feeling of permanence. That is not necessarily the effect that music has. Rather, it has the ability to lead us, if only temporarily, into a sacred realm. Music plays into the yearning many of us instinctively have – you know, the God-shaped hole. It is the art form that can most effectively fill that hole, because it makes us feel less alone, existentially. It makes us feel spiritually connected. Some music can even lead us to a place where a fundamental spiritual shift of consciousness can happen. At best, it can conjure a sacred space.

*You actually touched on that idea of spiritual ascension in 'The Secret Life of the Love Song' when you said, 'The love song is the sound of our endeavours to become Godlike, to rise up and above the earthbound and the mediocre.'*

Yes, well, I am not sure about that now. I think, these days, I would be more considerate towards the mediocre in us all. Well, maybe not the mediocre, but our ordinariness, our sameness.

It's interesting that one of the most common concerns from people who write in to The Red Hand Files is a feeling of meaningless or emptiness. Also a deep bitterness and cynicism towards the world, that the world and humanity is essentially shit. And a loneliness, too. I guess what I try to do through the songs and through The Red Hand Files is to make the case that our lives are more valuable than perhaps we sometimes think them to be, or, indeed, than we are told they are. That our lives are, in fact, of enormous consequence, and that our actions reverberate in ways we hardly know.

*Well, to be fair, many atheists would agree with that.*

I'm sure you're right. Still, there seems to be a growing current of thought that tends towards the opposing view, a sort of cynicism and distrust of our very selves, a hatred of who we are, or, more accurately, a rejection of the innate wonder of our presence. I see this as a sort of affliction that is, in part, to do with the increasingly secular nature of our society. There's an attempt to find meaning in places where it is ultimately unsustainable – in politics, identity and so on.

*But, hang on, are you saying atheism – or secularism – is an affliction? And that you equate it with cynicism? I mean, come on, non-believers can have a sense of wonder at the world – with nature, the universe, with the wonders of science, philosophy and even the everyday.*

No, I am not saying secularism is an affliction in itself. I just don't think it has done a very good job of addressing the questions that religion is well practised at answering. Religion, at its best, can serve as a kind of shepherding force that holds communities together – it is there, within a community, that people feel more attached to each other and the world. It's where they find a deeper meaning.

*What kinds of questions, in particular, would you say religion is more adept at answering?*

It deals with the necessity for forgiveness, for example, and mercy, whereas I don't think secularism has found the language to address these matters. The upshot of that is a kind of callousness towards humanity in general, or so it seems to me. And I think callousness comes out of a feeling of aloneness, people feeling adrift or separated from the world. In a way, they look for religion – and meaning – elsewhere. And increasingly they are finding it in tribalism and the politics of division.

*The decline of organised religion may be one reason for that, but there are others, of course, social and political.*

Well, whatever you think about the decline of organised religion – and I do accept that religion has a lot to answer for – it took with it a regard for the sacredness of things, for the value of humanity, in and of itself. This regard is rooted in a humility towards one's place within the world – an understanding of our flawed nature. We are losing that understanding, as far as I can see, and it's often being replaced by self-righteousness and hostility.

*That would seem to be the case. In another lecture from 1996, 'The Flesh Made Word', you talked about the influence of the Old Testament on your earlier songs and how, through that, your songwriting 'blossomed into a nasty new energy'.*

I think that's pretty understandable, given that the Old Testament is full of the most wonderful and violently outrageous stuff – powerful, at least it was for a young man of my apocalyptic tastes! Whereas in the New Testament, particularly the Gospels, the language is softer, but more penetrating.

*When you started to delve into the New Testament, how influential was that on the way you wrote songs? I'm thinking particularly of* The Boatman's Call *(in 1997), in which there was a definite change of tone and, indeed, a different kind of song.*

I think so, yes. When I reacquainted myself with the Gospels, in my thirties, I found the language so beautiful, it touched a need in me. It seeped into everything, especially my songs. There is nothing quite like the Gospels in literature – and the great human drama at its centre, the story of Jesus.

*I have always liked the passage where Jesus loses it and clears the hustlers and money-lenders out of the temple.*

Yeah, well, you would!

*Jesus the anti-capitalist! You also wrote about the particular resonance of the line, 'the kingdom is inside you and outside you', which suggests that it is also possible to have a private and unmediated relationship with the divine.*

Yes. That line gave me a sense that there was some personal agency around the idea of belief, rather than needing the church to deliver it to you. I liked that idea, because on a personal level, at that time, organised religion just didn't do it for me. Even when I was a heroin addict, I was in and out of church, trying to find some relationship with the whole thing. That line helped me form my own relationship with God or belief, something more flexible, and not feel that I had to go somewhere else to find it.

*A song I love from that period is 'Brompton Oratory'. How did it come about?*

Well, it is exactly as it says. I had broken up with Polly Harvey, and I was distraught, to say the least. The song is an explicit description of my situation – sitting in the Brompton Oratory in London, listening to the Gospel –

> *The reading is from Luke 24*
> *Where Christ returns to His loved ones*
> *I look at the stone apostles*
> *Think that it's alright for some*

– and just writing down the song as it happened. But it remained open-ended for a while. I couldn't work out how to finish it, so it just sort of hung around, part-written. Then a couple of months later, I was walking past the massive Pentecostal Church in Notting Hill and these lines sort of dropped out of the sky:

> No God up in the sky
> No devil beneath the sea
> Could do the job that you did
> Of bringing me to my knees

I was very pleased with that. Suddenly I had an ending to the song! Sometimes songs feel like little triumphs over your misfortunes. Little acts of revenge! I wrote the music to it in a flat in Basing Street, off the Portobello Road, on a tiny Casio synth I had bought down the market. The drumbeat is the 'rock' setting on the Casio slowed right down. I have nothing but affection for that song. I'm glad you like it.

*Well, it has that collision of the sacred and profane that is pure Nick Cave. As in the lines:*

> A beauty impossible to endure
> The blood imparted in little sips
> The smell of you still on my hands
> As I bring the cup up to my lips

Yes, that's a wicked little landmine hidden in the song. It has a lovely visceral charge! I love the little rising internal rhyme of 'cup' and 'up'. It's fun to sing.

*Have you heard Mark Lanegan's version?*

Of course! It is amazing – all those seasick horns, and his beautiful, ragged voice. It sounds like a New Orleans funeral march or something. It sounds like an act of love. He made that song his own.

*Given the circumstances of your life at that time, would you say there was a desperation in your religious seeking back then?*

I don't know about that, but I guess they were desperate times. My beliefs, such as they were, were very much a solitary concern. I had plenty of people to take drugs with, but very few who would accompany me into a church. It wasn't really desperation, though, but it was more than 'vague spiritual beliefs'. Ever heard of that term?

*No, where does it come from?*

When I went to my first rehab, they presented me with a list to fill in: twenty things that were indicators of whether I was a drug addict/alcoholic or not. One of them was 'Vague spiritual beliefs'. I always thought that was kind of funny – you know, you're damned if you do, and you're damned if you don't – it suggested that my going to church was just a symptom of my sickness. Maybe they were right.

*You have lived your life between extremes – heroin and God.*

I guess. Yes. I don't know. Maybe.

*And not one after the other – it's revealing somehow that you were exploring the divine even when you were using.*

I guess that's true. But it could be that using heroin and the need for a sacred dimension to life were similar pursuits, in that they were attempts, at that time, to remedy the same condition.

*Which was?*

A kind of emptiness, I guess, and a *hunger*.

*A hunger for what?*

More.

*Does that go back to your childhood? Or was it pretty uneventful in a typically small-town way?*

Well, in my child's world, growing up in Wangaratta was anything but uneventful. My memories of childhood are in their essence idyllic. I had the kind of uncomplicated, free-range childhood I wish I had been able to offer my own kids. Growing up in an

Australian town, in the sixties, we had an almost completely unsupervised existence. Mum would essentially shoo us kids out the back door in the morning and we would come back at teatime. I'd go charging around on my bike, collecting up my friends, a little gang of us, roaming around the town. It was like one of those idealised childhoods from a Stephen King novel or a Spielberg film – hanging around the swimming hole, jumping off the railway bridge into the river, climbing up on the foundations of new homes that were being built in my neighbourhood, flattening pennies on the railroad tracks, shooting rabbits, reconnaissance missions up storm drains, catching yabbies, lying on the hot concrete at the swimming pool, checking out the girls, smoking cigarettes. It was a kind of innocent and unbounded paradise.

*What's a yabby?*

It's a freshwater crustacean, a bit like a little crayfish. It lives in muddy dams and you catch it by tying a piece of meat to a length of string and dangling it in the water. When the yabby grabs the meat you carefully pull up the string, then you chuck the yabby in a pot of boiling water and eat the little fucker.

*What do they taste like?*

Muddy.

*I think it's fair to say that, in the past, you haven't been entirely kind to the town of Wangaratta.*

Well, ultimately I grew up. I went from a rascally little kid to a feral teenager and I started to look beyond the life I had. What had been, as a child, a kind of unbounded Eden started to shrink and feel cramped and stifling as my dreams got bigger. I just thought there was more life to be lived out there. Wangaratta was no longer enough.

I started having serious behavioural problems at the high school where both my parents worked. My father taught Maths and English and my mother was the librarian. It wasn't because I was depressed, or having trouble at home, but just because it was in my nature to cause trouble. My mother told me recently that one of the teachers had taken her aside and told her that she needed to get me out of that school, and out of *the town*, because it would be the end of me if I stayed there. Eventually, they packed me off on a train and sent me to an all-boys' school down in Melbourne – the big city. For better or worse that decision led to a seismic shift for me, an abrupt and absolute severing from my childhood. In Melbourne a different Nick Cave emerged, more problematic, more pissed-off.

*And, to a degree, you directed your pissed-offness at Wangaratta?*

As I started to get some notoriety with the band, I guess I made some ill-advised, disparaging comments to the press about Wangaratta – in particular about its over-zealous police department, some of whom had tended to get more than a bit physical with my two older brothers, on a Saturday night, when they had them alone in a cell. But you say dumb stuff when you're young – that is the very definition of being young, then as now, as far as I can see. But these days, I look back on Wangaratta with nothing but deep gratitude and awe at the unfettered freedom that town gave me as a child – a kind of exalted freedom and innocence I would never find again.

*Have you ever gone back there?*

Funnily enough, I started the In Conversation tour of Australia there back in the summer of 2018. And, of course, the local press had gone out of their way to remind the good people of Wangaratta that I'd called the town 'a shithole' and said some less than flattering things about the local police force. They even had a comment about it from the police chief.

*So how was that experience?*

It was an amazing trip, actually. A bunch of us went up there and we stayed in some weird motel just out of town. Susie came, too, and she walked down the main street of Wangaratta dressed in a long flowing gold lamé dress, everyone hanging out their cars and yelling stuff, honking their horns.

I stood on stage and opened the event by apologising to the people of Wangaratta for the awful things I'd said over the years and asking for their forgiveness. I think they found the whole thing pretty surreal and kind of funny – however, they absolved me of my sins and all was forgiven. It was a great night.

The next day I drove around just reacquainting myself with the place – out by the meat works on the edge of town, up and down the main street, looking for the fish 'n' chip shop, which was no longer there, and the shop where I bought my first pair of flares, also gone, and seeing the lovely old pubs where my teetotaller dad used to buy me a lemonade, then over the overpass, up Mapunga Avenue to my family home, which was still the same, and on towards the high school and the little creek that ran along the bottom where me and my mates found the body of this old dead guy.

*This is starting to sound like a Nick Cave song!*

Exactly, and then to the swimming hole where I spent so much of my childhood, which was completely unchanged except that someone had stencilled a giant Banksy-style Nick Cave on the pylons of the bridge I used to jump off.

Finally we stopped at the cathedral where I sang in the choir. The dean opened it up and took us around. It was Christmas time, and he showed me the plaster nativity scene – some vandals had tried to pull the head off the infant Jesus the night before. So when I got back to Melbourne, I sent a letter to the dean saying I would happily pay to have the baby Jesus' head reunited with his body. That led to a local newspaper headline: 'Former choirboy Nick Cave to fund repairs of partially decapitated baby Jesus.' I liked that.

*Priceless! And 'Sad Waters', an early song of yours that I really love, came out of your time there.*

Yes, 'Sad Waters' is a true description of the place by the river where we used to swim, and where I would spend so much time as a boy. The willows and exposed tree roots, where we 'plaited all the willow vines', that was the shallow wading area.

*It's an incredibly evocative lyric:*

> *We go down to the river where the willows weep.*
> *Take a naked root for a lover's seat.*

Well, thank you. It's funny you should mention 'Sad Waters', because I've never been so happy about a song. I remember going back from Hansa studio in Berlin, in the early hours of the morning, to my girlfriend Elisabeth's apartment in Schöneberg, and sitting on the bed and playing it over and over, with a big smile on my face. It had something that the best Bad Seeds music has – that profoundly casual, almost offhand way of recording something so that it retains its rawness and stark beauty. And I really like the lyric, too. The last verse is beautiful.

> *Mary in the shallows laughing*
> *Over where the carp dart*
> *Spooked by the new shadows that she cast*
> *Across these sad waters and across my heart*

*It's a beautifully seductive song: the strange, almost disconnected dreaminess of the delivery really evokes the sense of longing and languor that is such an integral part of childhood.*

Yes, and I have another song, 'Give Us A Kiss', that is also essentially sung from the point of view of a child, and describes first love and Wangaratta perfectly. And 'Red Right Hand', too, is basically set there. Those were innocent and uncomplicated days. The moment my parents put me on the train that would take me to Melbourne, things changed, you know, in that instant: things changed dramatically and for ever.

*Do you want to try to describe what happened to you afterwards?*

It's funny you should ask this, Seán, because I just finished *Boy on Fire*, Mark Mordue's biography of my early life. He sent me an early copy to see what I thought. Incidentally, I really tried to stop him publishing it.

*I didn't know that, but it's making me nervous!*

Ha! It was just that so much time had passed since I agreed to it, and so much has happened. At some point, I just thought, I don't want a biography written about me. I used every method of emotional blackmail at my disposal, because, well, he is a friend.

*I read a proof copy of the book and I thought Mordue came across as pretty reasonable. I'm interested to hear what you think of it.*

I don't know. I think mostly it's pretty much about a small scene in Melbourne back at a certain time in history, and I wonder who would find it that interesting.

*Hardcore Nick Cave fans, I guess.*

Maybe. The book revealed a lot about my father's death that I didn't know. I just knew the basic information around his death – the scant threads you pick up at the time that form part of your story, but are not necessarily accurate. Mark went into it in quite a detailed way.

*Did that upset you at all?*

It was jarring to read, for sure, but it made me think about the truths that we think support the story of our lives, but often turn out to be fictions or, at best, half-truths. It seems to me that much of our remembered past, especially around traumatic incidents, is based on assumptions and misunderstandings we collected at the time of the trauma and have gone unchallenged ever since.

*Do you think that is what happened to you with your father's death?*

Yes. And it's kind of understandable that in order to protect us, the young, from a huge, traumatic event, those who love us often tell us the bare minimum. As a result, we end up piecing things together from the scraps we overhear or hear second-hand. At least, for me, it seems that way. It made me think about what our lives actually are, in the end. What are they made of? Are they only semi-fictions, received information and false, or eroded, memories? Are they stories you've told about yourself so many times, and shaped and reshaped, that have very little relation to the truth?

*There's that famous Joan Didion line – 'We tell ourselves stories in order to live' – which gets to the heart of our need for narratives that make sense of, or impose order on, our meandering lives. I guess it's a way of making the cold, hard truths more palatable.*

Yes, and even our recent history is like that, insofar as we tell and retell a story so many times that it becomes a kind of fiction. It makes me think that maybe the traumatic events, the sharp, horrific pictures that live in our bodies, that leap up at us in the middle of the night, are the only authentic memories we have. The memories that are so devastating that they refused to be adjusted. The rest of our memories are a smattering of tall stories that exist to give our lives shape.

*Actually, it's fascinating, particularly in relation to other people's stories or received ideas about you. From talking to you, I think that's something you find frustrating.*

I find my own story, my own history, unbearable, mostly – at least, the one that is constantly trotted out. Not that I feel ashamed of it; rather, I find it wearying, exhausting. I don't like biography as a form, really. I don't tend to read it.

*Boy on Fire* does tend to put everything that happened to me, my various addictions and antisocial behaviour, down to the death of my father. That seems to be a little simplistic and probably only partially correct.

*Did you recognise your father in Mordue's description of him?*

Well, he actually comes across quite badly in the book. I knew my father as an inspired, larger-than-life, literary man – always passionate, gesturing wildly, telling stories. But it turns out that he wasn't much liked among my friends. They saw him as an authoritarian figure and a bit of a bully. Personally, I think that's unfair. He was certainly complex and inconsistent like most of us are, and also strangely competitive in perhaps not the most adult of ways. But, for all that, he was a great teacher. Many former students of his have written to me – and indeed wrote to him – to say what an extraordinary teacher he was and how his literature classes had a huge impact on their lives. Perhaps, at his best, that's what he was: a great and inspiring teacher. Not such a bad thing. I loved him very much, you know. I think my friends thought I was always trying to impress him and was never able to.

*Do you think there is any truth in that?*

I'm not sure. The story seems to be that my father died and I went crazy, hurtling wildly off into the world like a mortally damaged soul. But is that what actually happened? I don't know. I guess I have much of my father in me – the extrovert, the contrarian, all the manic impulses.

*That's certainly true! But did you recognise your younger self in the book?*

The character that comes across in the book is someone who was really out of control – a very problematic personality I didn't really recognise that person at all, but I'm happy to concede that we know very little about how we are perceived in the world. It's a biography, after all, which is a literary form that explicitly deals in degraded memories.

*Do you mean memories that have become less reliable over the years? Or even tainted somehow?*

Yes.

*On the other hand, perhaps Mordue's book tells a kind of truth, or tells a story that is true enough.*

Ha! Maybe. But in Mark's version it's like I was just eating up everyone who came near me and taking what I could from them creatively. Now, that is very much a matter of perspective. One of the criticisms aimed at me by people in the book is that I always needed a collaborator, as if that is some kind of weakness, rather than just a self-evident way of making better art – to be open to the ideas of other people, to be helped by other people. Some people he spoke to saw that as almost vampiric or something, but it's interesting, because that kind of criticism almost always comes from people who were not engaged in creating art themselves. They were mainly peripheral, perpetual onlookers who know nothing about what it takes to create something of value.

And if you were to ask me how I defined myself as an artist, I would say I was a collaborator, then and now. It's actually one of the things I am most proud of, that I have had sustained productive relationships with people that have ultimately been mutually bene ficial. I think most of the people I have worked with would agree. I always do my best to amplify and push to the front these people, you know . . . well, more or less.

*I think artists tend to take whatever they can from whoever they can in their formative years. 'Talent borrows; genius steals,' and all that.*

I think I probably just had more drive than a lot of the people around me and I suppose that drive may at times have appeared to some people as monstrous. Or, I don't know, cannibalistic. What I will say is that I can't remember a time in my adult life where I haven't worked every day, and sometimes at a furious pace. I've just kept ploughing on, really, and that's part of what you do as an artist. And I have a genuine love for the process of making things.

*I don't think you have to defend yourself here.*

No, I guess not.

*It's interesting that your mother said that you never shut up when you were a kid. Way back when I first met you, I thought you were shy and a bit awkward in your skin, but you definitely had a presence.*

Yes, people say that. Especially women. 'He was so shy.' Ha! But it was true. I was shy around women. They put me on edge and made me nervous.

*Did you find women threatening?*

No, it was more that they were just too fascinating, too intensely interesting. And men put me on edge, too, when I think about it. But for the opposite reasons.

*So the younger you was shy, but constantly craving attention?*

Yes. An egomaniac with low self-esteem and a sex drive! Definitely a problematic combination. But I'm not like that now, of course, you'll be pleased to know. I'm mild-mannered and compliant.

*Of course. So, in one of your lectures, you said, 'My creative life was an attempt to articulate an almost palpable state of loss that had laid claim to my life.'*

I wish you'd stop reading my old quotes at me. It's just fucking impolite.

*So much for mild-mannered and compliant! But was that the moment you finally acknowledged the 'palpable sense of loss' you experienced when your father died?*

I guess so. I was trying to work things out by confronting the idea that my father had actually died, you know, through writing, through words. I have since come to understand that there is little headway that we can make around grief until we learn to articulate it – speak it, say it out loud, sing about it, write it down, or whatever. There is no place to speak about grief in our regular lives. It's just not done, so we are left with these infernal abstractions that reside in the mind, and that, perhaps, unconsciously impact our behaviour. I think I wrote that essay to try to understand my own feelings of grief, to separate them from my feelings of concern for my mother. It was a belated way to acknowledge that my father's death may have had an impact on me, and not just my mother. At the actual time of my father's death, all I remember thinking was 'What are we going to do about Mum?'

*That's admirable in a way.*

Well, the circumstances around my father's death were, to say the least, difficult. The way I found out. The way Mum found out. For me, there is a sequence of intensely visual pictures around which the trauma of my father's death pivots. I cannot remember anything before or after.

*Can you talk about those particular images that linger in your memory from that time?*

Yes. What I remember is that I'd been arrested for burglary, some minor thing, and I was in the police station with my mother. We were in an adjacent room to the main station, and the policeman was interviewing me, asking me what I did for a living, and I said that I was 'a musician'. He was having difficulty spelling the word, so I was helping him by pronouncing it really slowly – 'muse-ish-yan'.

95

Next, I remember turning around and, through the glass window of the door, seeing Anita and my sister, Julie, walk past, both in tears. Next thing, another cop comes in and says to my mother, 'Mrs Cave, would you come out here, please.' I jump up and say, 'What the fuck's going on?' but they wouldn't let me accompany my mother out of the room.

Then a cop is opening the door to my room and I see my mum sitting there in the main station, with Anita and Julie, and I walk over to her and she looks up and says, 'Nicky, your dad's dead.' The one thing I remember vividly is that, while she was breaking the news to me, there were two policemen in the same room talking about a murdered prostitute, whose body had been found in St Kilda Gardens. Beyond that I recall very little.

*That's often the case when something so traumatic occurs – all this other stuff happens simultaneously at the absolute worst moment. There's a dreadful absurdity to it all.*

Yes, and I think we contain these traumatic memories in the cells of our body, in our blood, in our bones.

*When you describe it, it sounds like such a seismic event, which it obviously was, but you buried it somehow? Or transferred it?*

Well, I just focused on my mum and her pain. I have another little scrap of memory from then. I was driving back from the police station with Mum and she said, 'I loved that man down to his boots.' And I was thinking, 'Oh God, what are we going to do with Mum?' That is what I was thinking throughout it all. 'What are we going to do with Mum?' And not having a fucking clue what to do or how to cope. Being completely and utterly ill-equipped to be of any help. After the police station, I don't remember anything. Not the funeral. Nothing. Next thing, it's four months later and I'm getting on a plane to England.

*And years later, when you finally acknowledged the profound sense of loss you felt after your father's death, you didn't connect it with your heroin use?*

Well, I don't know, Seán, I was already using heroin before my father died. I was well on the way.

*Yes, and you went even deeper — into long-term addiction.*

Yes, that's true. And I really don't know how to talk about that. It's not that I don't want to; I just really don't know how. I mean, you take that drug and eventually you find you have a habit, in that if you stop taking the drug, you get sick. So you keep taking it and the habit deepens. Eventually, it feels like there is simply no other option: take the drug and feel good, or don't take the drug and be very sick indeed. It's not rocket science.

*Could we maybe discuss it in the context of your work? It's always intrigued me that heroin didn't seem to compromise your creativity.*

Well, who's to say that it didn't?

*It certainly didn't seem to dent your work rate. You were always very prolific.*

I guess.

*When did you finally get clean, by the way?*

I gave up about twenty years ago. I doubt I would have survived otherwise, even though I was, in the end, a reasonably methodical and conservative heroin addict compared to a lot of people I knew. I wasn't interested in just getting off my face. Well, I was to begin with, but not for most of the time I was on it. I was never interested in taking the kind of drugs that I felt got in the way of the work. I couldn't handle weed or psychedelics for that reason: they fuck with your perception of things. Anyone who can smoke a joint and write a song has abilities I don't fucking possess. Ultimately,

I had a different agenda to many drug users'. Some take drugs because they love the chaos and disorder; I took heroin because it fed into my need for a conservative and well-ordered life.

*Really? That's not just you putting a spin on it retrospectively?*

No. That's what having a habit is, surely. You wake up in the morning with a particular need, you are compelled to score, you score, you shoot up, and, in the evening, you do the same thing again. And that's basically how it goes – around and around. Year in, year out.

*And the ordered life you speak of, how did that go when you were on tour?*

Not great. (*Laughs*) It was actually very difficult, and the cause for all sorts of seriously calamitous situations. Most heroin addicts live constantly on the edge of disorder. The functioning addict lives a relatively ordered life, but take the heroin away and it just turns very quickly to extreme psychological and physical mayhem, where all manner of problems arise.

*Did you ever miss a gig because of your habit?*

I only ever missed one gig in my forty-five years, and I say that with a certain amount of pride, which was the New York show on The Birthday Party's second tour of the USA.

*What happened?*

Well, as I recall, we'd just played a couple of shows in Iceland, where you can't score heroin. I had just gone through three or four very nasty days without using, which meant I had been really sick, but also meant that when I arrived in New York, I wasn't sick any more – I was over the worst of my withdrawal symptoms. Anyway, we were all in a van coming from the airport, heading to the Iroquois Hotel in midtown Manhattan, and I thought I'd better score before I got to the hotel, so I just jumped out of the van and headed to Avenue A. When I got there I could see that there was police activity at either end of the block but there often was, and I thought, fuck it, I'll score anyway. Probably not the best idea I've ever had, but I felt pretty invincible in those days. So I scored a couple of bags of heroin and moved off happily down the street, heading back to the hotel. As I turned the corner at the end of the block a cop appeared out of nowhere, threw me against the wall, and said, fairly convincingly, 'I'm going to ask you one time. Do you have any drugs on you? God help you if you lie to me.' I say, 'Absolutely not, officer,' whereupon the cop opens up the jacket of a weird little lime-green three-piece suit I was wearing at the time and he finds the drugs, cuffs me and throws me into a van with a bunch of other junkies and general desperados. Everyone in the van is looking pretty unhappy because everyone knows they arc going to jail and that by evening everyone is going to be getting real sick — except me, of course, because I've already gone through my withdrawals in Iceland.

When we got to the police station, we're all put into a holding cage full of twenty or so other people, of which I was the only white person. I was also the only person wearing a tiny lime-green three-piece suit. At some point another load of people get thrown into the cage, all black, except one white guy, who sees me and starts screaming out, 'Fuck me! It's Nick Cave! I can't fucking believe it. I'm your biggest fan!' This is not so good, because I am trying my best not to draw attention to myself, which was hard enough, all things considered, so I tell him to leave me alone in no uncertain terms, but he keeps hanging around, just looking at me and shaking his head at the wonder of it all.

After a few hours, a cop calls my name and I go over to him, and through the wire of the cage he tells me I am allowed one phone call. This is good news because I have a gig that night and I need to alert the band to my situation. So the cop asks me for a number to call, I say I want to call the Iroquois Hotel, and the cop says, 'Okay. How do you spell it?' Well, under the general stress of the situation I can't even begin to think how to spell 'Iroquois'. I say, 'I don't know. Do you have a phone book?' and the cop just laughs and moves off and I don't get my phone call. This is not good because the band need to know that I won't be coming to the show tonight.

Eventually, they throw me in a cell with a Mexican guy, who is already starting to get real sick, cramping up and vomiting and stuff, which is not so bad because there is only one place to lie down, an iron bunk, and he is too fucked-up to fight for it, so I stretch out and wait for morning.

There was a row of cells and all the people in the cells were heroin addicts and everybody is starting to get sick and so the noise is really ramping up. Some guy in the next cell is screaming at the police the whole night, he's flooding his cell and abusing the cops, and everyone is yelling at him to shut the fuck up, and all the rest of it. Some transsexual in the next cell has managed to cut herself, the Mexican guy is getting sicker and sicker and is now rolled up in a ball on the floor of the cell, sobbing and praying.

The next day comes and I don't know what's going on – there is absolutely no information. At some point they bring me a pastrami sandwich, which was literally the most melancholy thing I've ever seen, and I'm eating it when Mick Harvey turns up with a carton of duty-free cigarettes. He had rung around all the hospitals and police stations and found me. He has a minute with me and I tell him that I have no idea when I am getting out and he gives me the cigarettes, leaves, and I just wait.

Eventually, we are all put in a big holding cage to await arraignment, I think. This cage is heaving with people and I'm sitting there, once again the only white guy, holding my carton of cigarettes, in my green suit. A strung-out black guy comes up to me and asks for a cigarette. I give him one. Another guy comes up and says, 'Dude, never give away anything in here. You charge a dollar a cigarette or these animals will eat you alive.' Something like that. So the next guy who comes up and asks for a cigarette,

I charge a dollar, which he happily pays. After a while there is a line of people all wanting a cigarette and all with a dollar in their hand. I'm finding this a little uncomfortable, to be honest, on so many levels, but sort of going with the flow. Later that day, they let me out, no one says anything, I don't have to go to court, nothing, and that's that – time served. 'Turnstile justice', they call it.

But, Seán, that's the thing: heroin addiction is all right until it's not. It quickly escalates – very quickly, actually. Chaos is always just around the corner. And these kinds of rock and roll stories may be funny but they obscure a lot of darkness and pain.

This is why personally I think heroin should be legalised. Users should be allowed to go someplace where they are supervised and given medical-grade heroin twice a day, where they can inject it, cleanly and safely, so they have the opportunity to lead relatively functional lives and avoid the danger and chaos that goes hand in hand with its illegality.

*I agree. Whatever the policy is here, it's not working. Just out of curiosity, did you feel you could quit at any time until you actually tried to and failed?*

In the beginning, yes, although I kind of suspected its grip was pretty tight. I remember being on tour in a motel in Brisbane with a girl and we couldn't score, and I started to feel a deep sense of unease – this just got worse and worse as the day went by, a terrible restlessness, a sickness – and I said to the girl, 'I think I've got the flu or something.' She shook her head and said, 'No, you've got a habit, baby.'

Ultimately, I went through many years, a decade, seemingly powerless to do anything about it. In the end, I found out that there was a choice that I could make about whether or not I wanted to go on living the way I was, but at the time, it didn't feel like that. It really didn't. I would get clean and then, two weeks later, a voice in my head, an actual voice, would start saying, 'Go on, go and score. It's okay.' And that voice would get more and more insistent and there was nothing I could do that would make it go away except go and score.

*What did that voice sound like — nagging, hectoring, insidious?*

It sounded like me.

*You do have a ferocious work ethic. Maybe that helped in the end.*

Yes, well, I always worked hard, if that's what you call what I do. It rarely seems like work. It feels like a kind of engagement with the better side of myself. And that's what probably kept me alive. I always did the work.

But, Seán, isn't all this kind of pointless? I really don't like talking about taking drugs. I just find it so, I don't know, tired and un-interesting.

*I can understand that but, to be fair, it was a big part of your life — and your creative life.*

Is that what we're doing here? Talking about my life? Reminiscing about the bad old days in the middle of a fucking pandemic?

*I don't want to reminisce. It's more about trying to put in perspective where you are now in terms of what you have come through.*

Let's leave that to the biographers. Back then, it was a different time and a different energy. It was mayhem. Violent. But work-wise, creatively, things are more intense for me now. They have reached a kind of fever pitch. There is a feeling that Warren, my band and my team are involved in something, or attempting something, in a way that isn't being done by anyone else and that hasn't been done before. There's intensity towards the work that is just growing as things progress. It feels like it shouldn't be that way, that there would be a natural easing off, a slowing down with age, but that is just not the case. Not so far at all. I don't know what's happening, but there is a kind of freedom, where I am no longer tied up, in any way, by the expectations of others – a sweet sort of unbounded freedom – where literally anything can happen.

*Well, it must help that you're living a more organised life now, domestically and creatively. And you have people around you who are efficient. That probably wasn't the case back then.*

There certainly is that. I have a small team of people – Rachel, Molly, Suzi and Beth – who are ferociously efficient and very smart and not to be trifled with. And Christina, who works with me on Cave Things. Amazing people. And Susie, of course, whose influence over everything is deep and far-reaching, to say the least. It's very impressive to see people working with that level of efficiency and dedication and competency. I like to be surrounded by competent people, where you just have an idea and it gets done. It's a kind of bliss!

*It just makes life so much easier.*

Yes there is something beautiful about walking into a room where everyone knows what they are doing. Personally, I have found that a disciplined and structured workplace encourages a certain kind of free-range creativity that chaos is just not conducive to. It actually allows for a kind of disarray of the creative mind – as I said, a beautiful freedom.

*Listening to all of this, I can't help thinking of the time we first met at that infamous NME interview in 1987 with you and Shane and Mark E Smith. As I recall, you were not long out of rehab then.*

That was just after my first time in rehab. I had just come out the day before.

*No way!*

Fresh out of rehab, and off to do an interview with Mark E Smith and Shane MacGowan. What could possibly go wrong?

*That really can't have been a good environment for you, considering what was going on that afternoon.*

It was not easy, Seán, that interview situation. I mean, those two guys were my heroes. They were the two people of my generation who could actually write! Suddenly, I'm clean and sober and they're like, 'What the fuck? You can't be serious,' as they sat there chucking down drugs and drinking themselves into oblivion. They were hardly sympathetic to my situation.

*The opposite, in fact. I could sense, even amid the mayhem, that you were having a hard time, but I had no idea how hard.*

I was like a snail with its shell ripped off its back. I was really hanging by a thread. You brought Shane there, didn't you?

*Yes, he was so nervous about meeting you he took two tabs of acid that morning. It was crazy, but not uncharacteristic.*

And Mark, Christ, he was fucking rabid. But, in a way, I was worse, a million times worse. I was straight and out in the world for the first time in fifteen years! I got through that day somehow, but it didn't last very long.

*I remember Shane was horrified when I mentioned that I'd heard you'd cleaned up. He wanted to turn the taxi round and go back home. Seriously.*

I can totally believe it. The first time I started drinking again after my first rehab, I met Shane in a pub in Portobello Road. I'd met him a few times in bars before and not had a drink. We had become good friends and, this time, when he asked me what I wanted, I said, 'I'll have a double vodka.' And I will never forget his face. I saw it light up like a child's. He was just so happy.

*I can imagine. Mad, really, when you think about it.*

I know. Incorrigible. But things are different now. When all's said and done, to be straight, and to be sixty-three, and still working in this business, on my own terms, there is something gratifying about that.

*Okay. That's it for looking back, I sense.*

Yes, that's it for looking back. But there's something else I want to say if I can find the right words.

The thing that happened that changed everything was that Arthur died. Talking about this stuff, the past, all these stories, feels like I am speaking about another person, a different life. It feels like I am recounting stories from across a deep divide. The stories hold no real value to me and all seem slightly beside the point. I can talk about these things, the drugs and all that, but the past has no purchase, no intrinsic meaning. It represents a whole life that has been severed and cut adrift from the life I lead now. That is why I tried to stop Mark Mordue's biography. I had a strange, unsettling feeling that the past no longer applied. The past had become irrelevant.

*Just to be clear, you were on a different path before Arthur died.*

Yes, but Arthur's death literally changed everything for me. Absolutely everything. It made me a religious person – and, Seán, when I use that word 'religious', you do understand the way that I am using it, right? We've talked about that enough for you to understand I am not talking about being a traditional Christian or something like that. I am not even talking about a belief in God, necessarily. It made me a religious person in the sense that I felt on a profound level a kind of deep inclusion in the human predicament, really, and an understanding of our vulnerability and the sense that, as individuals, we are, each of us, imperilled.

*You feel that we are imperilled?*

Yes. Insofar as anything can turn catastrophic at any time, personally, for each of us. Look at this pandemic. Look how unbelievably vulnerable we are. All these systems supposedly holding the world in place and we are laid low by a virus. Each life is precarious, and some of us understand it and some don't. But certainly everyone will understand it in time. And because of that, I feel a kind of empathy with people that I never felt before. It feels urgent and new and fundamental. For the predicament we have all found ourselves in − the predicament of an imperilled life.

*That sheds light on everything we've been talking about, really.*

Well, just to go back to music for a moment, and this is a bit off the point, I always heard that kind of compassion in Shane's songs and his music, and I loved him for it, but at the same time I never fully understood it. The genuine love he felt for people. I never understood it, but I do now. And I believe that is because I became a person after my son died. Not part of a person, a more complete person. Do you know what I mean?

*I'm trying to take in what you've just said.*

Well, it happened to you, right? You said how capsizing it was when your younger brother died. Do you not feel that something fundamentally changed inside you, on an almost cellular level?

*For me, there was a point I reached where I thought, I have to find a way to go on or I'll go under. That was a turning point, but it took a while to get there.*

You either go under, or it changes you, or, worse, you become a small, hard thing that has contracted around an absence. Sometimes you find a grieving person constricted around the thing they have lost; they've become ossified and impossible to penetrate, and, well, other people go the other way, and grow open and expansive.

But what I want to say is this: this will happen to everybody at some point — a deconstruction of the known self. It may not necessarily be a death, but there will be some kind of devastation. We see it happen to people all the time: a marriage breakdown, or a transgression that has a devastating effect on a person's life, or health issues, or a betrayal, or a public shaming, or a separation where someone loses their kids, or whatever it is. And it shatters them completely, into a million pieces, and it seems like there is no coming back. It's over. But in time they put themselves together piece by piece. And the thing is, when they do that, they often find that they are a different person, a changed, more complete, more realised, more clearly drawn person. I think that's what it is to live, really — to die in a way and to be reborn. And sometimes it can happen many times over, that complex reordering of ourselves.

So, to return to what we talked about at the beginning of this conversation — the religious impulse . . . It seems, for some of us, the religious experience awaits the devastation or a trauma, not to bring you happiness or comfort, necessarily, but to bring about an expansion of the self — the possibility to expand as a human being, rather than contract. And, afterwards, we feel a compulsion, too, a need to pass the message on like missionaries of grief or something.

*Were you angry at the world after Arthur died?*

No, I was in despair. I don't think anger was part of it. Not for me, although who knows what boils away inside us. Susie, of course, entered a circle of hell that is reserved solely for mothers who lose their children. It's a whole other level of loss and suffering, a terrible, terrible thing to happen to anyone. There are all sorts of feelings tied up in it, guilt and shame and self-loathing so primal, yet so complex, they are near impossible to unravel.

*I guess people in the main don't know how to deal with other people's grief and loss. It's something you almost have to learn for yourself.*

Yes, that's a very good point. We must not be denied the opportunity to learn from the experience itself. But as I keep saying, we don't have the language for it. Or maybe language itself is not up to the task, so it's hard to discuss. Perhaps the cultures that encourage people to dress in black and just wail, maybe that is the most articulate response.

*But you both came through somehow. That's the extraordinary thing.*

I think we both worked out that we could be happy and that happiness was a form of insubordination in the face of, I don't know, life, I guess. It was a choice. That's it, a choice, a kind of earned and considered arrangement with the world, to be happy. No one has control over the things that happen to them, but we do have a choice as to how we respond. There was a defiance there, in the face of the world's indifference and apparent casual cruelty.

*A defiance, but also an acceptance?*

Well, the thing I found helpful was the realisation that it is commonplace. Grief is as ordinary or commonplace as love. I sing about it at the end of *Ghosteen* when I tell the story of Kisa and the mustard seed.

*It seems to me like a kind of parable or a fable.*

Yes, it's the story of Kisa Gotami and the Buddha. Kisa has a baby that she thinks is sick and she runs around the village trying to get help, but the villagers can see that the baby has actually died, and they tell her to bury her baby in the forest. In despair, Kisa consults the Buddha. The Buddha tells Kisa to go around house to house and collect a mustard seed so they can make a potion to make the baby well again. But he tells her she can only get the mustard seed from the houses where no one has died. So Kisa does that, but, of course, every household she visits has had someone die. She comes back to the Buddha without any mustard seeds, but with the realisation that she is part of a great river of humanity, where everyone has suffered loss. Kisa then accepts that her child has died. She can then go and bury her baby.

*There's a lot to think about in all of this. I'm not sure where to go next, to be honest.*

Well, when I start telling stories of the Buddha, it's probably time to stop!

*I really appreciate your talking about this stuff, Nick. I really didn't expect you to.*

I really don't think we can not talk about it if we are talking about the creative process. It's simply part of the whole thing. The creative process is not a part of one's life but life itself and all that it throws at you. For me, it was like the creative process, if we want to call it that, found its real purpose. But that's another subject. Maybe we can talk about these things in short bursts.

*Yes, that's probably a good idea.*

You know, I was just thinking, and I don't know how to exactly say this, and please don't misunderstand it, but since Arthur died I have been able to step beyond the full force of the grief and experience a kind of joy that is entirely new to me. It was as if the experience of grief enlarged my heart in some way. I have experienced periods of happiness more than I have ever felt before, even though it was the most devastating thing ever to happen to me. This is Arthur's gift to me, one of the many. It is his munificence that's made me a different person. Susie, too. We've never felt more engaged in things. I say all this with huge caution and a million caveats, but I also say it because there are those who think there is no way back from the catastrophic event. That they will never laugh again. But there is, and they will.

# 7

## A Radical Intimacy

~

*We spoke on the phone a little while back, when you were just starting to work on some new material. You were feeling quite daunted by the prospect, which surprised me.*

Well, writing songs is daunting. It isn't a case of skipping through the fields, merrily picking up songs and putting them in your basket. It's a bloody business, particularly at the beginning. You start from a point of deprivation, of nothingness, of complete lack. And that's when you're confronted with yourself minus your ideas, the very things that normally insulate you from all the ingrained negative bullshit about yourself and your capabilities that lives inside you like a curse.

*Do those kinds of doubts still assail you, even after all this time?*

Yes! You'd think that after writing around two hundred and fifty songs or whatever it is, things would get better, but I haven't found that to be the case. It's the terror of aloneness, of not having the support of a collaborator. It's a condition of being.

*Is it the fear of the blank page?*

I don't know if it's that exactly, because the way I write songs is perhaps different from many songwriters. I don't write continuously. Instead, I'll put an actual date in my diary for when I will begin writing the next record. And that date is the starting point, the initial action towards making a record. I don't start with notebooks full of ideas, scraps of dialogue, cool lines, or even interesting titles – indeed anything collected during the time leading up to that date. I don't take notes in that way. Not for songs, anyway. All the lyric-writing gets done from the ground up in an allotted time. I start with a new, blank notebook, an idea-free mind and a considerable amount of anxiety.

*I'd assumed you were someone who writes all the time, but you literally begin with nothing at all, not even some rough ideas.*

Well, if I'm lucky I do have some basic images in my head that I can build things around. I had a lot of those images when writing *Ghosteen*, which we've talked about already. In that regard, *Ghosteen* was very giving – it was full of pictures that were there in my head before I discovered the words to bring those primary images to life.

*So did you have a guiding image in your head for these new songs?*

Sort of. I had a few such images, the main one being a vision of a giant ice sculpture of a man, most likely me, melting in the sun.

*As a starting point, that's pretty out there. Where did that image come from? Do you even know?*

I think it may have been prompted by the image of the toppled Edward Colston statue in Bristol. I think it was probably to do with that, but I can't be sure. But even still, the narrator as an ice sculpture, lying on his side, made of frozen human tears, melting in the midday sun, is not a bad start for a record. I've written records with a lot less.

*Yes, but why that image in particular?*

I guess because I relate to it. It feels like an image that sums up where I am at this point in time. It feels rich with intent, a generous image.

*So, metaphorically, you're a melting ice sculpture made of human tears? The deeper meaning of that image, when it arrives, should be intriguing.*

Indeed. That's what I have to find out.

*You certainly seem more positive now than you did when we had that earlier conversation, which, by the way, was one of the things that planted the seed for this book. It got me thinking about the psychological process of making a record, from the very first impulse to completion. In your case, it seems to begin from an acute sense of anxiety.*

That is very true. And, not only that, but the next part of the process, which is to find the words that can support these primary images, is where the real trouble begins. That's when the self-doubt really takes hold. That's where I was when we had that conversation a month or so ago.

*Can you talk about how that anxiety manifests itself?*

Practically, it begins with a lot of note-taking. I'm basically writing down lines that come to my head – ideas, images and so forth – but the problem with that is these notes, on their own, are not very promising. In fact, they are mostly meaningless – just piles of words that, at the time, seem to amount to little more than the evidence of my failure as a songwriter. And then, day after day, I find myself drifting into a really unhappy, even depressed state. What's even worse is that this chain of events has been repeating itself for thirty years or more – maybe even forty!

*How bad does it get?*

Well, for a start, I'm just horrible to be around. Susie will usually pick up on it early on and say something like, 'Ah, have you started writing songs again?' And I'll be, 'Why!?' And, she'll say, 'You've got that look.' And I'm like, 'Well, nothing is fucking coming!' And she'll say, 'Well, nothing ever comes until it does.' As far as Susie is concerned, I've been doing this for years, like a goldfish going around and around a fishbowl, saying, 'Nothing is coming. Nothing is coming.' The creative process can be so demeaning.

*So it's a pattern of behaviour. Maybe you should see a therapist?*

Oh, thanks! But, yes, I guess it is a bit odd that, even though I have made many records and I should know this always happens, no matter how inevitable or familiar it is, it can still plunge me into quite a distressing place, where I'm besieged by the worst, most counter-productive thoughts. It's actually quite extreme, because it affects everything: my relationships with people, my capacity for tolerance. It casts everything in a bad light. For me, it's the perennial drama of songwriting. And then suddenly it changes. The lights come on. Things start falling into place.

*What precipitates the change – just having a breakthrough of some sort on the ideas front?*

Well, the thing is, even though the notebooks are full of meaningless words, there are always little bits in there that in time begin to rise off the page. They start to shimmer. It's like those classic spy movies, where someone is trying to break a code. They're staring at random numbers or letters that seem to mean nothing and then suddenly something appears as if by magic out of the mess. You see a line run from one letter to the next, and it all begins to make sense. The code has been cracked!

With songwriting, there are always these little glimmers embedded in all the scrambled nonsense and false starts and failed ideas. They're buried in there like clues. What happens is that they suddenly present themselves, rise from the page, and begin to hold hands. Not all at once, necessarily, but quite rapidly, and then you start to get a creative momentum, a kind of collecting together of information that moves towards the basic framing of a song. That's the thrilling part. It's really the best part of songwriting. That's where I am now. The dross is falling away to reveal the songs.

*You do seem a lot more cheerful.*

Well, I've just drunk a pot of coffee, but, yes, I think I might be on to something.

*I don't want to make a big deal of this, but, as I said, it does seem surprising to me that you are still beset by doubts and uncertainty about songwriting at this stage of the game.*

Look, when you begin a record, when you begin to create the songs, all you have are small particles of the greater picture and they seem desperately inadequate. There's always going to be a lot of anxiety around that. Then they begin to fraternise, these tiny particles, and together they start to collect meaning, and, at some point, you know that maybe you have enough. Does that make sense?

*Yes, totally. So, to move away from writing for a moment, do you enjoy being on the road? It always seems to me like the most demanding and repetitive aspect of the musician's life — the constant travelling, the hotels, the sound checks.*

Put like that, it sounds dire, but it's not. It is in some way a natural state of affairs. The airports, the buses, the hotel rooms are all just part of the weird itinerant life of the rock star. Travelling the world but seeing none of it! You get used to it. I get a lot done on those bus rides because I've always had the ability to work under any circumstances. I wrote *Bunny Munro* on the bus. *The Sick Bag Song,* too. I love that book, by the way. *The Sick Bag Song.* Have I told you that? I'm really very proud of that book. As far as writing goes, for me, that's the one.

*What makes it so special for you?*

Well, I had never considered myself a poet, as such. I was a song-writer, and to me there always seemed to be a significant difference. Just because you're a poet and have a facility with words, doesn't mean you can necessarily write a good song lyric, and, of course, it works the other way round as well. I felt I was stepping into an area that I had no formal knowledge of – poetry. But I didn't just put my toe in, I attempted to write a book-length epic poem. I'm not sure what people thought of it. But I liked it. It's audacious and humorous and has a lightness of touch. A friend called it 'jaunty'. I took that as a compliment!

*Okay. But I'm really surprised that you don't write songs when you're on the road.*

Songs are too hard to write on a bus. They ask too much of you. You have to go too deep. When you write a book or a screenplay, or, indeed, an epic poem, you can quite easily fall into the slipstream of the work where the writing takes over and, in fact, becomes difficult to stop. I don't have that with songwriting, I'm sad to say. I never have. Songwriting is too confronting.

*What are you confronting, exactly? Your vulnerability? Your perceived limits?*

Let me try to explain it this way. In my experience, being on the road requires a certain amount of bluff and bravado. This bravado is not a posture: it is a survival mechanism. You don't complain. You don't moan. You push on through. Because touring is actually hard to do. I understand that it's not working down the coalmines, of course, but it has its own struggles. You stagger onto the bus for an eight-hour trip to the next town, and it's 7.30 in the morning, and you've had three hours' sleep, and you're still fucked-up from the sleeping pills you've had to take, because on tour you never just get into bed and go to sleep – you have to knock yourself out. And you look like shit and your voice has gone and your knees are skinned and weeping from knee drops and you've fucked your back, and you have a urinary tract infection, and last night's Mexican is still roiling away, you think you're getting the flu, and the hotel has lost your laundry, and you fucking hate everybody, and you look at Warren and he says, 'How are you?' and you punch the air and you say, 'Fucking awesome, man!' because you know he is in precisely the same condition. And you sit down and the bus moves off and Warren says, because he's ten years younger and terminally fascinated by the world and has had sixteen coffees, 'Fuck, I saw this documentary last night on Iranian New Wave cinema. Just *amazing*. Have you seen it?' and you say no, and then off Warren goes. The point I'm trying to make is that you don't want to then engage in some parallel occupation that makes you feel even worse, that picks away at your self-regard, makes you feel smaller or emptier or insignificant or a failure, or plunges you into a dark place that you have to climb back out of, or makes you cry, or makes you despair. Songwriting does that. Songwriting would be essentially the last straw. It's just too fucking hard. So you write a book instead, or a screenplay, or an epic poem, or design a T-shirt, or something.

*Sorry, I'm just not buying that. You love being on the road.*

Okay, yes, true.

*On stage, it seems like you have this whole other persona that you can step into at will: a more confident, more dramatic, more exaggerated self. Is that the case?*

I'm not sure it is a persona. I see it more as a manifestation of a kind of essentialness.

*So you feel more alive, more essentially yourself in some way, when you perform for an audience?*

Well, we come together around a shared objective, not just with the band but the audience as well, something that unites and raises the collective soul. There is also a loss of self, a sense of being swept up by something larger. Where can we access this feeling these days, you know, outside a church?

*So, for you, what is the shared objective?*

To be awed. To experience a communal sense of awe. I can feel it on stage and see it in people's eyes. And I experience it too. It's certainly something I have felt many, many times at other artists' concerts. It's about reaching an essential and shared state through music – sometimes for a moment, sometimes for an entire concert. We've all experienced that. Not just a physical release, although there is that, too, but to be held by an artist at the crucial moment of expression – to be awed, second by second, at the way a song or piece of music unfolds, to be held on the edge of tears by the drama of it all, and to be, as an audience member, an essential participant in the drama itself. That is a wonderful thing.

*Maybe you could tell me about some of the times you've experienced that yourself – as an audience member rather than a performer.*

With Nina Simone, of course, and The Saints, many times. Neubauten in their prime. The Dirty Three. I experienced it the first time I saw Crime and the City Solution in some shithole in Sydney in the late seventies – a kind of crucial beauty. Swans. The Cramps. Johnny Cash. Emmylou Harris singing at a Hal Willner event, Led Zeppelin in Kooyong Park in Melbourne back in the mid-seventies, Bryan Ferry singing 'The Butcher Boy' alone at the piano, Bob Dylan in a tiny club in Rio.

So thank God, quite literally, for music, because it's one of the last remaining places, beyond raw nature, that people can feel awed by something happening in real time, that feeling of reverence and wonder. Fucking Al Green running up and down the aisles, screaming his head off, a James Blood Ulmer gig in a tiny club in London, Martin Rev's legendary fifteen-minute gig upstairs at the Garage in Islington, back in the nineties. These are sacred moments.

*Sacred and profane, in most instances. As someone who can still vividly remember the implosive, often chaotic energy of The Birthday Party back in the day, it was really fascinating to experience the fragile intensity of the* Skeleton Tree *show I went to in London.*

Personally, I think there was an emotional intensity to the *Skeleton Tree* concerts that was unlike anything I have been involved with before. I feel proud of the journey I've made from the mayhem of the Birthday Party concerts to the kind of emotional purity of the *Skeleton Tree* concerts, just in terms of the distance that has been travelled.

*What struck me was how reverent the atmosphere was at the O2, which is not the most welcoming venue. It was a long way from the chaos and abandonment of those early gigs, the intensity of the aggression you directed at the audience back then.*

Well, the feeling was mutual. The Birthday Party did attract the most cynical, self-loathing nihilists you could imagine – the sort of people I have never really had any time for, by the way, even back in the day when I was one myself. I did feel a tremendous release when I went on stage, a kind of purifying rage, but I also hated it.

*What did you hate about it, exactly?*

Those early shows were so punishing, just physically punishing. The demands that the audience made on us as a group were extreme, to say the least. Half of them were there with the express purpose of punching Nick Cave in the head, and the other half were there to watch it happen. So, yes, a lot has shifted in that respect. The audience has changed dramatically. These days it is a whole different thing. I'm very happy about that.

*Back then, I guess, it was all about chaos as a creative energy.*

Or chaos as a way of life. Chaos as a matter of principle.

*Can that work for any sustained length of time?*

It just depends where and how it is used. In The Birthday Party, I had a very personal relationship with chaos, which essentially meant wilfully losing control of the outcome of a concert. I am talking purely about myself here. The band, thank God, was actually very tight and on the money – Mick saw to that – and that's where the intensity lay. The concerts only rarely descended into musical pandemonium, no matter how hard I tried.

   On stage, chaos can produce a thrillingly disruptive and confronting energy. I, personally, was very interested in that at the time. Neubauten used chaos beautifully, with their chainsaws and punch-ups. Some of the post-punk bands, too – The Pop Group, Suicide, The Fall. Being on stage for me was just an amplification of the general way of life I was living at the time, but it wasn't a great work ethic. In the end, after many years, I settled for chaos in the mind, order in the workspace.

*Chaos in the mind? That's not something I associate with you these days.*

I mean chaos as a bounty of competing ideas racing around in your head. Maybe what happens when you get older is that you don't have the same battles in the brain as when you were younger, when you just had shit flying all over the place, where you were grabbing at everything and were just so amazed at the workings of your own mind! Instead, you become more focused and just carve away all the non-essential stuff. And, of course, the concerts we do now reach for something entirely different.

*Do you ever feel the weight of the collective reverence the audience have for you when you walk out on stage?*

I don't feel anything but uplifted and energised by the audiences we get now. And I know how to get them to that exalted place, because I go there myself. Especially on the *Skeleton Tree* tour, I just knew what to do. It was thrilling. And, the Bad Seeds played so well. So fucking articulately!

That tour was amazing for me, for all of us. And it wasn't at all dependent on us going out and kicking ass in that traditional rock 'n' roll way. Some of the time, we were playing really quiet, slow songs that had an extraordinary effect. You could feel the deep connection. It's really something else to stand on stage and sing a song that is just trembling quietly on the point of collapse, and to look into the faces of people and to see that they are inside the song with you. It was very, very moving; it felt like there was a kind of radical intimacy taking place. We'd play 'Girl In Amber', say, and all these young faces would stare up at us, just lost to it and in love with the song in a way that older fans might feel about the fervent power of 'Tupelo'. I could feel that it had its own unique meaning to each person, that it spoke to them on some soul level, and brought them deep into that part of themselves. That's the thing – the essential component – that each audience member feels implicit in the experience. It was magnificent – the young and the old and the in-between, all experiencing it together.

*It was certainly a brave move to start with the slow songs – a real declaration of confidence.*

Yes, and we worked that out early on. The very first gig on that tour was in Tasmania and we played one new song and then just went in hard, and it really didn't work. It just felt like a lack of courage. After that, we played slow songs up front and the gig slowly built and built. We did that in arenas, too, the first time we were playing these big venues. I guess it was bold.

*Do you enjoy playing live more now that you are more adept at reading and responding to an audience?*

I guess that's a part of it, but there's also an aspect of performing that is very challenging – you know, just what it takes out of you. I mean, there is always a gut feeling of dread when there's a gig coming up, because it all feels so overwhelming, so daunting. The shows require an emotional journey that is often very taxing.

*Do the other members of the band feel the same? How is Warren before a show?*

In nearly every way, Warren's relationship to creativity is different to mine. He just loves to play. I would say that applies to all current members of the Bad Seeds.

*Is it fair to say that you have always needed a creative partner, a foil as it were?*

Yes, I think so. Throughout the years, that has tended to be the case. I could do it on my own, but I don't think I'd do it nearly as well. The people I've worked with have brought a huge amount to the table. That began with Mick, and then Rowland came along with his extraordinary guitar playing and musical inventiveness.

*Can I ask about your creative relationship with Blixa, which, to put it mildly, ended pretty abruptly?*

Well, Blixa is the least nuanced person I've ever met in my life. With him, everything is black or white. I admired that in a way, because he's able to make difficult decisions in the studio. I found that enviable because I was often indecisive. That brutality of thinking, that resoluteness, that German-ness, is what Blixa brought – alongside his distinctive guitar playing, of course.

*Did you ever write a song together?*

No, we never sat down and wrote together. In fact, most of Blixa's guitar was laid on the tracks as overdubs after the song was recorded. That was his preferred way of working. Blixa liked to spend a lot of time deciding what he was going to play and then methodically applying it to the song that was already there. And he did that in a very beautiful and considered way. He really thought about the song, the lyrical content, and what his contribution should be, conceptually, rather than just strumming along, which a lot of guitarists tend to do. I really appreciated that. Blixa never thought his job was to carry the song. He thought his job was to augment the song. In my experience, that's very rare.

*Given all that, his departure from the Bad Seeds must have been a difficult moment.*

It was, yes. The suddenness of it. It was typically Bargeld in its cut-throat ruthlessness.

*How did he let you know he was leaving the band?*

He sent an email. Out of the blue. 'I've decided to leave the Bad Seeds.' A weird 'Dear John' letter of the most rudimentary and unsatisfying kind, almost as if it had been written by a robot. I was stunned. I loved him. He was a giant. For me, he's very much a symbol of a certain, extremely fertile period of the Bad Seeds. And he took a lot more with him when he left than just his presence. He took a point of view, a way of thinking and a way of working. I think he just found that our way of making music had become too traditional. Having said that, his contributions to the records we were making, post-*Boatman's Call*, had become pretty inconsequential. In the end, he did the right thing by leaving. He ripped apart the band and allowed us the opportunity to change, to grow. It was the shock that we needed.

*Were there no signs that Blixa was unhappy before the email arrived?*

I think the last time I recorded with him, he stormed out of the studio. He was angry with me, or himself, or the world. It was often hard to tell with Blixa.

*What were you recording?*

We were recording a song for a Wim Wenders documentary about the blues that he was making for Martin Scorsese. Wim had asked various musicians to perform his favourite blues songs. I wanted to go against type and do a super-upbeat version of 'I Feel So Good' by J. B. Lenoir, mostly because, at the time, the thought of the Bad Seeds doing some slow, lugubrious oh-so-worthy blues cover filled me with horror. But these up-tempo songs are tricky and not as easy as they seem. They require a certain amount of technical finesse that Blixa, despite being one of my favourite guitarists, lacks. Plus, I suggested to the band that we base our performance on the Muppets – just totally frenetic and mad and super-whacked-out.

Anyway, Wim is there and he's filming away, and we're jumping about the place like fucking idiots, doing take after take, and Blixa is getting increasingly frustrated by the whole thing because, well, I guess he couldn't get to grips with the song. I don't know. Also, in certain situations, Blixa doesn't have a very well-developed sense of humour, to say the least. And he has a famously explosive temper. It's impossible to exaggerate the performative level of Blixa's fury. Eventually, he just leaps to his feet, throws down his guitar, and screams those immortal words: 'I didn't get into rock 'n' roll to play rock 'n' roll.' Just to be really annoying, I said, 'What about the Muppets?', at which point he marched over to me and shouted, 'Fuck the Muppets! You be a fucking Muppet!' Then he marched out of the studio and I think that was the last time I ever saw him, as a member of the Bad Seeds.

*Quite a moment!*

Yes and never one to waste a good catastrophe, I turned to Wim and said, 'I hope you filmed that.' But Wim is just standing there with his mouth open and the camera hanging by his side. And I'm like, 'Wim, tell me you fucking filmed that!' But he hadn't. I think he was being respectful or something.

*Did that sort of thing happen a lot with the Bad Seeds — tantrums, rows, fallings out?*

We all had our moments, for sure, but not as many as people would like to think. There were fights, of course, blood drawn on occasion, but we have been making records together for forty years and often under pretty extreme circumstances, with people at various levels of intoxication, so it'd be just weird if there hadn't been a few punches thrown at some point!

What was more problematic were the power struggles that were often played out in ugly, Machiavellian ways. There were terrible frictions towards the end of Mick's reign and in Blixa's time. Often, they appeared to be about something quite trivial — who decides who does what on a particular song — but in the end the bigger issue was always about dominance.

On some level it's just the nature of the beast, I guess. It is what I call the corrosive power of collaboration. Collaborations that work are the most glorious and productive of things. But if the collaboration is not attended to properly, with care and respect, it can eat away at itself. The work can be so intense, you can forget to be friends.

Ultimately, the struggles we were having towards the end of Mick's time in the band were rarely ever about the songs themselves but about his perceived status. And the more someone feels they are losing their position, the more bloody and fraught the situation can become, until bad decisions are being made just to soothe people's egos.

*Would you say that your double album from 2004,* Abattoir Blues/
The Lyre Of Orpheus, *was a kind of defiant riposte to Blixa's
abrupt departure?*

Oh, for sure. It is a very defiant record and it was very much a
refusal to take Blixa's departure lying down. It was a record full of
feral energy and big ideas. There was a kind of hostility to it, in its
very exuberance and its power.

*Given all that, would you say your creative relationship with Warren
is pretty unprecedented?*

Yes. It's completely different to my relationship with Mick or Blixa
or anyone else, for that matter. Warren and I write songs together.
We're a duo. I never did that with Mick. I mean, Mick might start
something up in the studio and I would sit at the piano and play
something with him, or sing, and a song might emerge. I think
that happened with 'Red Right Hand', for example. Many great
songs, in fact. But we never sat down together, Mick and me, with
the express intention to write a song. That would have required a
kind of vulnerability or openness that didn't really exist between
us. I don't think we really had that relationship. I don't mean that
in an unkind way; it's just a fact. Perhaps, at the very start, things
were like that, but certainly not in the Bad Seeds.

*Does Warren ever contribute to the lyrics?*

No.

*So there is a strict demarcation in terms of what you do?*

In regard to the actual music of the Bad Seeds songs, Warren and
I write it together, in a free and intuitive way. It is difficult to
untangle who did what, and we don't try to. As far as I'm concerned,
it is an equal partnership. When it comes to scoring music for films,
Warren is writing the majority of the stuff, because there is generally no lyrical involvement. I am happy to take a back seat. Ultimately,

though, I think Warren and I are at our most interesting when we are sitting down together at our instruments and improvising. That's certainly when we're at our happiest!

*You seem very close, apart from the musical collaboration.*

Yes. We're on the same side.

*Was that ever the case with your other collaborators?*

I went through periods of being really close with people in the Bad Seeds – Mick, of course, and Blixa, but over the years we drifted apart and lost our connectedness. But this happens, you know. I mean, we're not married to one another – we're in a band. Other factors come into play – wives, children, we form different allegiances, and the intensity of those earlier relationships tends to suffer. This is the natural order of things, to be honest. I think the real reason Blixa left the band was that his wife didn't want him to go on tour any more. She wanted to have a baby. It was as mundane, and as beautiful, as that.

With Mick, our relationship did fracture. We were civil to each other, but there were all sorts of power struggles going on. Sometimes that can create an interestingly dissonant energy within a band, but not in this instance. The power dynamic between Mick and Warren was unspoken but exhausting. Mick required a certain musical finesse. Warren was primarily concerned with feel. Mick was about control. Warren was about abandonment.

*What were you concerned with?*

My loyalty was to the song itself.

*Can you give an example of how that dynamic played out?*

We have a song called 'Babe, You Turn Me On'. On the original vocal I suspected there might have been a couple of tuning problems and I felt I should fix them up. Warren thought the song sounded beautiful, pure and simple, and we should leave it as it is.

Mick, on the other hand, got a copy of the lyrics, listened through to the song, and made a show of putting a red mark under every word he thought was out of tune. He did this with his famous exasperated raised eyebrow. That was essentially a power struggle between two people with very different ideas about what it was to make music. It had very little to do with the song itself. The song was caught in the middle.

*What did you do in the end?*

I resung the vocal, most likely, and the song was probably better for it.

*All in all, Nick, it's quite a singular road you've taken: the whole trajectory of your career, and particularly the shift in consciousness that has led to this new way of working – and being in the world.*

Well, maybe the image of the ice sculpture is in some way an acknowledgement of that shift: a toppled thing melting in the sun. Whatever that thing was, it's over and it's changing into something else. I'm not sure what, really, but much of what I assumed to be the fundamental substance of life no longer seems to apply. Or no longer has the same purchase.

*And that has freed you somehow – made you fearless?*

I don't really know how to explain this, but, yes, I suspect it is about freedom: the freedom to step beyond the expectations and limitations that are imposed on you – by yourself and others – and just move towards the things that hold meaning. And I think those expectations and limitations have something to do with the past, and the demands that the past makes of you.

*What do you mean?*

We're often led to believe that getting older is in itself somehow a betrayal of our idealistic younger self, but sometimes I think it might be the other way around. Maybe the younger self finds it difficult to inhabit its true potential because it has no idea what that potential is. It is a kind of unformed thing running scared most of the time, frantically trying to build its sense of self – *This is me! Here I am!* – in any way that it can. But then time and life come along, and smash that sense of self into a million pieces.

And then comes the reassembled self, the self *you* have to put back together. You no longer have to devote time to finding out what you are, you are just free to be whatever you want to be, unimpeded by the incessant needs of others. You somehow grow into the fullness of your humanity, form your own character, become a proper person – I don't know, someone who has become a part of things, not someone separated from or at odds with the world.

*You mean you get old.*

Yes, Seán, old and free!

# 8

## A Sense of Shared Defiance

~

Things have been crazy today. Is it too late to talk?

*No, not at all. So what's going on?*

Work is getting insane. Like, earlier this morning I was in the studio with Warren, watching the serial killer Jeffrey Dahmer fuck and dismember the corpse of a rent boy while we wrote music for it. Then, in the afternoon, I had to recite 'The Little Thing', a children's story I've written for three-year-olds, for an audiobook. After that I did a vocal to a song called 'Macca The Mutt', by an amazing jazz-punk instrumental band from Australia called Party Dozen. In the evening I finished working on my *Seven Psalms* record, which is a suite of petitions to God, a project I'm very excited about. I'll send it to you. In the car on the way home I designed a little bucket hat for my Shit for Kids label on Cave Things. And now I'm ringing you up to continue this epic conversation. Tomorrow I'll go back into Corin's studio and keep working on my ceramic figurines, not to mention The Red Hand Files that I have to do by Friday.

*I do sense that you thrive on this kind of work schedule, though.*

Well, it's all getting a bit out of control, but it's wild and lovely. I feel amped up. Maybe a little bit too much. What I'm saying is that there's an openness and freedom to things that I've never experienced before, but right now it just feels like a very busy week. What I really want to do is curl up on the sofa and watch Netflix with my wife. It's the small things, in the end, don't you think?

*Yes, increasingly so. Do you think this intense burst of creativity is fuelled by anything in particular?*

The pandemic has certainly given me the time to do a whole lot of stuff I wouldn't normally get the opportunity to do, because I'd be on the road. I'm just doing whatever I like. It's a liberation.

*Can I ask, does it also have to do with encroaching mortality?*

Jesus, you're a gloomy bastard – yes, I've got to design that bucket hat before I die!

Seriously, though, as I've said before, I feel free of presumptions, my own, most of all – and of others' expectations. There is no reason or no valid argument for me to lead my life in the way I have previously. The pandemic has put that idea to rest. I just want to make art with my friends, be with my wife, and see my kids.

*I like how you neatly sidestepped the question!*

About encroaching mortality?

*Yes.*

I don't really look at death in that way, I guess. The idea of encroaching mortality isn't a concern – the idea of death as a sort of endgame, something separate, waiting down the line. It doesn't feel like that to me. I guess I feel, day to day, and in a profound way, enmeshed in death, as if it is a clear and present state of being that manifests itself in a sort of vitality. I feel a certain receptivity to its positive influence or presence. Susie feels the same, you know, not that she speaks about it, but you can see it in everything she does, this invigorating force, born of a hard-earned understanding of the immediate and urgent proximity of death. I'm not trying to be morbid here, Seán, but death feels all around.

*No, I understand that, and it's good that you brought Susie up. I was thinking last night that maybe we could talk about Susie, as she has been this constant presence throughout our conversations. I sense she plays an important part in the narrative of your creative life.*

In my life!

*Did meeting Susie have anything to do with your decision to finally get clean?*

That's a long story. You sure you want to hear it?

*Of course.*

When I came out of rehab for the sixth time in, like, ten years, it was to marry Susie.

*Hang on. Six stints in rehab?*

Well, I'd been busted a lot and sometimes they give you the choice between rehab or prison. Or my manager at the time would kind of dump me in one, or I'd go in just to get everyone off my back or whatever, but, usually, I don't know, pressure was brought to bear, let's say.

Anyway, back at the beginning of our relationship, it was wild times for me. I was hopelessly smitten with Susie, but I also had a heroin habit. We were very much in love, but it was also extraordinarily dysfunctional, and Susie, who was four years clean from a multitude of addictions, was advised by an army of well-meaning people who loved her – her chain of command, I used to call them – to stay right the fuck away from me. I was definitely bad news and not the right person for her to have a relationship with, all things considered.

Then, one night, Susie disappeared off the map. She just vanished. I was beside myself, and went looking for her everywhere, running around to people's houses, frantic, ringing everyone up, but she had simply vanished. No one knew where she was, or they weren't saying. This went on for months but no sign of Susie. I was distraught, and any restraint I'd felt while I was with her went out the window, and I just descended into a very bad period of drug taking. Not good at all. And eight very dark months went by.

*Eight months? That's a long time. I had no idea.*

Yes, an eternity. Until one day, I was sitting in my house, in not what you would call showroom condition, and the doorbell rang, and it was Susie. She walked in and said, 'How are you?' and I'm like, 'Well, how do I fucking look?' and Susie said, 'Well, I've tried to stay away, but I can't do it. I'm here. I love you. You can do what you like, but I am here if you want me!' I'm very happy with this, as you can imagine. Well, that lasted about three weeks, and I remember one day looking at Susie sitting by the window in the living room and thinking I love this woman and I am definitely going to fuck this up if I don't do something radical. It was a moment of clarity. So I flew to a rehab in Arizona – I'd basically done all the British ones – and I got clean. And that was that. It was suddenly relatively easy. I had not been coerced. I had made my own decision. Or at least I thought I had. Of course Susie was clever enough to make it seem like I had made my own decision.

*And since then you have drawn her into your creative world, and are very open about her influence.*

Yes, I guess that is correct. Susie is my wife, but also a collaborator. She comes from a very musical family. She has an innate and maybe inherited understanding of music – much more nuanced than mine

– even though she doesn't play anything. She also has a highly evolved aesthetic sense that is very much her own. These things work together to make her very sensitive towards certain things – like the way I perform a song, say, or, generally, how I present myself to the world.

And to be honest, this is not always the easiest of creative relationships. Susie has a maddening tendency to question the original idea at the eleventh hour, right at the moment when it has found its way into the bloodstream of a project and is no longer open for debate. This, as you can imagine, can be unbelievably frustrating, although I must say generally turns out for the best.

*Okay, can you give me a recent example of that kind of thing?*

You know the film I just made of 'Idiot Prayer', the solo show I did at Alexandra Palace during lockdown? Well, it was originally called 'An Evening with Nick Cave'. That was what the team and I had always called it, and it had just sort of stuck, but when Susie found out that's what it was called, her reaction was, 'Wow! Could you even find a more boring title?' So, I'm like, 'Well, Jesus, babe, that's just what it's called! I can't fucking change it now!' And she's like, 'Okay, but I'm just saying it's boring.' So, after a while, I say, 'Okay, what about "Idiot Prayer" then?' And she's like, 'There you go.' That sort of thing happens a lot. So a good result, but exasperating at the time.

*Are you someone who takes advice easily? For some reason, I'm thinking probably not.*

I do find, in general, that other people's opinions are mostly problematic, *especially* if you respect the person or, indeed, are married to them. Most of the time, I just don't solicit other people's opinions if can help it, unless of course I know their opinion is going to be the same as mine. I prefer to go with the flow, provided it's my flow, if you know what I mean.

*So, given that, how would you describe Susie?*

A perfectionist.

*And yourself?*

An imperfectionist.

*And how would you describe your creative relationship?*

I would describe it as a family business. I see the combination of The Vampire's Wife and my own work and all the other stuff as part of the same operation. There's a constant cross-pollinating between the two. Susie takes ideas from my work that influence her designs, and I take ideas from The Vampire's Wife that influence what I'm doing. I see it all as the same thing.

*Okay, so how does that work practically?*

Well, The Red Hand Files, for instance – as an idea, it is very much an extension of Susie's Stuff page on her website, which is a kind of very personalised public service. Twice a week, she posts things on there that she thinks are cool or that have influenced her over the years – poets, writers, artists, actors, musicians, dancers, thinkers, designers and so on. It's strange and slightly monomaniacal. It's something we've been doing together for five years or so, and there are well over seven hundred posts. It has had a huge influence over The Red Hand Files.

Every now and then, when The Vampire's Wife brings in a new e-commerce tsar to ramp up sales, the first thing that happens is that they discover the Stuff Page, and mostly are genuinely mystified by its utility, or lack of it. They're like, what's it for? And, why haven't we monetised it? But Susie tends to ignore them and carry on in her own way, because she has her own fully developed and uncompromising vision. This vision was always there, by the way, but when she began the company it found its purpose and the whole thing just blossomed.

What I'm trying to say is that I am not just influenced by her, but emboldened by her.

*In terms of how she lives her life?*

Yes. By the singular force of her creativity, for sure, especially after Arthur died. There was this new, vital, mutinous energy that she found. Not immediately, of course, but after a while. It was like everything she did was an act of insubordination towards what seemed like the callous indifference of the world. It is quite something to witness, truly inspiring. So beautifully positive.

*I know you are involved in The Vampire's Wife, and not just in terms of the name.*

At the beginning I was very involved. I used to help choose the fabric, go to the fabric fairs, go to Première Vision in Paris, trawl through the Liberty fabric archives.

*There's a quote from a recent interview with Susie, which is pretty astute: 'To be honest, I find the word muse to be a little demeaning. I haven't really got time to be anyone's muse. However, I am a frequent visitor in my husband's songs, I seem to be always walking in and out of them. His songs look after me. And if I am to be a muse, then I am his and he is mine.'*

I have never been all that comfortable with the word 'muse', myself. I think the problem with it is that it kind of sanctifies a subordinate role – and the term 'muse' has been traditionally seen as a female role. There's something about that that feels a little uncomfortable, as if the muse has nothing better to do than lounge around as a locus of inspiration for the artist. Having said that, Susie is without a doubt my point of influence, and I spend most of my creative life journeying back and forth along the axis of her general wonderfulness.

And you're right. She is astute to say that about my songs – 'I always seem to be walking in and out of them' – because it's true;

I don't ever sit down with the intention of writing a song about Susie. It's more that, when I am in that shadowy creative flow, I find it difficult to maintain my own form, so welded am I into her being. I find myself adopting her perspective – flipping from one to the other. A therapist would have a field day with this!

Sometimes I am trying to manage several voices in my songs – my voice, Susie's voice and our shared voice, and of course the subjective or observational voice.

*Are you talking about voicing your shared experience? Or is it more than that? Is she somehow speaking through you in certain songs?*

By shared voice, I mean our entangled form. We are both distinct individuals, but there is definitely a melding point where we are indistinguishable. I'm not sure about speaking through me, although that is a nice idea. It's more that I am speaking for her in some way. I am using some of my songs as a way of articulating her essence or our combined essence. A song like 'Spinning Song' begins with a detached, neutral narrative voice, moves into my voice, and then the falsetto bit at the end is Susie's voice becoming our combined voice. Same with the Kisa Gotami story at the end of 'Hollywood'. In my mind, at least, it is Susie who is telling the Buddhist story of a mother and her dead child.

*In terms of this reciprocal creative dynamic, does she ever offer advice on song lyrics?*

Not directly. She doesn't sit down and write the lyrics to a song with me, because there is no room in the process for her, or anyone else, for that matter. And I don't physically help her design her dresses, because she has her own highly distinctive ideas about beauty and needs to get in touch with that. But I think, ultimately, my songs are gifts to her and I think her dresses are gifts to me. We are both waving to each other, through our work, that we are both still present in the world.

*Not drowning, but waving!*

Yes! So, a song like 'Night Raid' is a good example. It describes the conception of our twin boys in a hotel room in New Orleans:

> *They annexed your insides in a late night raid*
> *We sent down for drinks and something to eat*
> *The cars humming in the rain on the street below*

And the chorus has the heroic couplet:

> *And we all rose up from our wonder*
> *We will never admit defeat*

*That says it all, really.*

It very much sums up my feelings when I visit the Vampire's Wife studios in Lewes, because nothing I do in my own work makes me anywhere near as proud as when I see a dress Susie has created that just blows everyone's mind. It's a source of great pleasure for me. To me, each dress is a glorious victory over the disorder of the world – 'We will never admit defeat!'

*So how much are you involved in the practical stuff these days?*

Well, back in the early days, I used to hang around the offices a lot and watch the process of making an actual dress. I learned all this stuff about French seams and baby lock and shoulder pads and overlay frills. I found it really fascinating. Plus, I loved playing with the fabrics! I knew nothing about it, of course, but I did know what I liked. Susie uses me as a barometer, so to speak, much the same as when I play her my songs and I am alert to her body language and her expressions.

*It's kind of interesting that you're so involved in something you admit to knowing nothing about.*

Well, isn't it always the way? I find not knowing about something in art, that kind of adventuring innocence, whether it is songwriting, scriptwriting, dress designing, score work, sculpture or any other thing, a distinct advantage much of the time. At least initially, anyway, because you enter into the project naïve to the potentially destabilising and corrosive aspects of it. You just blunder in and give it a go!

But I'll also say that, from what I've seen, the fashion business is an extremely difficult industry to work in and famously difficult to keep control of. Susie spends a lot of her time fighting for the integrity of the brand or hanging on to the purity of its vision.

*And are you in a position where you don't have to deal with those kinds of issues, at least not to that extent?*

I think I've done my best, as a musician, to insulate myself from these forces – by being my own boss. Nobody tells me what I can or can't do, because there is nobody there to tell me. All aspects of my creative life – the work, the production, media, touring and so on – are done in-house and on my terms. They're pretty much impervious to the forces that could unduly influence them. I have a small, tight, loyal and highly efficient team that is entirely self-contained, with no outside interference. So I feel well looked after, protected, and safe to just play and explore. It is a position of great privilege. Susie's professional world is very different. The tension between art and business is much more fraught, shall we say.

But at the end of the day, Susie designs and produces the most beautiful clothes on earth – heart-breaking, ethereal, transcendent creations that contain her very essence, her very soul.

As you've probably noticed, I'm a fan.

*You should work in public relations.*

Oh, I do that, too!

*I should have guessed. It's quite something, this mutual blossoming of creativity and creative risk-taking.*

Yes, well, our work is a solace, to be sure. But it's a subject of which we need to speak cautiously, because, on every level, Susie and I would give up everything if things could be different. But they can't. Life is as it is. So both of us in our different ways decided we'd either fight or we'd fold. And, together and separately, we fought.

*And creativity is the essence of that fight, that shared defiance?*

Yes, that's right: creativity and a sense of shared defiance. Nicely put. Susie and I are essentially bound together by love and catastrophe, but there is also the shared project of grief: we both understand what we are going through, and we know how to tread lightly around it and to keep each other afloat.

You know, I could never have got through this whole thing without Susie, and I suspect she couldn't have made it without me, but neither of us would have survived without the work. We had to get up in the morning because something needed to be done. Arthur's presence within Susie is as real and existent as her blood and bones and is a complex and motivating force that mostly radiates outward in good and beautiful work. I say 'mostly' because at times it can turn on itself, become interior and paralysing. But that is rare, these days. Susie's work is more than an occupation; it is a last measure, a strategy for survival, and a way of being strong enough for those of us still here.

Actually, Seán, Susie has just come home. I'll call you tomorrow if that's okay?

# 9

# The Astonishing Idea

~

Hey, I sent you the lyrics to a new song last night.

### Lavender Fields

*I'm travelling appallingly alone*
*On a singular road*
*Into the lavender fields*
*That reach high beyond the sky*

*People ask me how I changed*
*I say it is a singular road*
*And the lavender has stained my skin*
*And made me strange*

*The lavender is tall and reaches*
*Beyond the heavenly cover*
*I plough through this furious world*
*Of which I'm truly over*

*And sometimes I hear my name*
*Oh where did you go?*
*But the lavender is broad*
*And it's a singular road*

*Once I was running with my friends*
*All of them busy with their pens*
*But the lavender grew rare*
*What happened to them?*

*Sometimes I see a pale bird*
*Wheeling in the sky*
*But that is just a feeling*
*A feeling when you die*

*Yes — 'Lavender Fields'. I was just going to ask you about it.*

We've started working on it and it sounds very promising. It's a beautiful song, really — six four-line verses sung over a circular chordal motif that never resolves, just climbs. You'll love it. About halfway through a competing choral melody, a hymn, emerges out of the song and takes over.

*Sounds amazing. I look forward to hearing it.*

But, listen, the reason I sent it is because you said something recently that I found quite strange at the time. You said that I'd been on a 'singular road' or a 'singular journey', or something like that. That phrase stuck with me, and that night, as I was sitting on my sofa, the song sort of fell out of the sky, almost complete, like a gift. Anyway, it was you who talked about the singular road, or journey, that got me thinking. So thanks!

*Ah, that's great — I knew some good would come out of this!*

I know, and it's very unusual, because I don't write songs sitting on my sofa — I watch TV on my sofa. I tend to write songs, as you know, at my desk or at a table. And songs rarely come complete, but slowly over time. But this one I wrote very quickly, in one sitting — with a lyric that was, well, kind of perfect. It starts with the semi-humorous lines:

> *I'm travelling appalling alone*
> *On a singular road*
> *Into the lavender fields*
> *That reach high beyond the sky*

*That's semi-humorous?*

Okay, not humorous, but mischievous.

*I'm really intrigued to hear this song, but what is it about exactly, and how is it mischievous?*

Well, the singular road is the hero's journey, or the artist's way, let's say – the monomyth where the artist travels to the dangerous unknown to collect the knowledge and bring it back to the world. The 'appalling' journey, so to speak. To cast yourself as the hero in your own song is, I don't know, Seán, an act of mischief, maybe!

*So 'Lavender Fields' is an archetypal hero's journey song?*

Well, I'm not sure if it's archetypal given that the protagonist only *thinks* he is on a hero's journey; he is actually just dying.

> *People ask me how I changed*
> *I say it is a singular road*
> *And the lavender has stained my skin*
> *And made me strange . . .*

Halfway through the song a hymn rises up that ushers the narrator into the 'kingdom in the sky'. And then, in the final verse, we see the narrator is dead and the lavender fields are the afterlife.

> *Sometimes I see a pale bird*
> *Wheeling in the sky*
> *But that is just a feeling*
> *A feeling when you die*

*I love the internal rhyme.*

I know! I thank God Almighty and all his cross-dressing angels for that one! So, not bad for a song I wrote on my sofa in about twenty minutes. I wish it were like that all the time. So, once again, Seán, thank you! Maybe I need to talk to you more often.

*I'm here for you. So do you have enough songs for an actual album?*

To be honest, we've been reluctant to say we are even making a record. It felt too early to be making such grand claims. Rather, it seemed like we were approaching it sideways like a couple of little crabs. We went into the studio a few weeks ago, immediately after lockdown had finished, with the idea to just jam, really, and to reconnect without any real expectations. We certainly weren't broadcasting to each other our intent to make a record, probably because we didn't want to scare it away with our presumptions. I think it was more basic than that. I think we just missed each other. I hadn't seen Warren at all for over a year. Through the lockdown, he was in Paris and I was over here.

*So, hang on, you just started a couple of weeks ago and already you have an album's worth of songs?*

Yes. We ended up with about thirty pieces of music from those three days and we went through them and selected the best ones – maybe ten really good pieces, a couple of which were really quite formed. That's when we allowed ourselves to believe we had an album. Anyway, we've just been in the studio again, basically listening to those pieces more closely, pushing them around a bit, and forming them into songs. Right now, I'm working on the words again, and if we do maybe another two or three days in the studio, there'll definitely be enough for a solid record.

*How is Warren? He must be loving this.*

Warren is on fire. We barely said anything to each other. Just sat down at our instruments and ten months of quarantine poured out of us. I think he spent lockdown living in his studio, out the back of his house, in Paris, going crazy. It felt very necessary, the whole thing, for the both of us.

*Well, it's good to know you got to that place after all the doubt and depression that you started from.*

As I've said, generally the recording process is a kind of pleasure because, for me, the heavy lifting has been done: I've thought a lot about the songs, or rather the lyrics, coming up to the recording. And even though they may not be fully written, I am pretty clear as to the intent of the record. So the recording becomes, for me, at least, the beautiful, unexpected and collaborative bringing to life of those ideas.

*A while back, when you were just starting to write down ideas, you mentioned Jimmy Webb as a reference point, those beautifully arranged grand ballads of his. Has that idea carried through?*

It has, but not in the way I thought it would. Certainly, thematically, the influence of the big ballads is there – everyone is saying goodbye, everybody's hitting the road, everybody is leaving someone behind. I'm pleased with that, because I've always loved those sorts of songs, the grand ballads with beautiful, sweeping arrangements, and, of course, Jimmy Webb wrote them better than anyone. But, to be absolutely clear, I'm not interested in writing songs in that traditional form. It's more about a particular way of telling a story and establishing a certain mood – that melancholy, heartbroken feeling that those songs evoke.

*I do think that, these days, it would be difficult for that kind of heart-on-the-sleeve, bittersweet, romantic ballad to have the same kind of resonance it once had. I wonder if it is possible to delve back into that tradition and draw on it without a certain degree of self-consciousness?*

I know what you mean. But it's interesting you should say that because last night I was talking to my son Earl, who's been living with us. He asked me about the album, and I told him it had a lot of big ballads that have a sort of Townes Van Zandt feel, a bit like a strange country record. Earl is a big Townes fan, and he was like, 'Uh, okay.' Kind of sceptical, you know. And then I played him some stuff, and, after a while, he said, 'How in any way is this Townes Van Zandt? This isn't country, it's fucking Kanye!'

*Even though I haven't heard anything yet, I'd be inclined to go with Earl.*

Well, that kind of big ballad storytelling is what I hear within the songs. It's in there somehow, but it's coming in contact with a radically different way of making music and, of course, Warren.

*So did you start with quite abstract ideas and images like you did on Ghosteen?*

Yes, we did, but maybe not so much this time. As I said, it seems that everybody in the songs is leaving or saying goodbye – chucking their bags in the back of the car and going out on the road. It's 'By The Time I Get To Phoenix' writ large. In fact, there is a scene in one of the songs, 'Old Time', where the two people involved are lying around a motel swimming pool listening to that very song:

> *A lunatic beauty under a watery moon*
> *You're melting by the motel swimming pool*
> *'By the Time I Get To Phoenix' on the radio*
> *Your moon to my shooting star*
> *I'm throwing my bags in the back of the car*

I love how Jimmy Webb songs are heroic in their way, but doomed, too. Often, it's the doomed hero journey.

*Yes, the existential male loner with a broken heart and a troubled conscience. There's a whole bunch of classic country songs like that – Johnny Cash songs, Merle Haggard songs, Bobby Bare songs – where the hero is in jail or on the run. My dad loved those songs and I remember hearing them a lot as a boy.*

Likewise. My grandfather worked in radio in Melbourne and he used to be able to get his hands on 78rpm records. Way back before LPs. We had an old-fashioned vintage crank-up record player he gave to us, along with a bunch of these records, one of which had a deep effect on me. I used to play it all the time as a young boy. I'd lie in bed listening to it, over and over. It was called 'Can I Sleep In Your Barn Tonight, Mister?' I think it was by Charlie Poole. That one song that I absorbed as a child had a huge impact on me and on my songwriting later on, and perhaps still does.

### Can I Sleep in Your Barn Tonight, Mister?

*May I sleep in your barn tonight, mister?*
*It's cold lying out on the ground*
*And the cold north wind is whistling*
*And I have no place to lie down*

*I have no tobacco nor matches*
*I'm sure that'll do you no harm*
*I will tell you my story, kind Mister*
*Though it runs through my heart like a storm*

*It was three years ago last summer*
*I never will forget that sad day*
*When a stranger came out from the city*
*And he wanted to stop for his health*

*Now the stranger was fair, tall and handsome*
*And he looked like a man who had wealth*

*Said he wanted to stop in the country*
*Said he wanted to stop for his health*

*Now my wife said she'd like to be earning*
*Something to add to our home*
*And she talked till I finally decided*
*That a stranger's to enter our home*

*Last night as I came from my workshop*
*Whistling and singing with joy*
*I's expecting a kind-hearted welcome*
*At the gate from my wife and my boy*

*Nothing did I spy but a letter*
*Placed in my room on a stand*
*And the moment my eyes lay upon it*
*I picked it right up in my hand*

*Now the note said Stella and the stranger*
*Had run away and taken my child*
*And I'm sure there's a God up in heaven*
*And he'll do as the stranger deserves*

That's exactly what we are talking about: a man on the road with a woeful tale. In fact, I took that and turned it into 'Song Of Joy' on the *Murder Ballads* album. I made the nocturnal visitor a serial killer, moving remorselessly from house to house, but it is essentially the same lyric. These early songs you hear live in your bloodstream.

The thing I love about many of them is that there is a momentum in the actual storytelling – and it's often the actual movement of the protagonist in the story itself. In the case of the Charlie Poole song, the lost, cuckolded man moving from house to house, retelling his tale of woe, generates a kind of narrative push to the song itself. Almost like the rhythm of the train tracks under a Johnny Cash song. It's very beautiful.

Jimmy Webb's 'By The Time I Get To Phoenix' is an example of this par excellence. The three verses that move from Phoenix to Albuquerque to Oklahoma, as the man moves further and further away from the woman he has left behind, and as she simultaneously goes about her daily business – it is a piece of lyrical genius, really, the way that song is constructed.

*Yes, and the same with 'Wichita Lineman', of course. It's such sophisticated storytelling. Jimmy Webb took it to a whole other level.*

He's the absolute master. I love how, in 'Wichita Lineman', the narrator goes about his work but everything becomes a terrible metaphor for the one he may have lost. In my view, it's one of the greatest lyrics ever written. Not to mention the actual song itself. The arrangement. My God! It's just perfect. Do you know his song, 'The Moon Is A Harsh Mistress'?

*Yes. That's a strange and beautiful song, but in a different way. Haunting, really.*

I love how he sings the first two verses about the moon so eloquently and poetically, and then the song changes key and turns suddenly super-personal, where he is barely able to contain his broken heart, and it becomes almost clumsy and garbled with the repetition of the word 'fell' in the final verse.

You can hear that same thing echoed in 'Galleon Ship' off *Ghosteen*.

> *My galleon ship will fly and fall*
> *Fall and fly and fly and fall*
> *Deep into your loveliness.*

*I love the to-and-fro of those lines. So did you hear those old classic songs when you were a boy in Wangaratta? Or later?*

Yes, but back then it was mainly Johnny Cash. *The Johnny Cash Show* was on the TV and we also had all those half-hour American TV shows like *I Dream of Jeannie* and *The Addams Family* and *Bewitched* and *Hogan's Heroes*. We'd watch them when we came back from school, before we were called for 'tea' as we called it.

*Oh, that's very Irish – 'Your tea's on the table!'*

Yes! Looking back, our childhoods were saturated with American culture, but those shows were a great unifying force for my generation of Australians. I loved watching them. I literally fell in love with Elizabeth Montgomery from *Bewitched* and Barbara Eden from *I Dream of Jeannie* and, of course, I fell crushingly, hopelessly in love with Carolyn Jones as Morticia in *The Addams Family*. I have an unsettling feeling that I married Morticia in the end!

*That does explain a lot. Apart from Johnny Cash, were you listening to a lot of country music as a boy?*

No, I really got into country later when I was fifteen or sixteen or so – Tammy Wynette, Dolly Parton, Glen Campbell, George Jones, Willie Nelson. I listened to that music a lot.

*As you get older, you realise just how formative all those early, almost accidental musical discoveries were.*

For sure. I think we probably find the things that we love early on, and never stray too far from them. I read somewhere that there is something that happens within the brain between the ages of sixteen and twenty-three that makes us super-receptive, particularly to music, and that's why we attach ourselves so strongly to pieces of music from that period of our lives. That certainly applies to me. To be honest, I simply don't have the same attachment to music now, or maybe I don't have the same fundamental need for it as I had back then. Even when I find something that completely blows my mind, there's an almost academic remove. I don't have the urge to play it over and over.

*Yes, I know what you mean. At a certain point, I stopped listening to music in the intense way that I used to, and ever since, I've found it hard to re-engage with it to some degree.*

Do you think that is attached to trauma, in some way? Grief can produce an emotional disconnect that is very hard to claw back — a kind of stoppage.

*Yes, that's definitely what happened in my case. When I was grieving, I looked for music to pull me out of the place I was in, but it didn't seem to work. Actually, it was more that I couldn't concentrate enough to actually listen properly.*

Well, I think grief reinvents us. When I say grief, I mean the second life we lead after trauma. It feels more essential. The way we respond to things is altered — we become, as human beings, more *precise*.

*Yes, and much more selective in terms of what we listen to, read, watch. I like to think we become more attentive and discerning, but maybe it's just that we have less patience these days.*

I know what you mean about music. These days I find music intensely irritating most of the time. I think that may have something to do with my age, and it may have something to do with trauma, but it may also be to do with the fact that much music these days is actually just intensely irritating! I mean, I guess it always was, but maybe back then I was stronger and more resistant to stupidity. I just ignored it. These days I am more vulnerable to it. It hurts more. I take it all more personally! I'm probably being unkind.

*You said to me a while back, 'My point of view is fading.' I've been meaning to ask what you meant by that.*

I said that? Hmm. I'm not sure that's true. I still, as you know, have a point of view on most things. However, I think the stridency of some of my cherished positions is softening. It comes with age, maybe, to be able to hold two conflicting ideas in your head at the same time.

I can tell you one thing that's happening which is sort of disturbing, though. When I'm reading a novel, I find myself questioning the 'why' of it. That's a new thing. Before, I never questioned the absolute indispensableness of fiction. Do you know what I mean? But now it's like, why am I reading this novel? What's the point of getting through to the end when there is so much other stuff that I could be reading? What's the point of persevering with this one story that's going to take up two weeks of my life? Part of it is that I don't like a lot of modern fiction, I guess. It all feels so morally obvious. And yet, before, even when I was reading a book I didn't much like, I would still read it through to the end because of a belief in the clear value of reading fiction, in itself. These days, I don't have the patience for it. I don't have the time.

*What was the last novel you read that you really enjoyed?*

I just finished Ben Okri's *Astonishing the Gods* recently and, quite frankly, I was awed. What a strange, unique and enchanting book it is, which kind of makes a lie of everything that I just said! But, in general, these days, I struggle with fiction. It's maybe just a slow dulling of the senses. I hope not. Or maybe I'm just concerned with different things now.

*I tend to return every few years to the books I really like. You read them differently as you get older, see different things in them.*

I don't do that so much. I did go back and re-read Flannery O'Connor recently to remember why we must value her, but that was only because her books had been taken out of a college library in America, due to some skewed and overly harsh charges of racism. I actually refer to it in one of the new songs. I haven't got a name for it yet.

> *I'm sitting on the balcony*
> *Reading Flannery O'Connor*
> *With a pencil and a plan*

*So at least you're engaged, even if you aren't reading contemporary fiction.*

I think that's the best we can do. We have a kind of duty to remain engaged. There are a few lines towards the end of 'Lavender Fields' that are about that.

> *Once I was running with my friends*
> *All of them busy with their pens*
> *But the lavender grew rare*
> *What happened to them?*

*So what did happen to them, do you think?*

I don't know for sure. It seems to me that some of my contemporaries just became disenchanted and cynical about things. And I kind of understand it, because sometimes the world feels like a fucking lunatic asylum, and the desire to retreat is irresistible, to step into the shadows and keep your head down for the duration – which incidentally doesn't feel so long away. But I think it is necessary to weigh in with our individual truths as we see them, whether they are right, wrong or hair-raisingly out of step with the prevailing trends of the day. Do you know what I mean? We owe it to ourselves. We owe it to the world.

*Yes, I agree, but surely it's also incumbent on us to question our received opinions from time to time and maybe shift our thinking accordingly. Wouldn't you agree?*

Well, of course, Seán. But I think it's also wise to hang on to the things that are self-evidently good for the world, especially culturally. There are stores of wisdom and beauty in the world worth protecting, even if they don't happen to chime with the prevailing mood. We will always move forward; that is the nature of an essentially progressive society, to renew and to build upon, and also to critique and discard. Not every new idea is a good idea, nor is everything we get rid of in our deification of the new. Things are not easily retrieved once they are gone. They remain lost. We need to stay alert to this and call out bad choices when we see them. Or, at least, present our truth as we see it.

*In what way do your ideas diverge from the prevailing mood?*

Firstly, I believe, as a general rule, that the vitalising element in art is the one that baffles or challenges our outrages. I believe art should be confronting and discomfiting, and do more than just affirm your point of view. For my generation, that particular idea was bred in the bone. As a young musician, I felt it was my sacred duty to offend.

*Yes, but times have changed, Nick.*

No shit.

*How do you feel personally about growing older and all that comes with it?*

To some degree I feel I have the distinct advantage of having made a long lifetime of terrible mistakes. Like most old people, I have been hurt more, I have suffered more, and I have fucked up more. I have also overcome things that are incomprehensible to younger people. I have experienced more by virtue of being in the world for a really long time. Older people may be broken down, but we are also vast repositories of experience and, if we have been paying attention to world, a certain amount of wisdom, too. This has value. It is worth something.

*You're doing pretty good, all things considered. You're making the most interesting and challenging music of your life.*

Do you think so?

*Yes, with* Ghosteen, *you redrew the parameters of what you do in terms of your songwriting and music. You reinvented the idea of Nick Cave.*

Well, I don't think I consciously reinvented anything. At some point, life just became a serious thing, but nevertheless that's good to hear.

*I wanted to ask you about something you said previously about waiting for a song to arrive at its meaning, of being patient in terms of the song revealing itself? I found that really intriguing. It stayed with me.*

I was thinking about that some more, too, and I was reminded of that beautiful notion of William Blake's – of Jesus being the imagination. And also that startling image from Matthew 27: 'Mary Magdalene and the other Mary, who remain standing there in front of the tomb.' That always makes me think of what it's like to experience the birth of a creative idea, it's as if you are waiting for the Christ to appear, to step from the tomb, and reveal Himself.

*That's quite an analogy. Do you see songwriting at its best as a kind of creative self-revelation?*

Yes, and in order for it to happen, you have to be patient. You must have faith. And often you must do the waiting alone. You have to have forbearance, a patient self-control and a tolerance of the process itself. And also an alertness. It is easy to lose one's nerve, to run away like the apostles did, to go and do something else, but we do that at our peril. That's when you risk missing the astonishing idea, the Jesus idea.

*The actual moment of creative self-revelation?*

Yes. But, of course, there's also the deceiving idea!

*I've never heard that term before.*

No, that's because I just made it up.

*It sounds impressive. But what form does the deceiving idea take?*

It's usually the residual idea that pretends to be the astonishing idea. As an artist, you really need to constantly be on the lookout for that. I would say, 'Beware the residual idea!'

*Are you talking about the leftover idea, perhaps from a previous album, that's still hanging around in the back of your mind when you begin a new one?*

Yes. Exactly. I tend to find that when I first sit down to write new songs there is a kind of initial flurry of words that appears quite effortlessly. They seem to be right there, at hand, so there is a cosiness about them, a comfortableness. And because they aren't too bad, really, you immediately start thinking, this is all going to be easy. But these are the deceiving ideas, the residual ideas, the unused remnants of the last record that are still lurking about. They're like the muck in the pipes, and they have to be flushed out to make room for the new idea, the astonishing idea.

I think a lot of musicians deal in residual ideas, because they're seduced by the comfortable and the familiar. For me, that's a big mistake, although I can understand the temptation to create something reassuringly familiar. And, in a way, the whole industry is set up to cater to that – to the well-known or second-hand idea. Record companies think, erroneously, that the general consumer just wants to hear more of the same. Now, that may well be true to a degree, but in the long term I don't think it's sustaining.

Audiences need to be challenged, too. They are also on a journey and it's up to the artists to, I don't know, light the way, so that we can all move forward.

You can very easily fall into the habit of writing certain things over and over again, things you think will be popular, in part because you know that if you make a record that is significantly different to the last one, you'll lose some fans. A genuinely new idea can feel strange and unsettling. It's upsetting in a way, but an integral part of the creative journey. You lose some fans, but draw in others.

*Does it ever concern you that you have inevitably lost some of your audience along the way?*

Well, the alternative is much worse. If you stick to the safe idea, it soon becomes overly familiar, and the audience will grow bored and ultimately resentful. Put brutally, the audience should never dictate the direction an artist takes. I say that with all the love in the world, but an artist does not exist to serve his or her audience. The artist exists to serve the idea. The idea is the light that leads the audience and the artist to a better place.

*What do you mean by 'a better place'?*

A better way of being, I guess.

*So you believe music can actually transform people's way of thinking, of being?*

Absolutely. In my opinion, that is its primary function.

*It's not enough that it just moves or uplifts the listener for a time?*

No, I think music can have a way of influencing the heart in a righteous way that enables us to do better, to be better. Especially when the songs get played live. Collectively, we can experience the music actually improving the condition of the listener. I see it all the time. I experience it myself as well. It's a very real thing.

*Yes, but surely that collective emotional experience is, by its nature, a fleeting thing. How would you possibly gauge its lasting effect in terms of it making the listener a better person — which, I think, is what you are suggesting?*

Well, art must have the capacity to improve matters or what is its point? I think music, especially live music, has the ability to lift us up to our higher selves. In the collective moment of a performance, people are united by the music. That, in itself, has a moral force. It can have a supremely positive influence on a person and their relation to other people. Our better selves are made up of a collection of transitory experiences that have elevated us spiritually, music being potentially the most transcendent and necessary of these shared experiences. If we are deprived of transcendent experiences, we grow smaller, harder, less tolerant.

*I'm interested in the notion of the residual idea that you mentioned earlier. Given the ambition and subject matter of* Ghosteen, *was there a surfeit of residual ideas hanging around from it when you started writing these new songs?*

Actually, no. That's maybe because, with the new record we're working on, I had to, in a way, navigate the presence of Arthur. Not that I can ever entirely do that, of course, or that I'd even want to. It's more that *Ghosteen* was a very popular record and I could quite easily have written more songs in the same vein. I had the language at hand and I knew how to do it. That would have been the easier option. It requires a certain amount of nerve to rip it all up and start again with something that feels new and, therefore, dangerous. For a start, your brain does not want to go there and it's telling you that. It's challenging to write away from the known and the familiar.

*Do you think that, on some subliminal level, your brain tells you not to take creative risks as an artist?*

I do. I've been thinking about this a lot. The brain enjoys its patterns and paths and wants us to do the things that are familiar. Like heroin, which is the big daddy of deceiving ideas!

What I'm saying is that you can't get to that truly creative place unless you find the dangerous idea. And, once again, that's like standing at the mouth of the tomb, in vigil, waiting for the shock of the risen Christ, the shock of the imagination, the astonishing idea.

*I can tell you've given this some thought, but it strikes me that you could reach that truly creative place and still be writing about Arthur, maybe on some deeper unconscious level. I imagine, in a way, it would be hard not to.*

Yes, that is so true, Seán.

The loss of my son is a condition, not a theme. It's a condition and, as such, it infuses everything. My relationship to words has changed, for sure, but so has my relationship to all things. My life is lived with a different intensity. Not the burning intensity of youth, but something else – a kind of spiritual audacity. I've noticed this in a lot of grieving people, by the way – a kind of zeal. It's what I see when I watch Susie go off to work, and it's what I hope exists in the last couple of records we have made – an audacity in the face of things, a kind of reckless refusal to submit to the condition of the world.

Maybe that's what I was trying to say earlier about getting old. I think the old become not just repositories of lived experience, but of the dead, too. I've lost my mother this year, as well as a good friend, Hal Willner, and they have joined an ever-expanding company of loved ones who have passed on. I think these absences do something to those of us who remain behind. We are like haunted houses, in a way, and our absences can even transform us so that we feel a quiet but urgent love for those who remain, a tenderness to all of humanity, as well as an earned understanding that our time is finite.

But with regard to Arthur, the new record is not about that, but it's still about that. Do you understand what I mean? It's not explicitly about that, even as everything I do will always somehow be about that.

*Yes, that's what I was trying to get at. It's really complex territory, Nick.*

It is. And I'm tired.

*Okay, I'll let you go.*

Oh, by the way, have I told you how I've taken up ceramics?

*Yes, you did mention it a while back, somewhat reticently as I recall.*

Well, it's now a thing, Seán, the ceramics; it's definitely a thing — but maybe for another time. You must come down to the yard and check them out.

# 10

# A Series of Ordinary Carnages

~

So, listen. I was thinking about what we were talking about in regard to the new record and the concept of departure, and I think I may have steered you the wrong way.

*Okay. If I remember correctly, you were talking about the grand ballad tradition and, in particular, the theme of departure, as being a kind of conceptual starting point for the record.*

Yes. That's right, we spoke about that. And I think some of the new songs definitely have a mood or a feel that is familiar to older songs from another time, another era – classic songs, or whatever you want to call them.

*So have you thought some more about the recurring imagery of people travelling and departing?*

Yes. And while there is a sense of departure in the songs, as we discussed earlier, I don't think the record is primarily about that; rather, there is a general feeling of moving towards something. A sense that perhaps the final destiny of the journey is at hand.

*Which is?*

Death, maybe. Or God, probably. Transformation, definitely.

*I knew it!*

I know! Anyway, that's basically what I rang to tell you. Sorry if I sound over-excited. I just think Warren and I have made something really good. It feels like a massive leap forward. It feels, I don't know, *free*!

*Free in what way? Musically? Lyrically?*

It feels like this record has almost completely shaken off *Ghosteen* – which is no mean feat – shaken it off and moved towards something new. It feels unfettered and unencumbered by what's gone before. Free from the past. I don't know, Seán, it just feels fucking *free*!

*You certainly sound energised.*

Yes, and I was thinking that the idea of arrival or destiny emerges, especially beautifully, in the song 'Carnage'. And, by the way, that's what we're calling the record: *Carnage*.

*That's a strong statement!*

Yes, it is, and I like the fact that it's full of other words – cage, age, rage, arcane, grace.

*Is 'anger' in there, too?*

And anger, yes.

*Is it an angry record?*

Yes, definitely. Sometimes it's seething.

*'Carnage' suggests slaughter, destruction and death. Why did you settle on such a brutally powerful word?*

Well, the record seems to be nested in a collective catastrophe.

*The pandemic?*

Yes, and that collective catastrophe is echoed, song by song, in a series of small carnages.

I was thinking about the song 'Carnage', itself, which deals exclusively with a kind of metamorphosis. It begins:

> *I always seem to be saying goodbye*
> *And rolling through the mountains*
> *Like a train*

And, I have to say, Seán, I was very happy about that. It's a great opening line, and so full of promise. That was a good day in the Cave household! It feels to me like it's the voice, not just of the narrator, but also of the living song itself.

*And to be clear, the narrator is you – not a character?*

Myself, Seán, always myself – even when it's a character it's just me in disguise. The first line was half lifted from a poem I wrote last year called 'The Spanish Lady' that begins like this:

> *All my songs are waving goodbye*
> *They are trailing behind them a smear of rage*

*That certainly sounds like you're acknowledging your anger and regret. Are the songs attempts to assuage that anger?*

Christ, you're starting to sound like my therapist.

*Do you actually see a therapist?*

I do, sometimes, yes. I remember one time, a couple of years ago when I was living in Los Angeles, my friend Thomas Houseago, who's an artist and is dealing with all sorts of trauma, suggested I should go and see a woman who practises somatic healing. Do you know about that?

*Is it to do with releasing all the negative stuff that you're holding in your body? Is that it?*

Yes, it's a therapy that focuses on trauma being trapped in the body, something like that. It all sounded a bit LA for me, but I'm willing to give anything a go – as you know! So I went along and met this beautiful, very serene woman – I've forgotten her name. She began by talking to me about all this deep stuff – Arthur and so on – and then asked me to lie down on a couch. She put a blanket over me, and I almost immediately fell into this extremely relaxed state. It was quite beautiful, really. Then she took me through my body and asked me where the locus of my feeling was and I said it was in my stomach. So she asked me to concentrate and to describe the feeling. Well, at that moment, all I felt in my stomach was a kind of bliss that kept building and building, and I told her that. I was sort of tranced-out, and I told her I was very happy and I said all I felt was a kind of euphoria.

So she told me to keep concentrating on that feeling in my stomach, experience it, and then I felt, clear as day, the letter 'A' appear on my stomach, which was really weird. I told her that I was seeing this letter 'A', and she said, 'Okay. Just stay with it.' Now, I assumed the 'A' was for Arthur, and I told her so, and she said just concentrate on this letter 'A' some more. So I did, and suddenly I said, 'No, it's not "A" for Arthur, it's "A" for *anger*,' and as I said it, suddenly this rush of rage went through my body. It was incredibly strong, my whole body vibrating with a terrible fury. It was insane. And she just goes, 'There you go. There you go.' And I'm crying and shaking and fucking roaring with anger. It was quite something.

*That sounds primal. Did it help?*

Maybe. But I guess what I'm saying is that you never really know what you are carrying around inside you.

I have absolutely no idea why I told you that story. You actually are like a therapist!

*Maybe I missed my vocation . . . Did you go back for another session with the somatic woman?*

Fuck, no!

*Man, I would have been back there every week! Anyway, we were talking about escape and arrival being the main themes of the new record.*

Yes, so what I was saying is that the song 'Carnage' is not just about escaping the past, but rather it is explicitly coursing towards a kind of ecstasy. In the second verse of the song, the runaway couple share a vision:

> *The sun, a barefoot child with fire in his hair*

And then the whole song sort of detonates in an ecstasy of annihilation!

> *And then a sudden sun explodes!*

What I'm trying to say here is that the record may seem to be concerned with leaving, in the classic style of a Jimmy Webb song, let's say, but is actually about arrival, or maybe transformation – a kind of changing from one thing into another. About beginning at one place and arriving somewhere else. Most of the songs seem to do that – you know, they are split in two by an event. It seems important somehow to acknowledge that on a personal level.

*Because it's rooted in your own experience of the before and after of a seismic event?*

Well, we've talked about this a lot, the idea that suffering is, by its nature, the primary mechanism of change, and that it somehow presents us with the opportunity to transform into something else, something different, hopefully something better. That God bestows upon us these terrible, devastating opportunities that bring amelioration and transformation. This change is not something we necessarily seek out; rather, change is often brought to bear upon us, through a shattering or annihilation of our former selves.

*I see. So, on a much bigger scale, this also relates to the collective experience of the pandemic.*

Yes, I think very much so. The album might even be dealing with this to a degree. I'm not entirely sure, though. It's early days yet and the songs have to settle in. No doubt they have a lot yet left to reveal.

*As always. And that will happen at some point when you finally get to perform them?*

Yes. It's all in the performing – performing in front of an audience. That's when the fullness of the songs presents itself. I think the audience draws forth the true intent of the songs. Not that the recorded versions are lesser forms, mind. I actually prefer original recordings to live ones as something to casually listen to. They're less histrionic, less demanding, but the live versions of the songs are much more experiential and communal.

Seán, just out of curiosity, I'm interested to know what you think of the song 'Balcony Man'?

*On first listening, I felt that it seemed to be speaking directly to this moment we're in: the pandemic and, in particular, our collective experience of suspended time.*

Yes. And, as you know, my balcony was where the work got done for this record, throughout this strange, suspended time. I hauled a chair and table out and did most of the writing there. I remember feeling this weird paradoxical disconnect of a beautiful summer and a dreadful pandemic. So much hope and so much hopelessness.

*There are some quite surreal lines in that song:*

> *I'm the balcony man*
> *I am two hundred pounds . . .*

Yes, it's the statue again, the ice sculpture, from another song, 'White Elephant'. But 'Balcony Man' is a much more playful song, wherein the narrator happily anticipates congress with his wife. It feels optimistic. And it has that almost orgasmic finale:

> *This morning is amazing and so are you*
> *This morning is amazing and so are you*

So all things considered, it's a radically optimistic little song seated in a disaster.

*Yes, and it ends with the line: 'What doesn't kill you just makes you crazier.' Is that optimism or an acceptance of life's absurdity?*

Well, in the context of the song, it's a light-hearted, good-natured pay-off, but not without some truth. I think it's fair to say many people's mental health has been tested through the pandemic, some-times to a devastating degree. You know, the jeopardy, the existential dread, the abandoning of our collective sanity, the ultimate shedding of our communal strength.

*Do you think that is what's happening, that our collective strength has somehow ebbed away in the face of this terrible crisis?*

Actually, I think it is more than that. I think the pandemic offered us an opportunity to improve the world and we blew it. We squan-dered it. Early on, many of us felt that a chance was presented to us, as a civilisation, to put aside our vanities, grievances and divisions, our hubris, our callous disregard for each other, and come together around a common enemy. Our shared predicament was a gift that could potentially have transformed the world into something extraordinary. To our shame this didn't happen. The Right got scarier, the Left got crazier, and our already fractured civilisation atomised into something that resembled a collective lunacy. For many, this has been followed by a weariness, an ebbing away of our strength and resolve and a dwindling belief in the common good. Many people's mental health has suffered as a consequence.

So many of the letters I received on The Red Hand Files have been extremely disturbing. People just trying to cope, not knowing what to think or do, hanging on by a thread, and others being completely overwhelmed, sent mad by loneliness. And there is a level of societal dissonance that is fuelled by the internet.

Beneath all this, there is a reservoir of grief. I pray that people find a way through it. Just hang in there and try to stay sane.

*I wonder if it is necessary to almost go under in order to come through stronger.*

You mean, in regard to grieving?

*Yes.*

That's an interesting idea, and I completely understand what you mean, but there is a very dangerous and seductive feeling to living life on the brink that I think should be resisted. In that very dark place, the grieving person can feel a proximity to the one they have lost that can be difficult to turn away from, or return from. That particular kind of grief can have a deadening and, I don't know, mechanising effect that, in some cases, can be permanent. I mean, Susie and I felt this within ourselves; for a while, there was a kind of zombification.

I don't want you to misunderstand what I am saying, but there can be a kind of morbid worshipping of an absence. A reluctance to move beyond the trauma, because the trauma is where the one you lost resides, and therefore the place where meaning exists.

*Almost everything about grief is so slippery and unmooring – and potentially treacherous.*

It is. And I think the pandemic has brought about an acute collective vulnerability. When we went into lockdown, we were brought together through our shared experience, but also atomised. For many people, I think it was too much to handle.

*Yes, it was such an extreme dynamic – a collective experience defined to a great degree by isolation.*

It was similar to the feeling I experienced when I lost Arthur. I felt myself, on one hand, swept up in a kind of commonality of human suffering, but also I was suddenly entirely alone, almost as if I had been marked or branded by the loss of Arthur. That extreme paradox can feel like a kind of madness. I have never experienced such aloneness. You are essentially beyond the reach of any assistance – all the best intentions people have for you. Susie was the same. We had each other but we were also unreachable, even at times to each other. We were together, but essentially alone.

*That must have been so destabilising, the sense that everything you took for granted and held to be true was suddenly being shaken to the core.*

I remember one time I was lying awake in bed next to Susie, and I had this feeling that the grief was pounding through my body with an audible roar, and despair was bursting through the tips of my fingers. I remember, in desperation, reaching across and taking Susie's hand and feeling the shock of that same violent electricity in her hand. It was so physical. That physical affliction is not often talked about, as far as I can see. We tend to see grief as an emotional state, but it is also an atrocious destabilising assault upon the body. So much so that it can feel terminal.

*Yes, and when you are deep in grief, there's no real comfort to be had in people constantly telling you that time will make things better. But I distinctly remember waking up one morning, having finally had a decent night's sleep, and thinking, it's going to be okay. There was a sense that something had shifted imperceptibility. Did that happen to you?*

Well, at first there was nothing but darkness, but, over time, Susie and I started to experience something like small fragments of light.

These points of light were essentially thoughtful gestures from the people we encountered. We began to see, in a profound way, that people were kind. People cared. I know that sounds simplistic, maybe even naïve, but I came to the conclusion that the world wasn't bad, at all – in fact, what we think of as bad, or as sin, is actually suffering. And that the world is not animated by evil, as we are so often told, but by love, and that, despite the suffering of the world, or maybe in defiance of it, people mostly just cared. I think Susie and I instinctively understood that we needed to move towards this loving force, or perish.

*Is that the prevailing message of The Red Hand Files?*

It's the prevailing message in everything I do. The Red Hand Files are an attempt to give something back to the world. They are an explicit affirmation of the value of being human. Each answer says, 'I matter. You matter. We are of consequence.' Perhaps The Red Hand Files probably deserve a conversation of their own, though?

*Yes, let's save that for later . . . I wonder if your current work rate, which is pretty phenomenal, has to do with Arthur's death? Is work a kind of salvation, if that's not too strong a word?*

Yes, that's right, the work is a form of salvation.

*Do you think you have a compulsion to write songs, even more so now?*

I feel compelled to create. It's a force beyond my control, really. And I do what I can to keep the whole creative project alive by constantly trying to surprise myself. In that way things remain interesting. However, given all that, I do like to think I could put it all aside at any point and just enjoy what this astonishing world has to offer, in and of itself.

*Have you seriously contemplated doing that?*

Yes, it has crossed my mind, but I suspect that for me the world is enlivened by the creative process. It enhances the way I see things and makes the world feel sufficient, even abundant. Without creative engagement in the world, without contributing to the spirit of the world, I think I would start to feel a bit like an onlooker or something. But maybe that would be enough, just to observe what the world has to offer. It's a rich and amazing place and perhaps it has wonder enough.

*That's quite a surprising – and refreshing – point of view.*

It's not just that I need, or even want, to write another song. The world can easily do without another Nick Cave song. But the songs do have a greater function for me. They're the way I measure my life, song by song, in order to continue a creative journey that will surely never really reach its destination, other than in what we talked about before: death, God or transcendence. The songs are like signposts left along the way that signify the journey itself – like a trail of breadcrumbs on the forest floor.

*I like the idea of moving onward but leaving signposts behind. Are they essentially saying, 'I was here. I created this'?*

They are certainly more than just melodies and words. The songs have tendrils that reach down into the lived experience that is the essence of the bigger journey, and they chart that journey. They're also very enriching for me and, for that reason alone, they need to be treated with great respect. They're part of the dynamic core of my life, and maybe to stop writing them would be to somehow abandon the active engagement with that life. The songs give my life character.

*So, for you, the act of writing a song is the core of that engagement?*

In a way, yes, and at the end of the day I have a certain amount of pride in the protean nature of the journey itself, its varied complexion. And, of course, its duration and how far the music has travelled. I mean, I'm very happy that there are songs on *Carnage* that I could never have dreamed of writing five years ago. They would have been beyond me.

*In terms of how they were written or the nature of the subject matter?*

Both, but you also want to contribute something to improving the world as well. Personally, I want to know I have done something of value within my allotted time, for others, that the songs have been of some utility to people. There is always that. I just don't believe our artistic gifts are given to us entirely for our own amusement. Songs are too valuable for that. Once again, Seán, songs are a force. They can make people better, they help people, and with that lies a responsibility.

*So when it comes down to it, it's not just about the work, but how it impacts on and enriches the lives of others?*

It's partly about the work, yes, but only partly.

You know, I touched on this in that essay we talked about previously, 'The Secret Life of the Love Song'. I wrote about how, when I was twelve years old, my father asked me what I had done for the world. How had I contributed to the world? It's pretty strange, really, when I think about it, that he would ask me that question. And, of course, I couldn't really answer him, because I was twelve fucking years old! But I did ask him what he had done and he showed me, with considerable pride, a short story he had contributed to a magazine when he was a young man. That right there is the weird self-absorption of the creative person, don't you think?

*It seems a pretty egocentric thing to do, but also revealing. Or maybe he was just incredibly insecure?*

Well, if my twelve-year-old son had asked me what had I done to contribute to the world, I hope I would have ruffled his hair and said, 'Made you, little guy.' Because it has to be about the ones you love, beginning with those closest to you and then emanating outward. There is the work, of course, and if we can free it from that sort of self-absorption or self-conceit, so that it becomes an expression of love, then that has extraordinary value. But it has to

172

be about love. And it took a devastation to teach me that, to make me realise I needed to define myself first as a father and a husband and a son – as part of a family – and then finally as an artist.

*How did you arrive at a balance between the responsibilities of family and the compulsion to create, which are often in conflict?*

I'm not sure I ever did, and I am not without some regrets around that. But I'm working on it. I'm getting there. I think so, anyway. And I'm growing old so it's inevitable really to consider what all this amounts to. But when I'm on my death bed and breathing my last breath with Susie beside me, I don't think I'll be saying, 'Darling, lean closer, I have something to tell you.' And she'll whisper, 'Yes, my love,' and I'll say, 'I wrote "The Mercy Seat".'

*Well, you never know . . . But, seriously, you did write 'The Mercy Seat' and it shouldn't be discounted. That said, I guess you inevitably write a different kind of song as you get older?*

I think my recent songs feel more lived in, like they have travelled further, because, you know, they have. They feel like they are more experienced and have accrued a bit more knowledge – at least, in my humble opinion!

*Surely getting older must impinge on how you perform on stage.*

Ah, shit, I'm only sixty-three! However, I haven't performed in a while and the performances I was doing on the last tour required a huge amount of energy. I haven't done a full knee drop for two years. That will be a challenge. The knee drop feels like a matter of professional honour. I love a good knee drop. It's the most beautiful of all onstage moves. Elvis, James Brown, Patti Smith, Al Green, fucking Jim Morrison – it's a beautiful sacred act – to fall to your knees and howl your heart out into the microphone. I would hate to be too old to do that.

*I know it's not very rock 'n' roll, but have you considered kneepads?*

Well, Iggy used them, I'm told, but that rather defeats the purpose. What a guy, though, Iggy Pop. What an extraordinary, singular performer.

*Yes. Primal. I'd love to have seen the Stooges back in the day, but I think there's something heroic about his later performances, just to be still doing it with such utter commitment.*

It's incredible, but you have to realise that something super-human takes over when you're on stage. It's like a kind of rampant potential. The adrenaline, the energy of the crowd, the sheer force of the music — it's like you change into another thing. Another entity. It's a metamorphosis. I have to say there are things that you can do on stage that would most definitely be ill-advised when off stage. All that indiscriminate sexual energy, the physical contact, the complicity with the audience in some sort of wild, ritualistic act.

*Do you think social attitudes have changed so much that the kind of raw, Dionysian sexual energy you are talking about might soon be considered inappropriate?*

I don't know, but no doubt it will all go horribly wrong one day! I have to say, being on stage, performing to a crowd, and being swept up by the wanton power of the music, of the performance itself, of the audience's own frenzy is something else. To think you can climb to the top of a fucking lighting rig and flail around, or crawl around the stage on your belly like a snake, or walk across the hands of the crowd — it's a kind of beautiful madness, a beautiful, dangerous madness. I don't know how you can rein that feeling in. I don't know how the audience can rein it in. It is a primal force. A consensual pact. And it has little to do with age, and more to giving oneself over to the potency of the moment.

*How do you feel about the tendency for certain bands to go on and on into old age, like, say, the Rolling Stones? There's a kind of heritage rock now that essentially feeds on nostalgia for the past that our younger punk selves would have probably railed against.*

Well, personally, I look at the Rolling Stones as an extraordinary experiment in longevity. Mick Jagger is still defying the odds, with all his hair and all his teeth. I haven't seen them since they played Melbourne in the seventies but I assume it still means something for them to get up there and put on a show. You have to respect that. Complacency is a sin, pure and simple. To be given the extraordinary opportunity to perform in front of people is a God-given privilege, and not to be squandered.

*It's funny, because I remember talking to you a few years ago and you said that, as you got older, rock 'n' roll was fraught with embarrassment. And then not long afterwards, you formed Grinderman!*

Ha! For me, Grinderman was a glorious, shameless, defiant embrace of the more problematic aspects of our natures – specifically, our explicit maleness. And despite that, Grinderman was greatly loved by men and women alike, as far as I could see.

*What was the initial impulse behind the project?*

In its perverse way, it was anti-rock 'n' roll. It was experimental. And, even though it was high energy and stayed within the form, I think we avoided the standard, go-to rock 'n' roll clichés. We were trying to show that it was still possible to make compelling, confronting and original music, using the traditional rock 'n' roll format.

*It was so over the top, too, especially the subject matter. I mean, 'No Pussy Blues' . . .*

Yes, Grinderman touched on some interesting lyrical ideas – the nerve-wracked sexuality of the music. I mean, the performance anxiety of Grinderman was really quite a marvellous thing – explicit, confrontational and deeply disturbed. It was actually too anxiety-ridden sexually to be hyper-masculine. I really liked that about it, the sort of gloominess of the sexual themes.

I remember being in Mark Knopfler's studio in Chiswick and Jason Pierce from Spiritualized came in to hang out. We played him 'Worm Tamer' – which was Grinderman's supreme specimen of a kind of sustained sexual insanity – and he listened to it and said, 'Have you any idea just how fucked-up this sounds?' We were very happy to hear that, especially coming from Jason.

*'Worm Tamer' has some, how shall I put it, interesting lyrics.*

Yes, it has to be one of the most sexually fraught songs ever recorded. It's like an Edvard Munch painting on amyl nitrate. The extreme coital horror! But after *Grinderman 2*, I think Warren and I kind of thought we had exhausted that idea of rock music, at least for the time being. After that, our music took a different direction altogether.

*I always felt there was a certain kind of stoical, old-school masculinity about the Bad Seeds.*

You could say that. You could definitely say that.

*When I did an onstage interview with you at the Roundhouse back in 2009 for your novel,* The Death of Bunny Munro, *you said that a lot of the male banter in the book came from listening to the lads on the tour bus.*

I suspect at the time I was trying to deflect the blame onto other members of the band. Mostly, I just tapped into my own most base and unfiltered impulses, to be perfectly honest. It wasn't overly taxing on the imagination. But you're right, there are very few corrective influences on tour, that's for sure.

*It's essentially a bunch of men going to work.*

Well, in our case, yes. You know, at one time, we did view the making of our kind of music as an essentially masculine enterprise, or at least I did. But that changed.

*Oh yes? Tell me more.*

I think that as the music has developed over the years it has become more feminised, in the traditional reading of that word. It has become more nurturing, more vulnerable, more empathetic, generally speaking. Not that there weren't those aspects to the music before, but a lot of the songs these days feel, I don't know, more generous.

*Yes, but you've never had a female musician in the band.*

Well, funnily enough, we found a female keyboard player, Carly Paradis, who was going to play on the *Ghosteen* tour. She seemed really good. She's been in the Bad Seeds now for a year and a half, learned all the songs – knows them better than we do, most likely – but she's never actually met anyone face to face, because of the pandemic. But we took her on because she seemed the best person for the job. She had an energy about her the other people we looked at just didn't have.

*It's a real shame you never got to tour* Ghosteen.

Yes, heart-breaking, really. I felt we were just going to blow the lid off the whole thing. We felt we had touched on something with the *Skeleton Tree* shows, something we'd stumbled blindly upon, a kind of radical connectivity. It wasn't like there was a plan or anything. We were met with an amazing response from people that just grew, night after night, into a frenzy, like the audience was hungry for something – desperate.

*Desperate for what, do you think?*

Meaning. Desperate for meaning.

*For the music to be meaningful?*

No, for their lives to have meaning.

*Was it difficult to go on tour at that time, to leave home and travel, in the wake of all that had happened?*

Listen, the *Skeleton Tree* tour was so . . . I don't know . . . before the tour began I had just sort of collapsed. I was bedridden for about six weeks with some weird flu. I was exhausted, depressed. Those were very dark days, and I had a kind of overwhelming pre-tour dread. I literally had no idea how I was going to be able to perform. I was so fucking sad about Arthur. So depleted.

Anyway, Susie had heard about a nutritionist and I met with her on a Skype call and she claimed she could get me back on my feet in two weeks, so I sort of put myself in her hands. I drank all this shit she prescribed and stopped eating certain things and started eating other things, and stopped smoking and taking sleeping pills, and, well, she got me back on my feet. She was a miracle-worker. Nevertheless, I was still scared. I didn't know if I could perform or not, even just get on stage, to be honest.

*That must have been terrifying.*

Yes, it was, but it's like anyone who has a job to do – you just do it, right? I've seen various band members go on tour over the years, crew members, too, under the direst circumstances and perform heroic acts of mettle and endurance. You pack your suitcase – some suits and a couple of boxes of hair dye – and you go and do your job. That's the way it is. It's not like you have any choice. But something happened on that *Skeleton Tree* tour that is difficult to describe.

*Can you try?*

Well, there was so much trepidation. And then the shows began in Australia, and there was something about walking on stage into the force field of the audience's concern and awareness and love that was so restorative to the soul. I find it difficult to explain . . .

It changed me. It really changed me. I feel very indebted.

*To the audience?*

Yes, to the audience, and the band, too.

*So you were aware of the audience's collective concern, the sense that they were willing you on, but also watching out for you. I wondered about that when I saw you play the O2 on that tour. It was palpable from where I was standing.*

Yes, I felt that, very deeply.

*How do you feel about that now, looking back?*

Nothing but the deepest gratitude.

*In that respect, it would have been fascinating to see how audiences responded to* Ghosteen *live.*

Yes, as you said, it's a real shame it didn't happen.

*But other things have, interesting things . . .*

Yes, including a mad fucking book I may yet come to regret!

*I was thinking more of The Red Hand Files and how they have developed during this strange time.*

Well, I started The Red Hand Files long before the pandemic. The Red Hand Files are in no way a response to the current situation.

*Yes, but the tone changed during the pandemic. When you started, it felt like you were just trying something out that might or might not work.*

Well, I felt that I had things to say that I couldn't say within the limitations of the song. The process of songwriting is so abstract and slow, whereas I felt a sense of urgency to engage, to converse with people.

*Most people would probably have done that on social media – not that I'm recommending that, mind.*

I spent a year on Twitter, not active, just following people, but in the end even that proved to be utterly dispiriting. I followed all these people, people I admired, people I had been interested in for years – podcasters, writers, journalists, public thinkers, social critics – and I found that the form somehow diminished almost all of them. Not all, but most. Initially, I thought it was like the Wild West or punk rock, but Twitter is really just a factory that churns out arseholes. I got off all social media in the end.

*Good for you. So where did the idea for The Red Hand Files come from?*

It was a combination of things. For years I'd wanted to do something that expanded the scope of what I could do as an artist. Something that wasn't confined specifically to music, or even art, but had to do with communication of a different type, perhaps a kind of open conversation. I'd been talking about it with my team for some time, the creation of a space where I could discuss ideas that sat outside my role as a musician, but I had no idea how to do it.

*You launched the website by posting a statement that still stands: 'You can ask me anything. There will be no moderator. This will be between you and me. Let's see what happens. Much love, Nick.' It still seems like an audacious thing for a rock singer to do.*

To be honest, sometimes I suffer a kind of professional vertigo when I think about The Red Hand Files. I think, what the fuck am I doing writing to a suicidal girl about how to deal with her feelings of loneliness? It just seems so ludicrous. Just the presumptuousness of it — with what authority am I doing this? But then I think, well, she asked in good faith, and if I send a reply, maybe she won't feel so lonely. So I do. And suddenly that seems okay. That's it, really, and, you know, it doesn't just benefit her, it benefits me as well.

*So it's pretty instinctive in a way, which somehow makes it more interesting — and risky.*

Yes, and I've become quite accustomed now to that queasy feeling of stepping into the unknown. I think I've learned to trust that sense of discomfort as a signifier that something important may be afoot, that change is happening. It's like the same dizzying effect I get when I write a line down for a song that appears at first to be quite possibly a very bad idea, but keeps drawing me back. These kinds of ideas are often the agents of progress and change.

The Red Hand Files brought about a significant change in my life. For better or for worse, they became the channel that allowed me to step outside my own expectations of what it was to be a rock singer, or whatever it is that I am. They freed me from myself.

*From the idea of Nick Cave that was out there?*

Yes, I suppose so. There is definitely something about the perverse nature of the whole experiment that is very appealing to me. It's not something I can rationalise, because it doesn't make sense on some level, unless you read the questions that people send me. As soon as you do that, it really does make sense. The people who write in have legitimised the project with their trust and openness. The question section, which only I have access to, is unbelievably moving. It's like the book of longing — so real and so raw. But it is hard to talk about without your having some idea of the kinds of questions I am presented with these days. I could maybe send you a selection of letters or questions and you'll see what I mean.

*That sounds good. Let's talk some more when I've read them. So I have to ask, what would the younger Nick Cave make of the older one?*

Oh, Jesus, I hate that question!

*Really? Why?*

I don't like the implication. It implies that the younger me would in some way be scornful of the older me, which I don't think is necessarily the case. In fact, the opposite would probably be true. I think if the younger Nick Cave were to look at the older Nick Cave and find out he was still doing more or less the same things, he would be appalled, frankly. And rightly so.

*Yes, but he might also be surprised by the dramatic nature of the change.*

Like everybody, Seán, I've been on a journey, and that must involve change, or what's the point of going on the journey at all? With hindsight, part of it is about shedding the foolishness of youth. That's what maturity is, but I also think I've maintained a consistent essentialness of character throughout, because many of the things I discovered and loved as a young man, teenager or, indeed, child, I still carry with me. They remain the touchstones.

*How would you define that essentialness of character?*

It has something to do with beauty and sorrow. Or maybe the proximity of one to the other. Something like that. And I remember feeling that as a child.

*As far back as you can remember, have you always equated beauty with sorrow?*

It's difficult to know where to start with explaining this, but it has something to do with a particular and singular idea about beauty. And that has something to do with a *need to see* – a kind of voyeurism – and also arranging the world in images.

*I'm not sure I follow.*

Well, for instance, I've always had a love of figurative art, narrative art and symbolic art, especially in painting. And, of course, I've written primarily narrative songs using vivid imagery. I seem to experience the world visually, through stories and symbols and metaphors. It all comes down to seeing, essentially, to the visual nature of things. That is the way I've experienced the world since childhood. And that is the way I write songs – as a series of highly visual images, often violent, mostly sorrowful. Warren, on the other hand, hears the world.

*Perhaps you can give an example of this way of seeing from your childhood?*

I remember one particular instance when I was really young, maybe five or six years old, and I was lying in bed between my mother and father. I used to climb into bed with them every morning and talk about things; it was my moment with them, while my brothers and sister slept. My father had been away on a trip somewhere and he told me there was a present for me on top of the piano. It was a massive picture book called *The Fairy Tale Tree* that was full of folk stories and fables from all over the world, many of them quite surreal, violent and sad. It had the most beautiful illustrations and, looking back, I think the pictures in the book took me away, somehow. I remember I used to lie in bed at night and see the strange images and creatures from the book marching past my closed eyes. They made sense of the world.

Each chapter in *The Fairy Tale Tree* was a branch of the tree, and each story was a nest on the branch of the tree – and telling you this now, I realise that this is the same imagery I used in 'Spinning Song' from *Ghosteen*. You know, even now, it holds sway. I treasured this book, read and reread it for years, and revisited it all through my teens, and I actually used some of the illustrations on the inner sleeve of the first Birthday Party record, I think – a picture of a red devil drawing water from a well.

Then there was the family Bible that belonged to my grandmother. She lived in Melbourne, and I discovered the book in one of her cupboards when we visited. Again, I was very young and the pictures fascinated me. I pored over that book, sitting on the end of the bed in her bedroom, just staring at the pictures. There was the pull of these vivid, mysterious illustrations, but also the idea that these books – the Bible, *The Fairy Tale Tree* – contained secret knowledge. Imaginatively, I'm sure the aloneness of the experience was important, too. But what I'm getting at is that these experiences from my childhood remain firmly fixed in my soul, as a form of melancholy remembering. You must have had books like that as a child, right?

*Yes, I remember an illustrated* Aesop's Fables *and a book of dark Nordic fairy tales with black-and-white illustrations that seemed really vivid and exotic. But it's telling that your formal influences were visual rather than literary.*

That's right. I was always more drawn to painting than literature, actually. For me, painting was the thing.

*I've noticed you often become quite animated when you talk about art.*

Really? I take a lot from visual art. I'm more energised by it, I guess. It's more instinctual.

*More instinctual?*

More natural. More in my nature.

*What sort of work were you making when you attended art school in Melbourne in the seventies?*

Crude figurative paintings, really – large, flat, compositionally awkward things. At the time I loved the work of Alan Davie, the Scottish painter who seems to be largely forgotten. He did big, spiritual, symbolist paintings – I found them very powerful. Also

Sidney Nolan, of course, I loved Sydney Nolan, and Brett Whiteley. I only lasted a couple of years at art school, though. I failed second year. They claimed my head was elsewhere; I guess they meant in rock 'n' roll.

*Was that the case?*

No, actually. I really wanted to be a painter. I just happened to be in a band as well. I guess in the eyes of the college this made me unserious.

*Apart from that, how would you describe your time at art school?*

Well, I went there from a quite traditional, all-boys secondary school, where I think it is fair to say that anyone who was interested in art was looked on with a kind of disdain and suspicion. So to go to art school was an enormously liberating experience. I did know something about art. I had paid attention in Art History at school, pored over art books, and spent time in galleries, but when I arrived at art school it was like stepping into another world. I was adopted by these older third-year students, and we would spend our nights sitting in the pub talking about art, exclusively about art and artists. I was very interested in what these students were doing, and they gave me advice about my stuff. They were fascinating individuals – radical, eccentric, compelling people – who had a certain heightened relationship to the world and spoke with such knowledge and passion about art. I remember feeling a kinship with them and thinking, this is what I want to be. I want to be an artist. I wanted to give my life over to this weird, introspective, obsessive occupation. I wanted to be a painter.

*Even though you didn't achieve that goal, the fertile environment you describe must have instilled in you a sense of creative potential.*

It did, mainly because the older students taught me so much about the world – about working hard, living a life outside the normal constraints, and finding your own voice.

*And, of course, you met Anita Lane.*

Yes, Anita was doing a foundation year in a different art college, and she was just out of this world, a ferociously talented person, unbelievably beautiful and so full of life. I had never met anyone like her. We would spend our days making things, and drawing, and painting, and just soaking up the world and each other. These were innocent, uncomplicated, dazzling days. We were all finding out stuff at a rapid rate. We were friends with Tony Clark, one of the teachers at Prahran College, who was a fascinating character, a kind of outsider himself, and, to this day, a wonderful painter. He turned us on to all manner of things that sat outside the conventional art narrative: late-period de Chirico, Alberto Savinio and outsider art, and the wonderful cat paintings of Louis Wain, and Pierre Klossowski, and Leonardo's shocking cadaver drawings. And books, too: Huysmans and Bataille and Strindberg. It was such a wild, vibrant year or two of my life, before things took a different, darker, more complicated turn.

*And yet you didn't finish art college. Is that a source of regret?*

To fail art school was devastating. Even though I gave up painting and threw myself into the band and all that rock 'n' roll had to offer, and started writing songs seriously, and finding a way of being on stage, and travelling around and making a name for myself, deep down inside I really just wanted to be a painter. Weirdly, I have always felt that I was in the wrong occupation – not an imposter, as such, just ill-suited to music as a form.

*That's quite an extraordinary thing to say.*

Well, it's not to say I'm not grateful for all that music has given me, or that music hasn't become a platform for true and authentic expression, or that I haven't developed certain talents, or come to the realisation that music is perhaps the most mysterious and purest of all the creative mediums; it's just that I have always felt I have a sensibility – an essentially visual relationship with the world – that is at odds with a lot of the musicians I am acquainted with. I am often mystified and in awe at the deep understanding my musician friends have of sound – of music.

*So were there particular artists you were interested in when you were young?*

I kind of loved everything back then, especially painting. Van Gogh, El Greco, Goya, Munch, the nudes of Renoir. I loved Piero della Francesca and Stefan Lochner and Rodin and Donatello. Titian, too, and Rubens. Oskar Kokoschka and Egon Schiele. Just the experience of walking into the National Gallery in Melbourne and coming across a work that broke you open because it contained the artist's soul. It's a beautiful, strange, almost perverse idea, to create a kind of essential impression of the self that hangs on a wall in a frame, trapped in paint.

*I've heard you talk passionately about certain classical religious paintings that you found compelling back then.*

I'd say there were three major religious works that had a huge impact on me from very early on, and to this day I still hold dear. The first is Grünewald's *Crucifixion*, which I saw when I was in my early teens. It's a kind of horror image, a torture image, that seemed so at odds with the placid image of Christ that was presented to me in my choirboy days. It was my secret, suffering Christ.

The second is the *Rondanini Pietà* by Michelangelo. It's his final sculpture, in which the figure of Christ has been quite literally hacked back to its essentialness and is just so shockingly human. I'm often encouraged by this sculpture in relation to the way a well-honed lyric can be chopped back to its inner spiritual shape in the editing process, when we are in the studio.

Finally, there is a plaster, rag and wood sculpture, *Christ and the Magdalen*, by Rodin, where a naked, voluptuous Magdalen has crawled up onto the crucified Christ. I saw this in a catalogue when I was young, and when I witnessed it for real, in the Musée Rodin in Paris in the early eighties, it just blew my mind. It was so tortured and sexual and sad. In some ways this image is the spiritual heart of *The Boatman's Call*.

Oh, and there is also a huge canvas, *The Beheading of John the Baptist* by Pierre Puvis de Chavannes, which was in the entrance to the National Gallery of London when I first came here. I used to spend hours sitting in front of it. I'm not certain why, but it kept drawing me back. I'm not even sure it is a particularly good painting, but it just had something that I connected with. I wrote the song 'Mercy' with that massive canvas towering over my head. I'm not sure that is such a great song, either. But those works had a kind of mystical hold even on my younger self that I think was beyond art itself.

*They had a mystical hold on you?*

Yes. Much like the poems of St John of the Cross or the strange erotic writings of Saint Teresa of Ávila, which live beyond poetry, or the works of William Blake or St Augustine. Their poems serve an ulterior purpose beyond being beautiful works of art. They are in service to the divine, and become ladders to spiritual experience. I didn't see things in that way when I was young, of course, but nevertheless I had an uncommon interest in these images.

*These are probably not the kinds of images that most young art students would tend to be drawn to. Do you think there was something about your upbringing that give you the confidence to be different, even contrarian?*

When I was a young man, I was definitely excited by things that flew in the face of what was happening within the scene I existed in. That's for sure. I enjoyed the dissonance that occurred when you took the other side, as it were. So, back then, I was a true contrarian in that respect. I mean, The Birthday Party, for all their chaotic nature, weren't anti-establishment or politically radical. As a band, we weren't concerned with the workings of the world as such, or with challenging the status quo. We were more concerned with disrupting our own consciousness, our own states of mind – more concerned with chaos than anarchy, if that makes sense. For me, it has always been about the nature of the human soul rather than the problems of the society we live in.

*You don't think the latter impacts on the former?*

For sure, but I also think the condition of the soul can be treated independently of the situation one finds oneself in.

Personally, I don't think my job as a songwriter is to inform people of the problems in our society. I have never seen my role as a musician as didactic or instructive. There are many musicians who do that job a lot better than I could, although I really don't think it is a good idea to get your politics from rock stars. In fact, rock musicians seem to me to be the least credible people on earth to be doing that. Thinking back, I guess that's probably one reason why we felt like such outsiders in Britain in the eighties. We came over here when Thatcher was running the country and everyone was outraged by the whole situation, but, as Australians, we had no real connection with that. We loved The Pop Group, for instance, who were politically extreme in their own way, but it was more the visceral chaos of their music we were drawn to. We were good friends, but we couldn't have been further away from them in terms of what motivated the chaos.

*Yes, and that was evident in your music. Would you say you are still a contrarian to a degree?*

I think we need to be wary of the word 'contrarian', or, at least, how we use it. While the idea of being contrary for the sake of it, for the simple pleasure of pissing people off, can certainly have a fortifying effect, for me that's not what it's about. I think contra-riness can be a kind of survival strategy, a way of dismantling the preconceptions of others. And a way of keeping your art alive. It's about freedom as much as anything else – the freedom of deliber-ately twisting away from the demands of your public. As an artist, you want to be fluid and impossible to define, even to yourself, and committed only to where your heart might take you, even if that is in direct conflict with the prevailing mood of the moment.

*The freedom that comes from constantly moving forward, from a commitment to creative risk-taking and reinvention?*

Yes, and as I was saying earlier, the new record feels free in that way. Even though it was a struggle to write, the finished thing seems to be something that exists completely on its own terms, and the more I think about it, that most likely has something to do with the pandemic.

*In what way, exactly?*

Insofar as the rules that govern our lives no longer apply. I am very familiar with this feeling. It is the compensatory gift at the heart of grief. The usual precepts collapse under the weight of the calamity: the terrible demands that we place upon ourselves; our own internal judging voice; the endless expectations and opinions of others. They suddenly become less important and there is a wonderful freedom in that as well.

*Well, 'freedom's just another word for nothing left to lose', as the great Kris Kristofferson put it.*

Ha! Exactly, Seán, exactly! Fuck, I love that song.

# 11

# A Beautiful, Desperate World

~

*I've been listening to your work in progress — both versions that you sent.*

Great. Do you want to talk about some of the songs on the album? I don't know if it will be of any value. It's still early days. It usually takes quite a while for me to get to know the songs. I need to take them out on the road and play them to people: that's where their meaning is revealed. But let's have a go.

*Okay. The first thing that struck me was that it feels, for the most part, like a reflection of the times.*

Yes, it feels like a product of the calamity of our time. In that way, it is unlike most of my other records, where the concerns of the day go largely uncommented upon. My songs are generally interested in matters of the heart, or the soul, and perhaps that's a kind of limitation — but in any case, the historical moment we've been experiencing, this shared tragedy, has been so acutely present it has been impossible to avoid.

*There are several songs which seem to reflect unease of these strange times.*

My experience of lockdown, apart from escaping into books and films and, of course, work, was that there was all this damn news – and it was always troubling, and it was always coming for you.

*And the social media chatter, of course, which amplifies and exacerbates the threat and anxiety.*

Well, I have to say, when I came off Twitter, the world suddenly improved. It became a better place to live in, and the quality of my life improved immeasurably, the sun started to shine and the little birds started singing in the trees. I wasn't feeling so ill in my body, so worn out and depressed by it all. As far as I can see, social media makes you sick.

*One song in particular, 'White Elephant', seems to be touching on that sense of political/cultural dissonance and rage.*

Well, 'White Elephant' is sung partly from the point of view of a very pissed-off toppled statue, or a defaced statue.

On one level, it's speaking to the attempted erasure of history, I guess. In this instance, history returns in a more monstrous form. As we start to tear down these symbols of our past, perhaps it enables the same kind of evil to rear its head again, in a renewed energised form, to be reignited as something even more sinister.

Obviously, there are statues that need to go, but there does seem to be a kind of collective derangement at work when you have demonstrators in Portland setting fire to a 120-year-old statue of an elk and, in Copenhagen, someone painting 'Racist Fish' on the famous statue of the Little Mermaid.

In my song, 'White Elephant', the Little Mermaid – the 'Racist Fish' – rises from the sea as a hideous monstrous entity, armed to the teeth, to become 'a great grey cloud of wrath raining its salt upon the earth'. I really wanted the song to have the same weird sexual energy that unleashed self-righteous fury can have – if you know what I mean?

*I'm trying to process it.*

The song, I hope, takes on a volatile subject and imagines a horrific scenario, without it being didactic or polemical. In the same way as a movie like *Taxi Driver*, say, can present a story and then step away, allowing the audience to make of it what they will, you know, without wagging a finger or talking down to people, or resorting to the morally obvious.

*There's a dramatic shift in tone with the line: 'I'll shoot you in the fucking face if you're thinking of coming around here.' I immediately thought of that armed white American couple on their lawn as a Black Lives Matter protest passed their house. That was part of the derangement, too.*

That's right. It feels as if there is something primal that is being unleashed upon the world that has been waiting for its moment for years, something that has found its oxygen of outrage.

> *I'll shoot you in the fucking face*
> *If you think of coming around here*
> *I'll shoot you just for fun . . .*

*The end chorus is quite dramatic: 'A time is coming/A time is nigh/ For the kingdom/in the sky.' It's like an apocalyptic Plastic Ono Band song.*

Originally, there was just a small coda at the end of the song but it just got bigger and bigger. It's a return to that idea of a promised land, with the same evangelical zeal, but in the context of 'White Elephant' that promise becomes darker, more ominous. Do you consider 'White Elephant' to be problematic?

*Only if you talk about it!*

I'll keep my mouth shut, then.

But, you know, I feel that the song addresses the idea that there is a bottomless rage out there that has been animated somehow and is now mutually sustaining – each side fuelling the other. The cosy arrangement that the Left and the Right have traditionally had has turned into something else entirely. It constantly feels like things are going to blow.

*Yes, in America in particular.*

Well, yes, but as with all these sorts of things it kind of spilled over into Britain, too – an attempt to map the American experience onto our own.

*The song 'Shattered Ground' seems to pick up on that sense of unease and place it in the context of a relationship. Is that correct?*

That sense of derangement is going on throughout the album, a feeling of unsoundness of mind that concentrates itself in this song.

> *And there's a madness in her and a madness in me*
> *And together it forms a kind of sanity*

The song pulls together a bunch of themes – madness, escape, the road, the moon, abandonment, aloneness, old age and rage – so much rage. The statue reappears, as well, toppled and seething on the shattered ground!

*So in what way exactly do you relate to the toppled statue?*

In this instance it's about the feeling of being out of time, perhaps, or the precarious nature of one's position in the world.

*So you feel out of time?*

Well, I love this world – with all its joys and its vast goodness, its civility and complete and utter lack of it, its brilliance and its absurdity. I love it all, and the people in it, all of them. I feel nothing but deep gratitude to be a part of this whole cosmic mess. I have no time for negativity, cynicism or blame. In that regard, Seán, I feel as if I am completely and hopelessly *out of time.*

*And you also feel precarious about your place in the world?*

Only insomuch as I suspect the world hasn't quite finished with me yet.

*That's for sure. So do you relate to some degree to every character you write or sing about?*

Well, of course. How could I possibly not?

*Bunny Munro?*

Yes.

*Staggerlee?*

Hell, yeah, *and* Billy Dilly!

*Okay, that is deeply worrying. So can we talk some more about 'Albuquerque'? It seems in a way the most traditional song on the album.*

By the way, that title is not fixed, so if you have any ideas.

*I really like the title – the word 'Albuquerque' has a poetry to it.*

Yeah, and it also has a lineage, I guess.

*There's that beautifully ragged Neil Young song on* Tonight's The Night. *But in the second version you sent me, you've taken out the actual line: 'You won't get to Albuquerque/unless I dream you there.'*

Yes, I was going to ask you what you thought about that. That line was just an ad-lib, actually. Albuquerque is, of course, one of the three towns mentioned in 'By The Time I Get To Phoenix', but it's also a kind of in-joke. Whenever I get pissed off with Susie, which is rare, I threaten to go to Albuquerque.

*That gives it a whole other meaning. I actually love the version in which you mentioned Albuquerque. It sounds really wistful — the sound poetry of the word gives it a certain resonance. I actually can't believe you took it out.*

Jesus! Okay, I'll put it back in — for you. We can maybe get a small choir to come in and sing that. I just wondered that, if I sang the place name 'Albuquerque', it might be distracting, but at the same time, as you say, it could be good. When we play it live, we could add in whichever city we are playing.

*Yes, but it wouldn't work in Bognor. Or, indeed, Brighton. You could only play it in towns with four-syllable names.*

That's true. Mind you, I could sing, 'Bognor, baby,' and that's four syllables. Problem solved! By the way, the word 'baby' is very handy in songwriting — something you may not know. It's a songwriter's secret weapon, 'baby' or 'babe'. Those much-needed additional syllables. I once had a German journalist ask me why I used 'baby' in my songs all the time. He said, 'Don't the women in your life have names?'

*Really?*

He thought the word 'baby' was infantilising to women.

*How did you respond to that?*

I said someone should have let Janis Joplin know.

*Can you talk me through 'Albuquerque' before we go off on another tangent?*

'Albuquerque' is a very simple song. It begins with a gorgeous tune picked out on the piano, which, believe it or not, is an improvised melody, but one that was so sweet we built the whole song around it. The song begins with a couple waking up in bed, to a shared memory.

> *This morning crawls towards us, darling,*
> *With a memory in its paws*

*Yes, but on one of the versions you sent me, you sing 'with a memory in its jaws'. That's a whole different register, really.*

Yes, and they're both good, but 'paws' felt more giving, I guess, like an offering. Anyway, the actual memory is Susie's, and it's one I have heard many times from her family members and repeatedly from Susie herself. She spent her early childhood in Malawi, in East Africa, and she used to swim in the massive lake there, which was full of fucking hippos and crocodiles. When she was three years old, she was sailing in a boat and she jumped out and started to swim towards another boat. She was very small, but to everyone's surprise, swam like a little fish. That image of a child swimming between two boats – in that perilous in-between – has always interested me. I've been waiting for a song to come along where it could find a home. I've imagined that scenario so many times and attempted to put it in so many songs that I feel the memory belongs to me. I don't know how to explain this without sounding nuts, but I suspect Susie and I share each other's memories. I think on some level I was there, too, at that lake.

The memory only begins the song, and then we are suddenly trapped within the present, unable to go anywhere, imprisoned in our predicament. It's as if this time we're in is also a state of suspension – a swimming between two boats – the only release being our dreams, our imaginations, our memories.

> *And we won't get to anywhere, baby*
> *Unless I dream you there*

*That line, and in fact the whole song, certainly has an added bittersweet resonance because of the stalled moment we are in.*

Yes, it's kind of an odd song, because, right now, I'm actually just so happy not to be travelling. And I do think of 'Albuquerque' as a stationary song – we're still on the balcony. Whereas a song like 'Lavender Fields', which we've talked about already, is a song of ascension, a spiritual rising towards death. In a way, it reminds me a lot of Stevie Smith. I love her so much, that woman, and I wanted to get that simple, repetitive uncanniness that some of her poems have.

*So she was in your head when you wrote it – or in retrospect?*

I don't know. That's hard to tell. She's always in my head. They all are.

*Who?*

My influences. They're always hanging around.

*Like who?*

Just fucking *everybody*!

*What do the lavender fields represent?*

Oh, you know, death. And all that goes with it.

*So, in your mind, what goes with it?*

Faith. Love. Change. Refuge.

*I was intrigued by the final lines of the song:*

> *Sometimes I see a pale bird*
> *Wheeling in the sky*
> *But that is just a feeling*
> *A feeling when you die*

*So the 'pale bird' is death looming. Are you confronting some of your own fears in that song?*

I'm not sure that's what you do when you write a song or make a record. I personally don't need songs to do that. I confront my fears all the time. I mean, death seems to find its way into this record a lot, but I don't fear death. It's more that I just don't want to lose any more people, because I love them and love having them around. But, of course, we can't make these cosmic covenants: we can't bargain with God. It's like asking the world to stop turning. So you learn to make peace with the idea of death as best you can.

Or rather you reconcile yourself to the acute jeopardy of life, and you do this by acknowledging the value in things, the precious nature of things, and savouring the time we have together in this world. You learn that the binding agent of the world is love. That's what I want to say, not just with this record, but pretty much everything I do.

*That ultimately there is love and there is hope?*

Yes. I think in a way my work has become an explicit rejection of cynicism and negativity. I simply have no time for it. I mean that quite literally, and from a personal perspective. No time for censure or relentless condemnation. No time for the whole cycle of perpetual blame. Others can do that sort of thing. I haven't the stomach for it, or the time. Life is too damn short, in my opinion, not to be awed.

# 12

# Anita Led Us Here

~

*Hey, Nick. How are you feeling? It was so sad to hear about Anita.*

Seán, this year has been so fucking crazy – Hal dying of Covid, my mother gone, and now Anita dying, too. Jesus. I'm not sure how to really process this. It's such a massive blow to everybody. Anita's amazing kids. Everyone's, I don't know, dumbstruck. Anita was really something else. It's just difficult to fathom that she's gone.

*Can I ask, had she been unwell?*

Yes, but I didn't realise quite how bad. But when I think about it, it's not that I didn't see it coming somehow. I think everyone who knew her felt that things weren't good, you know, not good at all. She rang me about a month ago. We'd call each other over the years and have long, intense, meandering conversations that basically just picked up where we had left off, and also these crazy, sporadic text flurries. Anita wrote the most extraordinary texts. I should show you sometime – long and beautifully abstract messages, really out there.

But this time when she rang me, she sounded maudlin. She said, 'I just want to say, I love you, I want you to know that I always loved you,' and I said, 'Well, yeah, I know that, and you know I love you, too,' and she was like, 'No, Nick, I just really want you to know that,' and she was coughing a lot and kind of slurred. It was a troubling call. After I hung up, I felt scared suddenly, fearful. Our phone calls were always strange and freewheeling, but this sounded different, and I called her back and said, 'Hang on a second, Nita, are you okay, here?' And she said, 'Yes, yes, don't worry. I'm fine. I'm going to bed.' But she wasn't well; she had many illnesses, including diabetes, chronic bronchitis, and she was still battling with alcohol on and off.

*I didn't know that. That's a tough one.*

I guess the thing I find so difficult with Anita is the realisation that, regardless of how deserving one might be, some things just don't turn out well. I know it seems like a naïve thing to say, but Anita was the best of people, one of the truly good ones, and she deserved better from life. She was, at heart, the kindest, most generous, most unorthodox and intensely creative person I have ever known, and she should have had an easier life. She should have had a happy life, but for her things just didn't go the way they ought to have, somehow. I guess she was her own worst enemy in a way. She could become consumed with paralysing resentments about stuff – her friends, the world, everyone. She felt a sense of personal betrayal that in the end, I think, just ate her up.

And it's hard to square this with her other side, because she was such a sparkling and beautiful woman, with a vibrancy of character that was so incredibly infectious.

*You were quite a couple back in the day. I remember seeing the pair of you from time to time, usually walking down Brixton Hill in south London. She always seemed to be laughing, vivacious. She definitely had a presence.*

Oh yes! Back then she led the way for us, creatively and aesthetically. As far as I'm concerned, we all tripped happily along in her wake. All those pictures you see of her, smiling, laughing – she was

201

just like that. She was almost pathologically inspired, ideas just pouring out of her. But as time went on, it was as if a certain darkness collected around her. The fact that she was found three days after she died alone in her house, in fucking lockdown, has been difficult to compute. These two opposing images of her.

*So she obviously moved back to Australia at some point.*

Yes, for most of her life she lived in a ramshackle, old weatherboard house that her mother left her. It was in Glen Iris – near where Barry Humphries grew up – with a scandalously overgrown garden in a typically pristine Australian street. Anita had a fierce, protective love for her three boys – two of her kids actually lived there, and also some kids who were kind of strays off the street. All sorts of people. Amazing, really, like the mythical mother figure, tending to these young people. She actually moved into an annexed back room, while the kids took over the house.

*Generous, but maybe a recipe for chaos?*

Yes, probably. Anita was a brilliant, fascinating woman, but she never learned how to negotiate with her demons, I guess. She battled with her health, her feverish mind, but despite all that, she still managed to radiate a kind of brilliance.

But I do want to say this, Seán – and I don't in any way want to undermine the deep void that Anita has left with a whole bunch of overly sentimental notions – that when I meditate, I feel there has been a kind of reinvigoration of the spiritual space.

*Do you mean the spiritual space around you when you are meditating?*

The spiritual space generally. I imagine Arthur and Anita there, Anita acting as a conduit for all the dead we know. I saw this as a vision several times just after Anita died. All the people who died when we were very young from heroin overdoses, and Tracy Pew and beautiful Lisa Craswell, my mother and father, and her own

202

mother and father, and Arthur, all these people, Hal and Conway and Bunny and Rowland and my friend Mick Geyer — all drawn towards the spirit of Anita that was now in its purest form. It was as if all the disappointment and resentment had fallen away and there was just a shimmering spirit that felt like a kind of point of assembly. It was really very powerful, very strong for a while, that image and that feeling of an energised spirit world.

*That's pretty wild, but I hope it is the case.*

Me, too. Before now, when I imagined Arthur in my meditation, he was always alone. When I talked to Arthur, he was alone. But when I imagine Anita, she is drawing everyone towards her, bringing everyone together.

*So what do you make of these meditative imaginings?*

Well, I certainly don't consider these things to be just a comfort or a panacea, that's for sure. In my opinion, in the collaboration between the living imagination and the potential of the spirit world – this dance between the two – each ignites the other, the dreamer and the dream.

*That sounds pretty Yeatsian!*

Maybe, but I am also aware that when we talk about these things, they are easy to demolish, they are easy to scare away. The argument is lost the moment it is put into words and enters the rational world. I get that. I know that. However, God cannot be defended, hence we must.

*Is that a well-known aphorism?*

No, it's one of mine, but it should be!

I think we need to remain attentive to these absences, to revere them, adore them, just as we love those who are present. You know, the rational, the verifiable, is not the only game in town and it can end up denying us these glimpses of eternity that many of us experience, to our bafflement, in some form or another. I find that by defending these tiny, fragile, indefensible notions – such as the very existence of God – there comes a great enriching of the spirit as we avail ourselves of the mysterious, the fantastical, the absurd. Anyway, I'm not sure how we got on to that!

*Anita led us here.*

She did. By the way, I was talking to a friend on the phone today, and we were remembering Anita, and he told me a very beautiful story. My friend's name is Marcus Bergner, and he's a poet, artist and professor who Anita and I have known since the old days, back in Melbourne. A wonderful guy. Marcus lives in Brussels now, and when he went back to Australia he would often stay at her place. He told me a story that happened six or seven years ago at Anita's son Carlito's eighteenth birthday party. Carlito is my godson, by the way. Like I said, Anita's rundown house on Bellavista Road had turned into a kind of drop-in centre or safe house for young teen-agers and street kids, and Anita helped them, attended to them and looked after them, though she could barely look after herself. Marcus told me that at the party there were dozens of these kids running around, gangsta rap blaring out, fires all over the backyard, under-age drinking and what have you – absolute chaos, teenage pandemonium. Anita and Marcus were basically the only adults there. At some point Anita turned the music off and called everyone together and gave a birthday speech about Carlito. Marcus said the scene was incredible. All the kids just stopped whatever it was they were doing and sat on the ground around Anita and listened to her talk. She spoke for about twenty minutes and the kids just sat there in a trance, captivated by her words, as she stood under the pine tree in the backyard, a huge bonfire burning behind her, talking about her boy.

You know, we often talk about the importance of art, that art is the most significant or consequential of gestures, our greatest achievement, the very best we can offer the world, all that. And sometimes I used to get angry at Anita that she sort of wasted her staggering talent, because she wouldn't apply herself and had no discipline. But, these days, I don't know. I really wonder about that. I regret it, you know, I really do. I think of Anita in that moment at the party, articulating her love for her boy to all those feral kids, who listened to her words because . . . God, I don't know what the lives of those kids were like, but you have to think there is nothing greater than that, nothing at all, that powerful, radical, caring instinct. There was a profound goodness in Anita, that's what I'm trying to say – just an astonishingly valuable human being. I'm so sorry that she's gone.

# 13

## Things Unfold

~

Hey, sorry I'm a bit late, Seán. I'm just out of a recorded Zoom conversation with Mick Harvey about the *B-sides & Rarities* album, which is coming out soon. Fans were asked to send in questions. It was a lovely conversation, but the questions they sent in were mischievous, to say the least. Beautiful people, my fans, just the best, but they are definitely mischief-makers.

*What kind of questions?*

Oh, like, what is one thing you would like to say to Mick now that you are not working together?

*What did you say?*

I said to Mick that I was sorry about the way I treated him around the time he left the band. I thought I had probably been unfeeling.

*These things happen with bands. It can get pretty brutal when things fall apart.*

Well, the band was sort of broken and extraordinarily dysfunctional and Mick needed to go – there is no doubt in anyone's mind about that, especially his! He was so fucking angry, raging, especially after a few drinks. But then again, it's kind of understandable. He had been pushed to the margins, I guess, and felt super-aggrieved about it. Warren and I had become very close, in both our personal and professional lives, and there were no honest conversations in those days. We were a band without a manager, so it was the law of the jungle to some extent. There were no band meetings, no sitting down and hashing things out, just a whole lot of very bad, unregulated energy and internecine strife. It needed to change. When Mick rang to tell me he was leaving, I made no efforts to convince him to stay.

*What did Mick think about your apology?*

He was probably wondering why I was apologising to him in a public forum!

The conversation was very warm and moving, at least for me. I love Mick. We went through a lot of stuff together for a very long time, two polar opposites who made a lot of wonderful music. It seemed to me a natural thing to at least mention that I had regrets about the way he was treated, and my part in that.

*Do you have many regrets yourself, Nick?*

Well, I can't imagine there is anyone with no regrets, unless they are leading extraordinarily unexamined lives, or they are young, which often amounts to much the same thing. So, yes, I have my regrets. Not that regrets in themselves are bad things, of course. They are generally indicators of a certain self-awareness or personal growth or distance travelled.

But, to go back to the conversation with Mick, even though I'm a very private person, for better or worse, I live my life in public, and I have found myself in a position where there is little I won't talk about publicly. Whatever filters I've had in the past have been dismantled over time. The Red Hand Files were responsible for that. They have created a kind of ever-creeping transparency by slowly prising me open. They changed me.

*It's interesting that often the questions are not about your music. They are often quite personal.*

Well, for a long time, I've felt hemmed in by the traditional music interview format. I wanted to take the conversation away from music specifically and locate it somewhere else. I wasn't sure where or, indeed, how to do that, but I just felt I had this other stuff going on in my head and nowhere to really articulate it. Then Arthur died, and that changed everything. I started getting actual letters from people, most of them just addressed to 'Nick Cave, Brighton'. For me, the interesting thing was that they were not just letters of sympathy, but letters from people who had lost someone. They essentially began, 'I know what you are going through. This happened to me,' and then told their story. Those letters were very powerful, because it was clear that people were fulfilling some sort of need in themselves, simply by articulating their particular story for somebody else to hear. Does that make sense?

*Yes, it does. Totally. They were reaching out, but also finding a way to address and articulate their own grief.*

Yes, and I sensed that inside their questions was a need to speak about their own suffering so that another human being could acknowledge it. This idea had a profound impact on me because I felt it pointed to a form of healing through the combined acts of telling and listening. Essentially, that became the basic premise for The Red Hand Files. For me, The Red Hand Files is not just about answering the question: it is primarily about *listening* to the question.

*I'm assuming you receive many more questions than you can practically answer.*

I get about fifty to a hundred a day, I guess, and part of my commitment to the project is to read each question and listen to what each person is trying to say. I am the only one who has access to these questions. This practice of opening my laptop and reading the questions feels like a form of prayer.

*Really? In what way?*

Prayer as a kind of concentrated listening. For me, prayer creates a silent, contemplative space where the soul has its place to speak. And, for me, prayer is not so much talking to God, but rather listening for the whispers of His presence – not from outside ourselves, but within. It's kind of the same with the questions that come in to The Red Hand Files. I think they are singularly and collectively trying to tell me something, which may just be 'I am here'. I think they reflect my own needs. There is an exchange of a sort of essentialness, wherein we attend to each other through a sharing of our collective need to be listened to.

*Is that essentialness, as you call it, to do with people being incredibly honest and open about their experiences?*

The Red Hand Files tell me, explicitly and repeatedly, that we all suffer. They tell me that suffering is the defining element of the human story. I know this to be true because I recognise myself in these letters – I have my own situation mirrored back at me, my own pain – and I also know that by engaging with these people, I get better. I think the benefits of the exchange are mutual. I certainly hope so. I try to present to the person who has asked the question the very best part of myself, because by being vulnerable and genuine these individuals are presenting the very best of themselves. I think the spirit of love exists within this exchange, in the same way as the spirit of love, the divine spirit, exists inside a live concert.

*So is there essentially the same therapeutic aspect to The Red Hand Files as your music?*

Yes, very much so. Music, of all the creative forms, best repairs the heart. This may be its actual purpose. It is within music that the

ameliorating spirit is most vibrant, and it can be accessed by literally anybody. I know this because it has restored me and been my
salvation. Music as a form radiates love and makes things better. It
is important to me that there is a practical and positive utility to
music — that it improves matters. And so it is a similar thing to The
Red Hand Files. They are at their best, like music, a sincere and
loving exchange that goes some way towards mutual restoration.
Both music and The Red Hand Files have been a saving force in
my own life.

*When you launched The Red Hand Files online back in September
2018, which was just three years after Arthur's death, what kind of
shape were you in?*

Well, I don't know what shape I was in — who can really tell? —
but in a very real way I felt the same need as some of the people
writing the letters to work out a way to speak about my own
catastrophe and articulate my own grief. I felt that this would not
only save me, but also help others. I really held on to that idea,
which meant that I was not going to avoid speaking about Arthur
because it was a difficult subject, or worry that it might make
people feel uncomfortable, or that it was bad for my career, or that
I didn't have the right vocabulary.

So, really, one of the reasons the project was created was an
attempt to find a language to set forth, in words, the travails of
grief. It was an attempt to remain open and vulnerable to the needs
of others, as well as my own. I didn't set out to do that, exactly,
but it quickly found its purpose.

*That theme keeps recurring throughout our conversations — things
finding their purpose or revealing their meaning through the doing. The
creative journey as a series of revelations, almost.*

Yes, now you point it out, that's exactly right. Most of the time, I
have no idea what I am doing while I'm doing it. It is almost
purely intuitive. That should be pretty clear. But I do have a strong

commitment to the primary impulse, the initial signalling of an idea — what we could call the divine spark. I trust in it. I believe in it. I run with it. The writing of this book, if that is what we are doing, is a case in point. It's something that is just unfolding before us. I have no coherent idea of what we are doing at this time, and I'm not sure that you do, either. There is a sense of discovery about it. Things unfold. This place of discomfort and uncertainty and adventure is where an honest, good-faith conversation can happen. It's all the same thing.

*I hope so! So, early on in* The Red Hand Files, *were the questions quite tentative? Or were they, for want of a better term, typical fan questions?*

At the beginning, most people didn't understand what I was trying to do. But like I said, neither did I. The early questions came in and most of them were about music. Who's your favourite singer? What are your inspirations? What's Blixa Bargeld like? All that kind of stuff. These were not the kind of questions I was interested in answering, so I began to write beyond the bounds of what you might normally expect a rock singer to talk about. I began to write about personal issues that affected my life and, explicitly, about the death of my son. This encouraged people to ask different sorts of questions, and not just to ask questions but to share their own experiences. This was very affecting — just in terms of the volume and intensity of feeling that came across. Quite quickly, the kinds of questions began to change and everything started to get a whole lot stranger.

*Who is your favourite singer?*

Elvis.

*Of course! So in what way did things get stranger? Do you mean more personal?*

It was more that I suddenly found myself answering questions that I had absolutely no authority to answer. You know, I'm obviously not a therapist, a public intellectual or a political thinker, far from it, but I do have my own peculiar relationship to the world that some people seem to find interesting, even helpful. I found that weirdly liberating.

*So three years and over 150 Red Hand Files later, how do you think this sustained engagement with strangers has changed you?*

I think it has succeeded in breaking down my own expectations as to what my role is – as a musician, artist and human being. As I've already said, at the outset I really had no idea of what I was doing, or of the implications professionally, or indeed just how profoundly it would impact on my life. But the format became so open and trusting, and the questions so raw and candid, that there was no walking back from it. It is simply mind-blowing. I'll send you something now from a woman from Fremantle who wrote last week, and it might make it clear what I am talking about. Just take a bit of time with it. I'm going to email it to you and then I'll call you back.

> Nick, my 22-year-old son died of an overdose 5 months ago. He was a beautiful sensitive boy who was studying classical piano at WAAPA and wanted to become an expert in fortepianos. He was an anxious child and I worried about him a lot. I'm wracked with guilt about him and have bad PTSD from the trauma of his sudden demise. He'd been clean for two years and was doing so well in his life. He was so kind, so sensitive, so compassionate. Everyone is devastated. I know guilt is part of grief. How did you and Susie deal with it? And the trauma?
>
> Here's a poem I wrote about his death. I was trying to capture the shock and emptiness.

## young death

when young death shines a flash
on your
2am
the cop says
takes the breath right
collapses your
stills your
stops the

your knees
and your brain

you drive in
and greet young death
he's he's he's he's
on a hospital
tube in his
on a
under the
in the
bedroom that marks his growth and
he was a baby here once
there's his
height
see?
pencil marks on the
cosmo 2, 3, 4 and a half, 6, 7, 9¾, 10, 13,
and his precious
that filled the house with
mute
sister's drawings on the
chair where he
there he lies
still

tube in his
grey pallor
it is your
it is not your
hold him for the last
small sob falls
frozen
want to
want to
forever
young death kisses
wraps you in cold
your son
watching
your son
wanting
reach out and touch
it's ok Mum
it's ok Mum
here
the light is beautiful
i'm happy
really
you kiss him one
you kiss him
last time and return
to his Dad
hold hands breathless
wait
for dread dawn to break
your sleeping daughter
to wake

Tiffany, Australia

*I'm not sure what to say. I really need to take that in. It's so viscerally powerful and so formally brilliant – those unfinished lines and missing words. It just plunges you back into the trauma of losing someone, the wild unreality, the shock.*

Isn't it incredible? Not just a wonderful piece of writing, but an act of enormous courage, and it articulates so beautifully, so complexly, so terribly, 'the night of . . .' that so many of us have.

*Yes, 'the night of . . .'. Exactly.*

And Tiffany is new to grief, yet brave enough to place herself inside the trauma itself. Because, you know, grief is not just an amorphous fog-like state of being. Grief actively revolves around a point of torture, a moment of realisation, an actual tangible thing. Tiffany dared to step into that moment, unprotected, with eyes wide open, and write it down. When I read it, it moved me to tears – as many of the letters do – because of the sheer openness of it, and, God, I don't know, the *bravery*. The power of her poem made it safe to turn around and face my own point of trauma.

*I see. It helped.*

I don't know, Seán. There is such courage in the world I am awed, and I think this extraordinary woman will be all right in the end. She has found the facility and the fearlessness to say the unsayable, to broach the forbidden, solitary horror of her moment in Hell and communicate it to someone else. I love this woman. I love that she has done that. I have to say, it's a total honour to be the recipient of such a letter, a letter that can be passed on to the world as, I don't know, a public service of immeasurable value to others. There is a responsibility around The Red Hand Files that I had no idea I was getting into. And, Seán, there are so many of these letters, thousands of them. It has become a thing of fundamental importance in the way I live my life. Questions or even criticisms of whether I have the authority to answer questions like this fall by the wayside.

*How do you feel about the weight of responsibility that comes with a project like this one? Do you ever feel burdened or weighed down by it?*

It can be challenging. The care and the feeling of responsibility have grown, as has the sense that they are of some help, so I feel duty-bound to do my best to respond to the questions. I do get anxious if I haven't had the time to give them my proper attention. There's also the danger of just getting it wrong and the whole thing blowing up in my face. And sometimes I go through periods of limiting the amount of questions I read at any given time, because it can be exhausting, even debilitating. But beyond all that, as an exercise in existential meaning, they are invaluable. And for me they're also a source of genuine happiness.

*Have you had any negative responses to The Red Hand Files, or people questioning why you were even doing it?*

There was a certain amount of pushback from some people who wanted me to retain my mystery – whatever that was – and to be untouchable, remote, like a rock star should be. Others were just pissed off by some of the answers I gave. Or, as I've said, they didn't think I had the authority to be talking about certain things. But, largely, The Red Hand Files were welcomed by people, and, quite wonderfully, it has grown way beyond my fan base. A lot of people write in who don't really know my music at all, or are not even interested in finding out about it. They just find the exchange interesting, or even helpful. That is hugely gratifying.

*How do you respond to people who say you don't have the expertise to deal with what are often quite complex, sensitive topics?*

Well, obviously there will always be people out there who find the whole enterprise dubious, people who think, 'What gives this *rock star* the right to dispense life advice or expound half-arsed wisdoms on important matters?' And, on some level, they have a point: what does give me the right? I've gone through many dizzying confidence crises about that since I've been doing them, when it felt like I was literally free-falling through the whole idea. But I am ultimately saved from all that by the questions themselves. When someone is suffering – maybe because they've been fired from their job, or their marriage has broken down, or maybe someone has lost a kid and they want me to help them, possibly as a last measure – I just think, fuck the detractors, and I get on with the job.

*Were the In Conversation events driven by a similar impulse to engage with, and maybe help, people to articulate their experiences of loss?*

Maybe, yes. I do remember early on talking to Andrew Dominik about doing the In Conversation events and The Red Hand Files, and I was kind of upset by his response. I thought I was doing something of value and he said, 'Dude, you're grieving.' It was as if I had somehow gone mad and was out there making a scene in public, live on stage. And maybe he was right, but I don't think it was only that. What I was trying to do was forge a relationship with my audience through our mutual vulnerability. I wanted to encourage audience members to ask a question, often of an extremely personal nature, or tell a story, which I would listen to and respond to as honestly as I could. Sometimes it worked and the evenings were really powerful; other times it didn't work so well and it ended up feeling more like bad stand-up with a musical component!

But you give these things a go, for better or for worse. And, in a sense, Andrew was right, because if Arthur hadn't died, I would not have been doing any of these things. But grief gave me a reckless energy. It afforded me a feeling of invincibility and a total disregard for the outcome, a sort of fearless abandonment to destiny. The worst had happened. I still feel that to this day.

*I can understand that. Can you talk some more about that sense of reckless energy and invincibility you felt?*

Put simply, I felt protected by Arthur.

*Insofar as he was watching over you somehow, that he was there with you?*

Yes, I felt protected by Arthur's actual presence, imagined or otherwise.

*Did you ever feel Arthur as a physical presence?*

Yes, it felt to me, sometimes in a very real way, that I was in his presence, that he was close by, and he was saying to me, 'There is nothing to fear.' Throughout those In Conversation events, I felt him standing on stage with me. I don't know if you can understand how empowering that felt.

*I can only imagine. So is Arthur a kind of guardian angel?*

Well, he does protect me, but he is not a guardian angel. Arthur is my son and he died. He exists just beyond my vision and my reason and a whole sea of tears – as a promise, maybe, or a wish.

*Can I just ask what Arthur was like?*

Oh God, Seán. I don't know. He was just such a great little kid . . . I'm sorry . . . I can talk about Arthur in some ways, and other ways, I just can't go there.

*Okay. I understand. When you say he exists as a promise, what do you mean by that? A promise of what, exactly?*

A promise that the intimations of the presence of those who have passed away are more than just mere wishful thinking. And, like I said, Seán, this is *beyond reason*. I don't know about you, but for me there is forever a struggle between the rational side of myself and the side that is alert to glimpses or impressions of something otherworldly. And, of course, I know there is no coherent argument to be had here. My rational self has all the weaponry, all the big guns – reason, science, common sense, normality – and all that far outweighs the side of me that only has suspicions and hints and signs of something else, something mysterious and quietly spoken. But, even still, it feels, under the circumstances, that to dismiss the existence of these things that live beyond our reasonable selves outright is, at best, ungenerous. Don't you think? I mean, I don't blindly succumb to these feelings, but still I remain watchful for that promise. This is how I have chosen to live my life – in uncertainty, and by doing so to be open to the divine possibility of things, whether it exists or not. I believe this gives my life, and especially my work, meaning and potential and soul, too, beyond what the rational world has to offer.

Arthur is a reminder that I don't really have to conform to the rules the world has laid down for me, because the world feels chaotic and random and, well, indifferent to any rules. When I call Arthur to me and I feel him around, as an optimistic force, a hopeful force, I don't have to be afraid. I am aware of how that sounds to many people, but this is, at the very least, a survival strategy – and grievers know. Generally, they know.

*Do you mean they are more aware of, or have more access to, some wisdom that lies beyond the here and now?*

It seems to me that people who are grieving, especially the recently bereaved, live their lives at the edge of a potentiality, adjacent to death, in a kind of poetic twilight world. I say this not only because I inhabit this world myself at times, but because in The Red Hand Files I am confronted with the same story, time and time again – 'I feel his presence' or 'I sense her all around'. Now, we are repeatedly told that these kinds of 'feelings' or intimations are a delusion brought about by our desperate need, or that they are somehow a denial of the finality of death, or, worst of all, they reveal a lack of intellectual integrity. Now, we know that. We fucking get it. But these feelings, indefensible as they may be to rationalists, are real and loving and nourishing, and go some way to being a bridge to normality. They may well be delusions, but these poetic intimations guide us back to the world. In that respect, they are as real and true as anything else, and perhaps the most beautiful and mysterious things imaginable. In my view, we deny or dismiss them at our peril.

*Because to do so is to somehow limit your chances of healing or moving on?*

Well, grief can lead some people to dark places from where they simply never return. I have seen it often. People constricting around an absence, growing hard and mad and furious at the world, and never recovering. There is nothing to lead them from the abyss. And beyond that, too, I think the point-blank rejection of all spiritual matters as mere nonsense has its own problems. I'm talking about the outright rejection of religion by some who basically see it as a kind of inherent evil. That stance is a denial of all the potential good religion brings: the comfort, the succour, the redemption, the community. This thinking can bring its own kind of nothingness – not always, of course, but often. And, as we are seeing, people find a version of religion elsewhere, in tribalism, in their identity, in politics, for God's sake, in possessions. Look at our glorious secular world as it stands today. To me, secularism can also feel like a kind of hardening around an absence.

So, essentially, what I am trying to present is the idea of grief as a gift. Grief as a positive force. Grief that can become, if we allow it its full expression, a defiant, sometimes mutinous energy. I was running on that energy through the In Conversation events and maybe that's what Andrew was talking about.

Anyway, to answer your earlier question, those events were raw, unguarded versions of The Red Hand Files, and it was interesting to stand up on stage and do a show, the success of which was completely predicated upon the questions the audience asked. That said, in the end it felt too close to performance for me, like a gig, strange and unstable as it was.

*So, at some point, the performative aspect in some way undercut the energy and made it less risky?*

Something like that, yes. And, weirdly, those times, which were only a couple of years ago, seem strangely innocent to me now. Back then, they felt generous and free, but I honestly don't think I could do something like that now. Not in the same freewheeling way. Things have changed so much, even in this short space of time. Talking in public in itself has become a fraught thing to do. It's looked at by many with suspicion. You know, who would stand up on stage and speak their mind unless they had bad intentions? The Red Hand Files suits me better. It is a one-on-one exchange, witnessed by many, completely on my own terms.

*And of course you get to have the last word.*

Well exactly, Seán.

*Yes, you have managed to protect yourself from the usual enmity and abuse that characterises other social media platforms.*

I'm certainly alert to the vulnerable position you put yourself in by even having a point of view – the fraught nature of being out there in the public space.

*Does Susie help you with your responses to The Red Hand Files?*

She is totally supportive of the project and she has seen the positive change in me since I've been doing them, but Susie is generally more sensitive around certain matters than I am. Susie has a strong online presence, and she knows the way these things work. She understands the precarious nature of an opinion. She would certainly be more wary of some of the things I discuss, because ultimately she's protective of me. That said, I often don't show them to her before I send them out.

*You don't? That seems odd, given all you've just said.*

Well, it takes a lot of time and effort to write a Red Hand File, and a lot of thought, and I am personally not as squeamish about the outcome as she is. I write what I feel, as honestly as I can, and any pushback that I get happens entirely online, which I'm not aware of.

*You've made a conscious decision not to engage with social media.*

Yes. Ultimately, I don't use social media because I don't have the time for it. It makes great demands on us, not just on our precious time, but damaging emotional demands, as far as I can see. I personally find the dissonance and narcissism of social media energy-sapping and counter-productive. I need to look after my inner world as best I can. That is a seriously high-maintenance job in itself!

*Back in August 2020, you responded to a Red Hand Files question about 'cancel culture', which you linked to the rise of social media. I'm suspicious of the term 'cancel culture', to be honest, and the way it can be used to shut down debate, but you wrote about how 'the refusal to engage with uncomfortable ideas' was having 'an asphyxiating effect on the creative soul of society'.*

Yes, I agree that terms like these are woefully inadequate and unhelpful. They are constantly employed by the worst of people, on both sides of the political spectrum, to dismiss a phenomenon that actually requires serious examination. People can question the existence of cancel culture or they can rebrand it as a culture of accountability, but I don't think anyone can question the stifling and deadening effect of the fear of cancellation – or even just getting it wrong – on art, writing, public discourse and even comedy. It has made the world of ideas so relentlessly uninteresting.

*So you don't accept that there is often a social justice impulse behind it?*

Yes, I do. There are a multitude of problems that need our attention. The world can be desperately unfair, and we need to move forward in solving these problems, as we always have. I just think the methods are wrong and do more harm than good.

But it's understandable that certain people behave in this way. We are, as a species, meaning-seeking creatures. That is what defines us.

*What do you mean by 'meaning-seeking'?*

I just think the traditional institutions in which people once sought meaning and validation have been eroded, certainly in this country. It is natural for people to look for meaning elsewhere, to look for unity and a sense of belonging. Ironically, I think the rise of woke culture is akin to a fundamentalist religious impulse. Come to think of it, it may reflect an unconscious desire to return to a non-secular society.

*Go on, I'm intrigued.*

Well, it's as if autocratic ideas of virtue and sin have come into play, and, as a result, prohibitions and punishments have been put in place, enforced by a kind of moral callousness that, in my view, is akin to the very worst aspects of religion – the fundamentalist, joyless, sanctimonious aspects that have nothing to do with mercy. Cancellation is a particularly ugly part of its weaponry and can end up as a kind of sadism dressed up as virtue.

I do happen to think the impulse behind it is sincere and, in a way, I understand its primary motivation; in fact I share it myself – the basic religious impulse that is a need to belong, a need for meaning and a desire for social reform. Unfortunately, there is a performative aspect to the theatre of cancel culture that is essentially vindictive. It is a posturing that has devastating consequences on people's livelihoods, in fact their very lives. This, Seán, is not good.

*Are you concerned about being cancelled yourself?*

No, I'm not. As I said before, I'm relatively insulated from that kind of thing. That is the beauty of The Red Hand Files.

*Recently you mentioned that many of the letters had become pretty dark and disturbing. I think it was around the start of the second lockdown.*

Yes, that was difficult. We know the pandemic was a struggle for many people and, at that time, there were a lot of very despairing letters from people who seemed to be clearly unravelling. It was tough to read them.

I also have five or six people who I would describe as heretical thinkers, shall we say, who write in all the time. I feel like I know them very well, but it's impossible for me to tell what condition they are in. Sometimes the letters are shockingly abusive, at other times full of strange, arcane information, some just flat-out conspiracy theorists. Their lives seem chaotic, but they are fascinating people. I always look forward to reading their letters, and worry when they haven't written – even if, sometimes, one of them may have what appears to be a manic episode and send dozens of letters on the same day.

*I was struck by how many of the people who contact you are so incredibly open about their own experiences of loss, grief and despair. It must be difficult at times to respond to them.*

You know, I've found that nothing is difficult to answer if you respond to a question in good faith. You just have to remember to answer the actual question as best you can. Something is being asked of you and the question itself validates the response. By the way, grief is not the hardest subject to talk about.

*So what is?*

Any question where you have to mount an argument and do it in a few paragraphs without coming off as strident or conceited or like you're pushing an agenda. This is difficult for me, as you know. And, in attempting to do that, you also know your answer may be very porous and open to criticism or condemnation or ridicule. You understand in advance that there will be a certain amount of people who will respond negatively. Now, I don't mind criticism at all, but my intention is not to provoke. That's important. Negative responses take up mental space. They require time and energy they often don't deserve, time and energy I would rather put elsewhere.

*I'm sure some of the letters must get to you from time to time.*

Yes, they can be very upsetting. I mean, I'm not a naturally empathetic individual. I don't think it's in my nature to be that way, to be honest. My mother's stoicism is bred in the bone and, believe it or not, I still feel uncomfortable with public displays of emotion! So that kind of empathy or compassion for others – and myself – is something I've had to learn. I've definitely changed in that respect, and some of that is to do with reading certain letters that have just overwhelmed me. Someone asks you something and it's so vulnerable and immediate and honest that you can't help but love them.

*I know there have been times when you have asked yourself why you were doing this. Have you found the answer to that question?*

Yes, I think so. Initially, you create solely for yourself in order to discover what you are. Your art places you in the world. This is very exciting – you feed off the world, off other artists, off your collaborators, off everything around you. By sucking up the world, you become full of potential and powerful with art. But at some point, for me at least, this energy must be redirected. You have to turn it around and pour it back into the world as an act of service.

*So you're saying that it's your duty to do good, which is an essentially moral, even Christian, interpretation of the artist's role?*

Well, music is one of the last great spiritual gifts we have that can bring solace to the world. It becomes a sort of duty, in my opinion, to use your music, not for your own aggrandisement, but for the betterment of others. As far as I can see, that is our purpose as artists. The Red Hand Files have come to belong in that tradition

– as a small gesture of service, and, maybe, as a form of spiritual sustenance and kindness that may go some small way in helping people with their lives.

*Is there a point with The Red Hand Files when you will have to say enough is enough and just stop?*

Well, I figure that the people writing in will let me know when it's reached its end. Right now, I'm committed and the questions keep coming, more than ever. The Red Hand Files keep me anchored at the better end of my nature. It's similar to meditation in that way. When I stop meditating for a couple of months or so, my life changes, and it tends to slip back into chaos, low-level depression and anger, without even my realising it. The Red Hand Files require me to look at the world in an empathetic way. And, on some level, it feels as though I have no choice: I am compelled to keep it up. I have a duty.

*When you were younger, people bought into an image of you as a dark and dangerous, self-destructive figure. You have certainly confounded them of late.*

Well, good, I'm glad. But, as you know, I really don't see the young man in The Birthday Party as a separate entity from the person who made *Ghosteen* or does The Red Hand Files. That's not how it goes. What I mean is, we may shed many skins, but we are essentially the same damn snake.

*But surely your outlook is entirely different now?*

Well, the young Nick Cave could afford to hold the world in some form of disdain because he had no idea of what was coming down the line. I can see now that this disdain or contempt for the world was a kind of luxury or indulgence, even a vanity. He had no notion of the preciousness of life – the fragility. He had no idea how difficult, but essential, it is to love the world and to treat the world with mercy. And like I said, he had no idea what was coming down the road. He was entirely innocent of all that.

# 14

# The God in the Cloud

~

I had this phone conversation last night with Warren. It was strange. It was about what went on around the actual time of Arthur's death, because Warren was at my home in Brighton at the time. Maybe I was prompted to call him because of Tiffany's poem, her letter to The Red Hand Files, or the fact that you asked me some questions about the period following it, and I just couldn't remember. So I called him to find out what happened.

*Yes, I think we were talking about the difficulties you had finishing* Skeleton Tree.

We were, and I was perplexed about everything that happened around that time. My memory of it all is very unreliable, to say the least.

*You mentioned that and, you know, it's hardly surprising, Nick.*

I guess. But I do have certain memories of the night Arthur died – a chain of events, really, of the kind that I think probably mark out the time following all tragedies of this kind. I'm referring to the actual night it happened. Yet when I try to recall what happened after that night, it's almost like there is a rupture that time and memory poured itself into. Everything disappears.

*I think that is not uncommon after a devastating event.*

Well, for me, the night it happened feels acutely real and then everything afterwards goes kind of blank. The conversation with Warren was interesting because it was clear I'd completely forgotten significant chunks of time. Like I said, I remember the night Arthur died, some severe and shocking impressions, but it all just blanks out after that.

*Well, people tend not to want to revisit the moment of the actual trauma itself – and probably for good reason. Are you sure you even want to talk about this stuff?*

Fuck, I don't know, Seán, but after talking to Warren, I'm just kind of mystified by how little I remember, just how much I have forgotten. Like, the day Arthur died just rears up out of nothing. I remember I was watching TV, and Arthur rings me, and I answer, but it's not Arthur; it's a stranger who had found his phone and his rucksack and shoes in a field near the black windmill outside Brighton. The stranger also says that there is police activity at the cliff near the windmill. Then there is this sudden roaring panic, and we are calling 999. Asking the operator what is happening at the cliffs! The police won't tell us anything. Then the police come to the house. Susie and I standing on the doorstep, seeing the police car pull up, and the detectives stepping out and walking towards us with their composed faces, and us just knowing. The cops standing in the kitchen and telling us the news – our boy has fallen off the cliff, his body is in the hospital, he is dead, and my head starts roaring the loudest noise in the world, and Earl's legs collapsing from under him and Susie catching him – the escalating confusion – the sudden horror. Then all this deafening confusion and the noise in our ears – then I remember the trip to the hospital, walking into the hospital, and then waiting and waiting. And then being taken to some makeshift annexe, and seeing Arthur's body laid out, with a sheet over him, and him looking so calm and beautiful, a clean white bandage around his head. He looked so angelic. Arthur always so alive and full of agitated, mischievous energy, and here he was at peace, more beautiful than we had ever seen him, and just gone.

And later, ringing Luke and Susie's mum and my poor old mum and my sister in Australia – everybody coming around. Luke appearing and wrapping his arms around his dad trying to calm him down.

*I don't know what to say, Nick. I just can't imagine . . .*

But it's what happens, right?

*Yes, it is, but still . . .*

But, Seán, I don't remember much after that, for quite a while. Mostly, I just recall sitting on the back step of the house away from everyone and smoking and feeling the roaring body shock of it, like this alien force was going to burst out the ends of my fucking fingers. I remember feeling like I was physically detonating, like if I made any sudden moves I'd literally explode, so stuffed was my body with despair. And then sitting next to the bed, with Susie lying completely still in the dark, like a stone, her eyes closed, and saying, 'I am here, babe, I'm here,' but really I'm not, I'm not there at all, I'm in a million fucking pieces, everywhere else, all over the place.

So, the other day, when you asked me what happened around that time, like I said, I just didn't know. Everything just got sucked into that night itself, this great obliterating force, extinguishing everything else, so I don't remember what happened within that time. Days went by, weeks, months, I don't know. You were asking me and I was thinking, 'How come I don't know these things? Like, when did I go back in the studio again to do *Skeleton Tree*? And when did I make the film with Andrew Dominik?' Basic stuff. But apart from the sequence of memories that presented themselves horribly over the weeks following Arthur's death – things like having to choose the coffin from a catalogue, certain hysterical, screaming friends, the coroner's inquest, Arthur's body in the funeral home after the autopsy and the devastating funeral – it felt like our lives had been poured down a fucking hole. All of us.

*It's what happens, and it's obliterating and no one is prepared for it.*

Well, fuck it, I rang up Warren last night and asked him about it. He remembers everything: he was there in my house through the whole thing, and he really wanted to talk about it. He actually said at the end, 'I'm really happy we've had this conversation, finally.' I mean, he just helped me remember stuff. He brought it back.

*So, in a way, he had been waiting to have that conversation?*

Well, Warren always said through it all, 'I'm here if you ever want me, you know, or to talk to me about anything. I'm here.' But he wasn't ever going to initiate the conversation; it's all so hard, so impossible to navigate. Although I have grown to understand that it's a good thing for people to probe a little bit into the way grieving people feel, maybe ask them questions. There is a lot of hesitancy around this because it feels invasive, but the bereaved need encouragement to speak sometimes. They are prone to silence because they're worried about the effect their sadness will have on other people. And this silence becomes habitual, but also builds up like a terrible pressure. Anyway, Warren was always there. We just didn't talk about it much. Neither of us had worked out how to do that.

*Now that you've spoken to Warren, is it all coming back to you?*

Yes, kind of. I mean, Warren told me that three or four days after Arthur's death I went around to his house. He was obviously really surprised to see me, and I said, 'Look, the music and the work are the only things that have ever saved me in the past, and I need to do it. I need to work.' So he was like 'Okay. Just let me know when you feel ready?' And I said, 'Now. I'm ready now. Get your synth and your laptop and let's go down to the basement.' And he's like, 'What? Now?'

So, basically, we went down and tried to do something with the songs we had for *Skeleton Tree*. From talking to him, I think Warren regarded it as an act of survival on my part. You know, obviously, I didn't know what I was doing. I just recall being confused about the subject matter of the songs 'Jesus Alone', 'Girl In Amber', 'Magneto', 'Distant Sky'. I was deeply disturbed by this, suddenly thinking are all these songs about Arthur?

*Yes, it's quite uncanny. So did you actually start working on the songs there and then with Warren?*

Yes, basically just discussing how we would approach each song.

*That must have been so strange for him.*

Yes. Right. Of course. It would have been very strange. I hadn't thought of it like that. And then – I'm not sure exactly when, but Warren says it was October, which was three months later – we actually went to La Frette Studio, outside Paris, to put *Skeleton Tree* together. By then, that lunatic energy I had when I went around to Warren's place, whatever it was, had dissipated completely. I was just deeply depressed. It felt like I was walking through treacle, or walking against the wind. Throughout the entire *Skeleton Tree* session I just felt dead, but I knew if I didn't do the record then, I never would. In retrospect, I was clearly in no condition to be there at all.

*Maybe, but you were in no condition to be anywhere at all. Your survival instinct was telling you to work, which is also totally understandable.*

Maybe . . .

I was in a very strange place. I mean, when we were recording at La Frette, I stayed by myself in a little house that belonged to Olivier, the owner of the studio. It was by the Seine, just a fifteen-minute walk from the studio. I'd wake up there after another crazy, sleepless night, completely exhausted, and I'd do press-ups and vocal exercises and take freezing showers, all this weird shit that I never do. I was just trying to, I don't know, activate myself or something. Then I'd walk through the woods like a zombie, through all these spider webs, on the way down to the studio, and just do my best to work on the record. But I'd do nothing worthwhile, actually. Everything sounded feeble. My limbs felt so heavy. Then, in the evening, I'd finish the session and walk back up through the woods to the house, and when I got in the door, I'd just collapse again. All night, taking pills, and suddenly and appallingly unanchored from Susie.

*There's really no escape from that kind of overwhelming despair. It's utterly dislocating. I can't imagine anything worthwhile coming out of that recording session.*

No, nothing I produced in that studio was of any value, as far as I recall. I remember Olivier had this big black wolfhound called Luna and I just played with him. He was like the only thing I could understand. He loved me and he was always excited to see me when I arrived, jumping up on me, with his big muddy paws. A lot of the time, I just played with the dog. Maybe I thought the spirit of my boy was in the dog. The only thing I did there was sing 'Skeleton Tree', which is the only song on the album written after Arthur died. I just felt emptied out and utterly diminished by my own state. I'd ring Susie half a dozen times a day, checking on her. I really shouldn't have been there. I shouldn't have gone away. I feel so bad about that. Susie was looking after Earl and I was making this fucking record, and playing with a dog. I didn't know what I was doing.

*Well, you were trying to get through as best you could, and you can't really rationalise those kinds of decisions in retrospect. But can I ask how the band dealt with all this? It must have been unsettling for them.*

Yes, Warren told me it was a really strange time for them, because I have always gone into the studio prepared, with all my notes and stuff. But this time, I didn't have anything. Basically, the band members were like, what are we supposed to do? In the end, Warren pushed that record through. I mean, no one really played on it as far as I could see. Marty played some bass, but tentatively, sparely, and some of that was replaced by bass synth. I remember Jim setting up his drum kit and just sitting there not playing anything because the songs were so tremulous in themselves. I mean, Jim being reluctant to play says a hell of a lot, because he's such a monumental force. I think the atmosphere was such that I don't think he, or anyone else, really knew what to do with this music that suddenly had a new context – and one that was so devastating. George played a bit of acoustic guitar, I guess, thank God. Basically, that record is more or less in the raw state that Warren and I created together at the studio we used in Ovingdean.

*That makes sense in terms of the stark, atmospheric power of the music.*

I think it was difficult for the band to know what to do with that music. You couldn't just stick a drumbeat on those songs. The music was so formless and fragile. It had changed its intent essentially and taken on the form of the trauma itself.

On the previous album, *Push The Sky Away*, most of the songs came out of the band playing together, just jamming. *Skeleton Tree* was the first record not born that way. It's just me and Warren sitting in a room.

*So 'Skeleton Tree' itself was the only song on the record written and recorded after Arthur's death?*

Yes. I wrote that after Arthur died, in my office out the back of my house, which was a typical Nick Cave office with a big desk, notes and books everywhere, and pictures pinned to the walls – a big, chaotic, creative, self-absorbed space that backed onto our main house. That's where a lot of the Arthur thing played out for me, because I would go into that room to be alone and sit on the step on the street at the back of the house and just think and smoke. I wrote 'Skeleton Tree' in there, at the little upright piano, but afterwards, I couldn't go back into that room. The thought of the office made me physically sick. It felt like a terrible, obscene indulgence. It's empty now. I've never used an actual office again since Arthur died. I just sit at a table somewhere, in the kitchen or the bedroom, or indeed on the balcony, and do the work I have to do.

*Do you still use the studio in Ovingdean?*

Yes, we still use it. Ovingdean is the next town along from Brighton. We've used it for years and still do. It has a nice piano. It's where we did all the initial recordings for *Skeleton Tree* and *Ghosteen*, too, as well as all the film soundtracks, just me and Warren sitting and jamming together. Each day, driving past the black windmill and cliffs. And right next to the studio is St Wulfran's Church, where we buried Arthur.

*I didn't know that, Nick. So Arthur is nearby?*

Yes. The studio looks out over a new field that the church acquired and started to fill with graves. It's called Daphne's Field. Arthur's was the second grave to be put in. The first was an old airman. Arthur's grave is right there. You can see it out the window.

Those were very dark times, but I found that proximity really helpful in its way, to know he was nearby. I'd just walk up from the studio and sit by his grave.

Anyway, talking to Warren last night, I realised that I had literally lost a year. It appears we did six movie soundtracks in a row in that studio in Ovingdean overlooking Arthur's grave in Daphne's Field, just sitting there making instrumental music.

*It's a wonder that you managed to do that, to create in the face of what happened. Did it help in any way?*

Well, yes, because it was something to do.

*I'm guessing you haven't listened to those recordings since.*

No, but I'm sure a lot of the music we made was really very beautiful. Very beautiful indeed. Warren says we kind of burnt ourselves out doing so many film scores. We took a few years off from score work after that. We began doing them again more recently, amazing stuff – the score for Andrew Dominik's new film, *Blonde*, for example, is off the planet. And also a lovely documentary about a snow leopard, *La Panthère Des Neiges*.

*Just to go back to* Skeleton Tree, *though, as I've said before, when I first heard it I assumed that some of the songs had been written in the wake of Arthur's death: maybe 'Jesus Alone', 'Girl In Amber,' 'Distant Sky'.*

No, none of them were, but I can see why you might think that. Else Torp came into La Frette and sang the beautiful vocal on 'Distant Sky' that lifted the song somewhere else entirely. She really elevated that song.

And with 'Girl In Amber', I took out a line I didn't like and put another one in there instead: 'You turn, lace up his shoes, your little blue-eyed boy.' It changes that song and shifts the intent somewhat. But, actually, that is a song I wrote with Anita in mind. Or maybe an imagined version of Anita – the 'girl in amber', who is listening to the same record from back in the day, while never being able to escape the promise of her youth. It was largely ad-libbed, but in the end, it became something else. It found its true subject – Susie, trapped inside the dream of her absent child.

*That's quite a shift from just a single line alteration.*

Yes, and, really, nothing else is different, not even the vocal, apart from that one line, which we just dropped in.

*So when did Andrew Dominik begin filming you in the studio for*
One More Time with Feeling?

Some months later, early 2016, I think.

*In a way, that film is a study in grief. Throughout, you look altered, distracted.*

I was actually much better by then, but I do think, for a time, I lost agency somehow. I think that's what happens: you essentially become a person who needs someone to tell them what to do. That's what comes across to me in that film. I was literally being told what to do – 'Go and stand over there on that X on the floor and sing this song.' 'Sit down here and answer these questions.' 'Get in this taxi and look out the window.' That sort of thing.

*I'm amazed you got through the filming, to tell the truth. I guess you just had to surrender to the process.*

Yes, you surrender. That's exactly what you do. As I say, maybe making a film is basically about following instructions.

*Was it in any way a tense shoot because of your state of mind, your fragility?*

I don't know. I mean, I love Andrew, I love his work; he's a great filmmaker and a dear friend, really, one of my very best. I was sort of happy to put myself in his hands, but he claims I was actually quite difficult to work with and antagonistic towards him. Or maybe antagonistic towards the whole process of filmmaking in general, which may be true. I don't know. I haven't got the patience for that kind of thing at the best of times, and Andrew can be an exacting force, to say the least. He doesn't fuck around.

But I put a lot of trust in him with my whole family's situation, and so I was very preoccupied that the film wouldn't feel exploitative.

*Yes, I can imagine, but it's a beautiful, haunting film.*

Even though I cannot bring myself to watch it, just as I cannot bring myself to listen to *Skeleton Tree*, I believe Andrew made a beautiful, respectful film, and I will always be indebted to him for that. It was an extraordinary act of love. He made that film for Arthur. And I think a lot of people benefited greatly from it. There really is nothing in the world quite like it. I think he also went some way towards redeeming the *Skeleton Tree* album, which may have some good songs on it – 'I Need You', 'Girl In Amber', 'Distant Sky', 'Skeleton Tree' – but, for me, has a vacuum at its heart. I have to say, I don't much like it as a record. I don't know, it feels somehow cursed. When we played *Skeleton Tree* back in the studio at La Frette, on the last day, it felt sort of unholy. I think Andrew's film gave it the human context it needed. I don't know, maybe the record is okay, but to me it feels like a peculiar form of punishment.

*'Cursed', 'unholy' – these are strong words.*

Yes. I suppose so.

*So during all this, were you basically thinking, 'If I keep myself busy, I won't lose my sanity'?*

I'm not sure. Essentially, I think grief needs to be measured by action. It's not so much about working on your feelings. Your feelings come and go. They retreat and change and can ultimately surprise you. But you need to put some structure and method in your day, as best you can. I mean, that seems sound advice for any situation. You have to construct a series of actions around your day in order to survive: you exercise, you go down to the sea for a swim, you meditate, you make breakfast for your kid – you do all the small things that maintain order. Or you go and make a dress.

That's what Susie did, and that's what she still does to this day. Her energy comes from a strange veneration of Arthur, a glorification of the spirit of her child, but she is also warding off a kind of perennial sadness. It is also a way of staying present in the world so that she can look after her family.

*I guess everyone's grief is similar in its intensity, but the grieving itself takes different and unpredictable forms.*

Well, Susie, at first, was strong, because she really does have a warrior spirit, but after a while the grief started to make her ill. She suffered from terrible migraines – awful annihilating episodes that lasted two or three days, and sometimes every week. She's got them under control now, but it took a long and worrying time. For a while, Susie was either lying in a hushed and darkened room or crashing around making her dresses. She built The Vampire's Wife entirely on the mad energy of her grief.

I just want to say, the level of suffering she endured as a mother is unfathomable, even to me, but within that fucking roaring maelstrom of her nature, she is essentially a fighter. I mean, she managed to design a series of dresses that literally influenced the whole fucking fashion world – and still does. I am amazed by that accomplishment in itself, let alone that she did it under extreme duress. Under the circumstances, I am awed.

*Ultimately, I think, it takes an uncommon strength of character – and will – to come through what you both experienced.*

Well, maybe strength is the wrong word for it. I don't think strength has much to do with anything. It seems to me that you just take the next least-wounding step. And strength suggests there is also weakness. Is it a weakness to be bedridden for days on end because you lost a child? Is it a strength to keep your chin up and soldier on? I don't think these terms are applicable. People often say to me, 'How do you stay strong?' They say it to Susie, too: 'You're so strong.' But we are not strong. We survived because we remained together. It is as simple as that. When one crashed, the other stepped up. That is important.

And, you know, we live a wonderful life now, but it is as fragile as anything can be, and tumbles down often. A sudden jolting scene on TV, or a glimpse of a kid on the street, or nothing much at all, can trigger a kind of collapse. Indeed, for quite some time – I'm talking many, many months – we were hardly there at all. All we had was an instinctual determination to stick together and not fall completely apart at the same time. And to look after those still left to us.

But a mother experiences grief differently to a father, as far as I can see. It's almost a different state of being. I think mothers, in general, need to know everything that happened to the one they have lost. I mean, everything. Fathers cope in a more circumspect way, with a slight precautionary remove. Susie had to know every detail of what happened, every second leading up to Arthur's fall, and what followed, so that she could be with Arthur, posthumously, accompany him through those final hours and minutes and seconds, when she was not there to save him.

*You both somehow managed to go beyond the trauma and the grief to the place where you are now. Did you make a conscious decision, as I think you once said to me, to defy it?*

Look, I'll tell you this, because I'm feeling a bit tired. Talking like this about the raw details of what happened to us, I don't know if it's really much help to anyone. I feel like I'm getting it all wrong, that I missed out stuff. And to talk about it seems sort of diminishing. But I need to say this before I go. The life Susie and I have is full and replete with meaning. I love Susie more than I ever have. She feels the same about me. Our love is often joyous, which doesn't mean we don't shed our share of tears. I don't know how we got to where we are, because, in truth, I don't know where that is. I do know we shall never recover fully from the death of our son, nor should we. We are marked by it, and Susie carries a sadness that lives just below the surface of her loveliness, and perhaps that's what also makes her the astonishing and oceanic woman she is.

I do know that Susie and I apportion meaning to the smallest things, in a way we never did before, and we get enormous comfort from this. Grief comes and goes, but it no longer scares us. We can collapse together, or apart, in the knowledge that tomorrow we will be back on our feet. I know that mostly I am happy and life is good. I don't mean that casually or trivially. I mean that life is actually good. People are good. I rarely see badness in people; rather, I see layers of suffering. I think people can do both terrible things and wonderful things when faced with the true understanding of their own powerlessness, vulnerability and lack of control. And I think Susie and I are acutely aware of the precarious nature of not only our lives, but all lives – their rareness, their preciousness – and that it can all disappear in an instant. In the light of that knowledge, we find gratitude to be a simple and essential act. And Arthur showed us that – the necessary and urgent need to love life and one another, despite the casual cruelty of the world. Love, that most crucial, counter-intuitive act of all, is the responsibility of each of us.

*You see the world as essentially good.*

Well, in Revelations, there are those beautiful lines: 'Look, He is coming with the clouds/And every eye shall see Him.' I feel the goodness of the world must be experienced to some extent through the mechanism of suffering – the God in the cloud – if the notion of goodness is to hold any kind of truth or real substance. Beneath the surface, simple happiness is rarely simple at all, and most often hard-earned, and the price can be high. How Susie and I arrived at this place, I don't know, Seán. Like I said, I don't know what this strange place even is, but it was reached with baby steps, and through darkened rooms and countless cigarettes and a multitude of kindnesses from so many people, and many lessons learned along the way – just like anything else.

# 15

## Absolution

~

*Nick, how are you? I've been thinking a lot about our previous conversation. We kind of went in the deep end.*

I'm fine, Seán, just working away on my ceramic figurines. Going in every day. It's unbelievably addictive. And such fun to be learning an art form from scratch.

*Yes, I wanted to ask you about that.*

Well, yes. I had fixed a date to visit the studio of Corin Johnson, a sculptor friend of mine, who was going to teach me how to make ceramics, but my mother died on the day I was supposed to go there. I was just about to ring Corin to cancel, but Susie, who is alert to the symbolism in everything, thought I should still go to the studio, as planned. You know, for my mother. She felt it would be good for me to do that.

*That first day in the studio must have been very strange.*

Well, yes, it was. But there is something very direct and elemental about working with clay that draws you in and takes over, calms you. I got lost in it. It was exactly what I needed at the time.

*Since then it seems to have become quite an epic undertaking.*

I know. Very much so.

*So what prompted you to take up ceramics?*

Well, through early lockdown I got it into my head that I wanted to make a clay figurine in the Staffordshire style. I don't know if I've told you, but I've collected Staffordshire figurines for many years — these mass-produced ceramic sculptures that were hugely popular in the Victorian era. They usually depict gentle pastoral or biblical scenes and were mostly made for the middle classes to have something colourful to put on their mantelpieces.

*Do you have any previous experience of working with ceramics, maybe back in your days at art college?*

No, but when I was a schoolboy I used to make clay figurines, sweet little things that I created before I was 'corrupted' — my mum's word — by my time at art school. My mother loved my little figurines and had them displayed all around her living room.

*What was the subject matter?*

There was a Mexican peasant with a dead rooster, a clown with an accordion, a mermaid, a drunken satyr, a boy riding a lion, a group of wailing women — stuff like that.

*So you had already found your themes!*

I never thought of that, but, yes, now that you mention it. Even as a schoolboy, I realised I was pretty good with clay, that I had some affinity with it. So when I looked at one or two of the simpler Staffordshire figurines from my collection, I thought I could probably make one. They looked naïve and simple — and doable.

I rang Corin and asked him if he knew how to make ceramic figurines and if he could maybe help me make one. He has a studio in Camberwell, and he very kindly took me under his wing and taught me.

*So what was your first day like?*

Well, not surprisingly, my first attempt was a disaster. I tried to make a saint boiling in oil that doubled as a spill vase, but it was not what I wanted, to be honest. However, I just fell in love with the feel of the clay. The action of pushing my fingers into this elemental stuff had a kind of trancelike effect that delivered me to some other place – sort of part childhood, part outer space. I felt that I had stumbled upon a medium that truly spoke to me. It felt liberating, and also very healing.

*When you say it truly spoke to you, in what way, exactly?*

I think mainly because I was creating a *thing* – a physical object that I could hold in my hands, that I could look at, and that would exist in and of itself at the end of the process. Weirdly, the whole thing felt in some way like unfinished business.

*What – in terms of your decision to suddenly drop out of art school?*

I hadn't thought of it like that, but that's exactly right. It kind of took me back to art school. The moment I started modelling the clay, I knew I could render something that was convincing, that I had a facility with it. Even though the first couple of figurines I made were by no means a success, I quickly found my footing. I just got on with the medium very well, and Corin, who is a brilliant sculptor working mostly in stone, was a great teacher.

*It also sounds therapeutic, like you could turn your mind off and just engage with the creative business at hand.*

Yes, therapeutic, but also extremely confronting as it turned out.

*How so?*

Well, my initial engagement with the process soon became pretty intense, in unexpected ways. When I'm working on these figurines, my dreams become more vivid and powerful and sensual – my hands pushing around clay, everything made of clay, everything turning into clay, the whole world made of clay! I have these feverish nights and I wake up in the morning and head back to the studio in a strange state and continue working away.

*Christ, that does sound intense.*

Well, the work itself is extremely concentrated and has the effect that all work does, when you find your flow, of radically compressing time. I'd often leave the studio exhausted and go home and try to sleep, and the dreams would start again.

*I know you've been going in there a lot.*

Yes, I've been working pretty solidly for a year now: four days a week, morning till night. The project has just expanded beyond all expectations.

*I do sense, Nick, there's an obsessive element in everything you do creatively.*

Do you think so? I think it's sometimes hard for me to rein things in, to bring things under control, but I am getting better at that. I don't see that manic exclusionist impulse as a strength or a virtue any longer.

*A 'manic exclusionist impulse'?! Do you mean the idea that many artists have that everything has to be subservient to the work?*

Yes! And I used to think it was a sign of my fucking undying genius or something, that it had to be all and ever about the work, and that the damage I did to my personal relationships was part of the necessary and heroic sacrifice an artist needs to achieve true greatness.

*I think it's called egomania.*

Yes, but you learn in time that this is just nonsense. In fact, you learn all sorts of things: that personal chaos is not a necessary condition for creating good art; that the pram in the hallway is as much a source of inspiration as anything else; that being strung out on drugs doesn't necessarily make you a better artist. These days, that kind of compulsive mania I once had I find almost embarrassing. That said, I do still lose control over certain impulses from time to time.

*Yes, I remember countless times when I'd call you and you'd be in the ceramics studio, going to it or coming home from it – and that was all you wanted to talk about.*

Well, at first, it was pure pleasure: simple and innocent, sitting in Corin's studio, making these things. It was almost as if I was doing it to connect to my mother, but it quickly became something else entirely. As the clay took over, it became, I suppose you could say, compulsive – although I prefer to say engaged – and the project just grew and grew. That's just the way it is sometimes; it's a new discipline and you just have to put the work in. I mean, we've had to approach this project we're doing now, this book, with the same kind of energy and commitment. Otherwise, things never get done.

*That is certainly true. I don't know if you realise it, but the intensity of your commitment can be quite daunting sometimes.*

Really?

*Well, yes.*

I didn't know that. I just can't do things in any other way. It's not so much the creative impulse itself that is so compelling, but rather doing something that feels challenging and vulnerable and new, whether that is ceramics or a different-sounding record or The Red Hand Files, the In Conversation events, Cave Things, this book, whatever. There is a risk involved that generates a feeling of creative terror, a vertiginous feeling that has the ability to make you feel more alive, as if you are hotwired into the job in hand, where you create, right there, on the edge of disaster. You become vulnerable because you allow yourself to be open to failure, to condemnation, to criticism, but that, as I think the Stoics said, is what gives you creative character. And that feeling of jeopardy can be very seductive.

*So after that first not-so-successful day, what happened next?*

I woke up the next morning feeling a kind of exhilaration. I felt invigorated by my day in the studio, and I suddenly knew what I wanted to do. The idea came to me almost fully formed: to make a series of figurines based around the Devil that were meditative in nature, much like the Stations of the Cross.

*So the Devil, rather than Jesus, is the central figure throughout.*

Well, yes, but to be honest, my interest in making a figurine of the Devil was that he is traditionally depicted in red. I was excited by the idea of using a bold red glaze for the central figure, because the colour palette for a typical Staffordshire figurine tends to be quite subdued. So I began to work on a series of what were essentially benign, pastoral figurines that told the story of the life of the Devil, from his conception to his terrible death.

*Are you close to finishing the series?*

Well, here's the thing – the actual modelling is one thing, because you're working with the clay, making the objects themselves, and it's a kind of bliss. But the glazing is a whole different story. Glazing is a fucking unmitigated nightmare. You can spend almost a year getting the figurines to a high standard, and if you don't get the glazing right, you derail the whole enterprise.

*Something tells me you're quite a perfectionist about this kind of stuff.*

Well, I don't know about that. I just need things to be done in the right way. Like, the first real problem was finding the right white. The sculptures are essentially made from white clay with certain aspects of the figures, faces, say, or hair or articles of clothing, picked out in colour. I had great difficulty finding a translucent glaze that energised the whiteness of the fired clay in just the right way, and that did not flatten or diminish it.

*Did you succeed?*

Yes, in the end. The one that worked for me had a lovely, glassy feel that sort of trapped the figurines inside it, as if they were pressed against the glass, looking out. I was so happy. And so was Susie – she was very happy, because I stopped boring her to death talking about white glaze.

*Yes, I can see how that might be the case.*

At one point, she told me I'd turned into a 'white ceramicist'.

*Ha! I have to say, glazing sounds anything but calming and healing.*

It's intense. And then there's the issue of the colour itself: finding the right skin tone and the right red and so forth. This stuff is really important, because I wanted the figures to be coloured purely symbolically, like a Munch painting, say, where the use of colour always had its metaphorical intent. This departs completely from the typical Staffordshire model, which is essentially decorative.

*I'm going to stop you right there.*

Okay, but here's the thing: the glazing process requires a certain amount of holding your nerve. It has also really affected my sleep; my dreams have become all mangled up with colours, scary and blood-drenched. I was actually waking in the middle of the night having panic attacks about choosing the wrong colour of red. At one point, I was so stressed out I broke out in a fucking rash all over my body.

*Jesus, you need to get back to the piano. Seriously.*

Yes, the anxiety level is off the charts. But, personally, I think I have made good choices with the colours and I'm just looking forward to finishing them when I have the time.

*So can you talk me through the over-arching narrative – the protagonist's journey?*

Well, it essentially traces the life of a man – a man with horns, the Devil – in eighteen ceramic figurines that grow in gravitas as the series proceeds. It begins with the Devil's birth, which is a beautiful little sculpture of a baby awakening nestled against a red foal. Next, the child inherits the world. Then – I need to get this in the right order – he grows up, is initiated into the world by a sailor, seduces a woman, fights a lion, goes off to war on a horse, comes back empowered by the war and decked out in medals, takes a bride, kills his first child, becomes separated from the world by his evil deeds, grows old, falls into a state of abject misery and remorse, dances his final dance, and dies a bloody death in the arms of two sailors. Eventually, his body is found by a spirit-child, who kneels and extends his hand in forgiveness.

*It sounds kind of epic and even allegorical. Can I ask, are the ceramics also related to Arthur in some way?*

I don't know if they are specifically to do with Arthur. It's certainly a presentation of a life and, in that life, a child is killed. In the final sculpture, the Devil has died and there is a child kneeling down, holding out his hand towards the dead body in a gesture of atonement. It is entitled 'Devil Forgiven'. So it has something to do with Arthur, but that was not its intention.

*I ask because sometimes I wonder if the level of commitment, even compulsion, that drives all your recent projects may not be to some degree a survival strategy – a way of engaging on some deep level with Arthur's presence as well as his absence.*

Maybe something is happening in that respect. I don't know. I certainly don't go into any project with Arthur as a kind of intention or destination, but generally he finds his way there.

*Or you find your way to him?*

Yes, Arthur always seems to be patiently waiting at the end of the idea. But it's a similar thing with Susie, actually – the songs themselves are doorways that she seems to be forever walking through. I don't have too much control over the process. I'm not sure what to do with that, to be honest. I wish sometimes I had more of a say in the work I create, that I was less of an onlooker, less of an enabler.

*I'm not sure you have to do anything with it, other than let it happen. You're engaging with something mysterious, ineffable.*

Yes, that is certainly true. But, listen, you came over to the yard and visited the studio a while back. You've seen them in their unfinished state. What do you think?

*I haven't seen the finished objects yet, but I actually loved some of the unfinished ones – the pure white figures that had just a flash of red. There was something humble and revealing about them – and their stillness. They were much more understated than I had expected. I found them quietly beautiful, but compelling. They stay with you.*

To me, they are soul objects. They were something I needed to make, because I needed to see them, to bear witness to them, so they could relate back to me the larger and unambiguous meaning of my predicament. The plain and explicit nature of them presented something to me personally that *Ghosteen* and *Carnage* couldn't, perhaps because of music's impressionistic and abstract nature.

*Can I ask what it is that they reveal to you about the larger and unambiguous meaning of your predicament?*

It's difficult to put into words.

*Is it something to do with forgiveness, maybe – an allegory about forgiveness?*

Well, yes, although the word 'allegorical' suggests that there is a secret meaning beneath the work. As I essentially created the figurines in order, from the birth of the Devil to his demise, the message they presented seems unequivocal to me, and anything but secret. I was actually dumbfounded at how directly and explicitly they spoke to me. It was a shock to the system, but, as I say, it's really difficult to articulate what they mean.

*It's such a different endeavour to songwriting or performing, but just from how you talk about it, it's palpable that it has energised you in some way.*

I think it's because it's a visual art form. I can see the results. A ceramic figure is an actual thing you can hold in your hand, not an abstraction. I experience the drama of it through the eyes and the heart, both. What I am trying to ultimately say may be an abstraction, but my figurines are objects that exist in space, and, for that very reason, they are also vulnerable to the judgements of others.

*That's revealing. Are you nervous about putting them out into the world?*

I don't know, but my friend Thomas Houseago said something interesting, coming from his experience as a sculptor. He said that there is no one to protect your work. That's the predicament of sculpture: the object simply exists in its vulnerable state, to be judged by others. People stand in front of it and say things about it, and the sculpture itself has no recourse. It is defenceless. And it's up to the sculptor to be the defender of these figures.

*I'm not sure how you could do that other than deciding not to exhibit them.*

Well, I have to find ways to defend them if need be. What I'm trying to say, I guess, is that these figurines are more than the sum of their parts. They are easily attacked because they are made with a whole heart. They are not ironic or sardonic, and they set themselves up as objects of consequence. They are narrative, they are religious, they tell a story that asks something of those who look at them.

*What do you think they ask of the viewer?*

I think they can serve as precise meditations on what constitutes a life, insofar as they tell a story of a broken life that collects meaning through misfortune and transgression. And running like a current through each of them is the need to be forgiven. I hope that the sculptures are light enough at heart and sufficiently unassuming to ask this question: can we be forgiven? I think that question is fundamental to all our lives. In fact, it may be the question that our lives pivot around or, indeed, the whole world revolves around. Can we be forgiven? And it is, of course, a religious question, not least because the secular world has failed to find a way of adequately asking it. Now, Seán, it's not that Susie and I discuss these matters, or even really acknowledge them, but I think this need is at the very centre of our lives – a need for forgiveness. I would say it is a motivating force.

*This is very much in keeping with everything else you have said about the religious nature of your work and your life. You imbue both with an extraordinary depth of almost metaphysical meaning.*

Well, it could be that you need to view my work, my relation to the world and, indeed, my position on things within a religious frame, or it all may not really make sense.

*I totally understand that now, but to be honest I'm still grappling with the idea that the figurines need to be defended somehow.*

Okay, let me put it another way. You know how artists or musicians often talk about their works as their children – this song is my child, this book is my child, that kind of thing. I've used that metaphor myself, on occasion. But the thing is, these figurines actually are my child. Like the songs on *Ghosteen*, they are inhabited by my child. He lives inside them. In that respect they require defending, or protecting, with the same vigilance as one would defend or protect a child.

*So how do you do that once they have gone out into the world?*

I think you have to have faith in your own intuitive process. That is really all you can do. I would say this to all people who are trying to become musicians or writers or artists of any kind: learn as much as you can about your craft, of course, but ultimately trust your own instinctive impulses. Have faith in yourself, so you can stand beside whatever it is you have done and fight for it, because if you can invest it with that faith, then it has its own truth, its own honesty, its own resilient vulnerability, and hence its own value.

*So do you feel that way about your songs, that they need protecting or defending once they are released?*

No, not so much, because a song is sent into the world and, if you're lucky, it is absorbed into the bloodstream of the world. The audience takes stewardship of the song. The song becomes their property. I don't see myself as the protector of my songs. That is the job of those who love the songs.

*What do think you are essentially trying to say through these ceramic sculptures?*

Well, they have, piece by piece, been making clear their intentions, and to be honest I am shocked at how direct and insistent the message is – just the power of these little figurines.

*And what are they saying?*

Ultimately, the figurines are not saying anything, they are not declaring anything, in the same way that all my work for the last six years is not saying anything. It is *asking* for something. *Skeleton Tree, Ghosteen, Carnage,* The Red Hand Files, the In Conversation Events, the live shows, even this book we are writing – they are all asking for the same thing.

*Which is?*

Absolution.

*I haven't heard that world since I went to confession as a boy. Do you mean forgiveness or something deeper?*

Yes. I am asking to be forgiven, to be released from my own personal culpability.

*I'm not sure how to respond to that. Do you mean in regard to Arthur?*

Yes.

*Again, I'm not sure what to say. Surely you don't feel culpable in that regard.*

Seán, I'm not being morose or blaming myself explicitly, but when I look at the work and the way I live my life in general now, it becomes increasingly clear that it is an attempt to . . . I don't know . . . Look, this is hard to say. Let me try it another way.

When I think of Arthur, when I sit and actually experience him, I feel a weight in my heart. And I think maybe Arthur feels sorry for what happened to him and the hurt we feel about his death. This worries me a lot, because I think it is somehow his ongoing spiritual condition. It preoccupies me, sometimes overwhelms me. I feel it. I feel it because, in a way, I feel the same. I feel that, as his father, he was my responsibility and I looked away at the wrong time, that I wasn't sufficiently vigilant.

I know Susie feels this, too, and it tortures her, as a mother. And the work that I do – the records, The Red Hand Files, the sculptures – and the work that Susie does, too, with her gorgeous, heart-breaking, ghost-like dresses, – there is not a song or a word or a stitch of thread that is not asking for forgiveness, that is not saying we are just so sorry.

So, I think, in a way, all our work asks for that burden to be taken away from us, our culpability. Do you understand what I mean? Not just to be taken away from us, but from Arthur, too. I'm not sure what else I can say about that, just now.

*I think I understand, but it does seem like you are being unnecessarily hard on yourself. Do you feel you have, to some degree, attained the absolution that you seek?*

Well, in my experience, art does have the ability to save us, in so many different ways. It can act as a point of salvation, because it has the potential to put beauty back into the world. And that in itself is a way of making amends, of reconciling us with the world. Art has the power to redress the balance of things, of our wrongs, of our sins.

*I think that is the first time you have used the word 'sins'. So you do believe in sin in the Christian sense?*

By 'sins', I mean those acts that are an offence to God or, if you would prefer, the 'good in us' – that live within us, and that if we pay them no heed, harden and become part of our character. They are forms of suffering that can weigh us down terribly and separate us from the world. I have found that the goodness of the work can go some way towards mitigating them. For instance, I can tell you that when Andrew Dominik made *One More Time with Feeling* I felt, to my very core, that it was a form of, I don't know, exoneration. I felt a burden had lifted from me.

*You felt more at peace with yourself?*

Yes. And I know I've spoken to you about this in the past, but nearly every day I would have to drive past the cliff where Arthur fell. It was utterly devastating. Most times, I would drive the long way, all around town, just to avoid it. But after making *One More Time with Feeling*, after it had come out and received such a positive and thoughtful response from ordinary people, well, I was driving past the cliffs, and suddenly I had this intense lifting of the heart, a freeing of some of the helplessness I felt, a kind of positive confrontation with the point of trauma. It was as if in making the film we had done something for Arthur, made something out of this tragedy. It was like I had done something to bring him back into the world, something more than just burying his ashes in a field somewhere and then moving on. I don't know, it's an odd thing to say, but I felt almost happy. I passed the cliffs and experienced a kind of inner peace, an internal silence and calmness, as if I had been released from something. I think all the work I do now, varied and frantic as it is, moves towards that need for inner peace, that need for release.

*I see.*

You know, at night when I try to sleep I close my eyes and see these ceramic figurines parading past in sequence – the newborn nestled in the foal, the infant with his ball of fire, the child holding the red monkey, the Devil riding off to war through a field of flowers and returning on a black horse down a road of skulls, on and on they go, the Devil with his bride and the golden rabbit, the child on the sacrificial altar, the Devil separated from the world, on and on, the Devil sitting on a wall, his tears pooling around his feet, his final chilling, operatic death, and at last his body washed up on a beach and a ghost child crouched with his hand reaching out in forgiveness – this parade makes a certain sense and brings enormous comfort. It draws my story out of the darkness, out of the chaos, to stand in testament to something. Or when I am in the studio and trying to sleep and the new songs circle round in my head, and all the strange, dreamy images leap up from the songs like visions – it's the same thing. They bring a form of deliverance. They bring an order to the world and a kind of peace. They bring their story. Art has its way. This is, in the end, its gift.

# Epilogue

~

*So now some months have passed and you've just finished the UK*
*Carnage tour with Warren. Given the circumstances, I'm guessing it*
*was probably the strangest tour you've done.*

Yes, it was unusual for many reasons. The music was so very different
from anything we had attempted live before and the circumstances
around the concerts themselves were so deeply surreal. It was like
we were journeying into the unknown and in the process working
out how to actually perform again.

*Because of the atmosphere in the venues or the challenging nature of*
*the music?*

Both. The first gig, I walked out on stage and realised to both my
terror and delight that I didn't know how to perform these kinds
of songs. All my normal patterns of performance had disappeared.
Like, I didn't know what to do with my hands! And there was
barely any physical contact with the audience – everyone sat quietly,
eerily in their seats. The music itself was so radically reduced, so
intimate that there was nothing to hide behind. Not even the
habitual self.

There was also a strange kind of reticence in the audience – to the process in general. Clearly, people felt extremely vulnerable, even endangered. For the vast majority of the audience, it was their first public gathering in a long time. They were essentially learning how to be an audience again.

The first show in Poole, I felt literally stunned, caught in the audience's headlights. And Croydon was like that, too, but there was also something wonderful about it, an aliveness and a danger. By the third gig in Aylesbury something clicked and I took a deep breath and stepped into the music itself. Suddenly, I just knew.

*You knew what to do?*

No, I knew how to be.

*When I saw you perform in London, I noticed almost immediately that your whole way of moving on stage was very different — much more gestural and expressive.*

Much of the music was slow and floating and hypnotic, so I had to learn how to calm down and have some faith that it was going to be all right, that I didn't have to perform in the way I would normally. And to a degree, we had done that on the *Skeleton Tree* shows, playing with the idea of intimacy, but back then I was insulated by the sheer animal power of the Bad Seeds. On the *Carnage* tour, though, we took the idea of intimacy to a new level. And after a few shows I began to really love that feeling of perilous vulnerability that comes from the presenting of our essential selves to the audience.

*Could you feel a sense of release from the audience as the songs unfolded?*

Yes, you could feel things loosen up as they found the confidence to be an audience, and the way their energy intensified was staggering.

*Even at the Royal Albert Hall, where the atmosphere can often be restrained by the imposing nature of the space, I really felt that sense of release. There was a tentative mood at the start of the show, but it suddenly shifted around the third song.*

The interesting thing is that the show we had originally planned for *Ghosteen* was monumental – a ten-piece choir, big light show – then the pandemic put an end to all that. The *Carnage* tour may not have had that full-on visceral force, but it had something unique because it was so radically intimate.

*Just out of interest, how long did you rehearse for?*

A week.

*So you made the album relatively quickly and then went out on the road after just a week's rehearsal?*

Yes. Generally we find too much rehearsing becomes deadening. You need to learn the songs, of course, but then you find that everything changes when you play live, anyway. It's like that wonderful Mike Tyson quote: 'You think you have a plan until someone punches you in the face.' It's a bit like that. You think you're familiar with the songs until you walk on stage and suddenly some that worked in rehearsal just fall flat, while other songs burst into life.

*It's interesting that many of the towns you played were not on your usual touring itinerary. Often, when I'd call you for a chat, you'd be on your way to a gig in Stoke or Stockton or wherever. What was that like?*

That was an unexpected pleasure and a kind of education. Because Covid prevented us from leaving the country, we ended up playing all sorts of unfamiliar, to us, places in the UK – Blackpool, Ipswich, Bradford – and these towns, the excluded places, the overlooked places, were so completely open to the whole thing. Portsmouth, what a great gig! Stoke, too.

*Were the actual theatres different to the usual venues you play?*

Yes, some of the older ones had posters of old-school entertainers like Dick Emery, Ken Dodd, Bob Monkhouse and the Two Ronnies on the wall. You knew they'd trodden those boards as well. There was something almost vaudevillian about the whole enterprise: driving from one town to another, sitting in the dressing room applying my make-up, coming off stage and slapping on the Pond's cold cream, just like I remember, as a child, my mother doing when she took off her make-up. Then, afterwards, heading back to the hotel without seeing anybody. There was this beautiful sense of repetition about the tour. It seemed old-fashioned, almost quaint. Very un-rock 'n' roll.

I remember when Barry Humphries did Les Patterson and Dame Edna at the Meltdown show at the Royal Festival Hall, he arrived on his own with an old suitcase that, I guess, had all his shit in it, his dresses and his wigs and the like. And when we were all partying backstage after the show, he suddenly appeared out of his dressing room, with his make-up off and his battered suitcase, and slowly walked out of the venue. It was very affecting, that image of him heading off on his own.

*A lonely, melancholy existence in many ways.*

Well, yes, but wonderfully poetic.

*So that's where you're heading, Nick – the end of the pier.*

Looks like it.

*I have to ask you – did any of the new songs reveal their deeper meaning on the tour?*

Well, of course. All of them. The songs off *Carnage* really went somewhere else entirely. But somewhere different night after night. For instance, I had no idea that 'Carnage', the song, was so emotive until we played it live. For me, it was extremely affecting. It was hard to keep my shit together. 'White Elephant' tapped in to a kind of inner rage that was overwhelming some nights. 'Lavender Fields' became less of a death trip and more of a gentle spiritual song of comfort. 'Hand Of God' was just fucking nuts.

*My wife's niece went to the Cardiff show and she loved it, but she was a bit freaked out by 'Hand Of God'. She said you sounded like a religious cult leader.*

Really? I can't tell you how happy I am to hear that. 'Hand Of God' does have that evangelical spirit, for sure. I've often thought, on stage, how easy it would be to become a cult leader.

*Are you considering that as a way forward?*

I don't know. Would you join?

*Fuck, no.*

Would your wife's niece?

*No way.*

Okay. Maybe not.

*How was 'Balcony Man' live? It's a strange song.*

Pure music hall, pure panto. People were hanging over the balconies screaming stuff out. And then we encored with an epic 'Hollywood' that took on a dark, satanic groove that just kept building and building, my beautiful back-up singers getting real deep and strange. All the songs found themselves in unexpected ways. You know, for me, a record is never a thing in itself; rather, it's just one part of a larger experiential event that terminates in a live concert.

*For me, there was something self-consciously performative about the show I saw. It was almost like an art performance in places.*

Oh, well, that's good – I think? Susie came to the Sheffield gig and sat in the wings. She loved it. She said it was her favourite show she had seen of mine, but I suspect that was because she didn't have to worry. When she goes to a Bad Seeds concert, all she does is worry that something bad is going to happen: I'm going to fall off stage, or get hurt in some way, or a fan is going to get crushed, or the stage is going to collapse, or we'll all get wiped out by a meteor or something. Which, in all fairness, could happen.

*Warren was carrying a lot of weight in those shows.*

Yes, it was a Nick Cave and Warren Ellis show, after all; it's not like having the Bad Seeds there, where he can just pick up the violin and launch into something and it's all copacetic. He had a whole different role. I think he took the responsibility very seriously. He was waking up in the night in cold sweats, worrying about fucking it up, the responsibility.

*How did you feel about that weight of responsibility? As you say, there was really nowhere to hide on stage.*

Oh, for me, it was wonderful to share the responsibility. It was liberating. And, my God, it was also very beautiful to be in that suspended, trembling space inside the music, just lost to it, like a musician, you know, like a fucking *musician*.

*There's a beautiful circularity to the fact that the two of you created many of these songs on your own in that intense, heightened space in Malibu and then, a few years later, ended up playing them on stage in a very different kind of intense, heightened environment.*

Yes, it's been a long journey and the songs have travelled far. In the end, there was a purity to the way they presented themselves in this particular time, after all that has gone on with us as a civi-lisation. They brought with them a kind of reverence and humility.
They brought with them a kind of reverence and humility It was as if we were mirroring back a shared experience. I felt that strongly.

*Considering the factors at play, did you ever feel at risk yourself?*

I wasn't overly concerned with catching Covid; I just didn't want to have to shut the tour down because someone in the group or crew caught it. That would have been it.

*So, given the Covid restrictions, how did you spend the time between the actual performances?*

It was literally the same thing every day – me and Warren, Ton the tour manager and Peter the driver travelling from town to town. We'd play out the same scenario, journey after journey, usually beginning with us trying to find a decent place for coffee before we hit the road. Then Warren would check his phone, look at it for a few moments, and go, 'Aw, no.' And I'd say, 'What is it, mate?' And he'd show me a picture of a one-armed monkey or a bear with no teeth or a legless eagle from Ellis Park, his wildlife sanctuary in Sumatra.

We'd do that for a while, and then he'd read out some of the comments posted on Instagram about the previous night's gig – usually fans going crazy about the show, which was lovely to hear. I'd write for a few hours until we got to the next city, where we would inter ourselves in our hotel rooms until the show. We'd have a meal after the show, having no direct contact with anybody else, and then head back to the hotel to sleep. We did thirty-two concerts like that. Two months almost. In a perverse way, it was a kind of uncomplicated bliss.

*That's one way of putting it. Did you not go stir crazy after a while?*

Well, I went for one walk outside in the whole time, in a park in Amsterdam, where Warren, who'd probably had one too many coffees, relayed to me the entire contents of a six-episode documentary series he'd watched the night before about American involvement in the Middle East leading up to 9/11. He did it in one sentence that didn't have a single full stop, and without any encouraging noises from me whatsoever.

*I think I've seen that documentary.*

Then, on the way back to the hotel, he told me Bobby Gillespie's entire life story! Oh man, I've still got to read Bobby's biography. I hear it's good, but it's sitting there on an ever-growing pile of books to be read. Christ, there is so much to read. Do you find that?

*I do. I always seem to have two or three books on the go. But don't you read more when you're on the road?*

I read a bit, but mostly I write – and listen to Warren! We haven't seen much of each other throughout lockdown, except for making the record, of course, so it's been strengthening for our relationship. The music we played was vulnerable and personal and very bonding. Sometimes I would sing a song like 'Ghosteen Speaks' or 'Lavender Fields' and turn around, and Warren would have tears rolling down his face. There was something about the unadorned nature of those shows that felt truly redemptive.

*It sounds extreme, when you think about it: the intensity of the shows and the strange, suspended downtime in-between with nothing much happening and nowhere to go.*

There was a weird, slightly haunted sense of repetition to it, but I had things to do, mostly. I'm pretty good at being alone.

*So what did you do to fill in the time between shows?*

Oh, I meditated, I wrote lots of stuff, read a bit, thought about things, talked to you, dyed my hair, conversed with the dead.

*Sometimes I don't know whether you're being serious or not.*

Yeah, neither do I. It's a problem I've had all my life.

But, Seán, maybe it was the nature of the music on the tour or the long time spent quarantined in hotel rooms, or Anita dying, or my mother, but the past seemed to rear up in a way that felt quite confronting. Anita was on my mind a lot.

*Are there things you wish you could have said to her, maybe?*

Well, yes, of course. But I will say this, with Anita as with Arthur and my mother, too − they always knew I loved them. They knew. There is no doubt in my mind about that. I always talked to them in that way. That is a great comfort to me, for sure.

*You do seem preoccupied by Anita's passing, which is understandable, of course.*

Well, it's what we discussed when we talked about her before, just after she died. I remember the last time I was around her house in Bellavista Road, the Christmas before the pandemic, I think. She was showing me the stuff she'd been doing: an amazing painting on an old carpet, a lovely drawing of Raphael, her eldest boy, sleeping, and a couple of dolls she had bought from charity shops and redesigned, painted different faces on them, sewed new costumes for them. They were beautiful, eerie things, but I was sort of distracted at the time and so was she and maybe I didn't pay enough attention to them. I know Anita cared a great deal about what I thought about the things she did, but I guess on some level I always felt that she had been given this extraordinary gift and yet somehow the world had been denied the full extent of it.

*By her lack of ambition? Or self-belief?*

It was to do with a certain artistic or creative reticence that I saw in her and, at the time, assumed was down to a lack of motivation. I remember some years ago I posted her a catalogue of Odilon Redon's pastel drawings and a set of pastels and paper, with a letter saying, 'You are this good.' I was literally begging her to draw.

So, basically, I thought she should have done more. And then, after she died I heard from Mariella, a mutual friend in Melbourne who had cleaned up Anita's house and collected up all the bits and pieces, that Anita actually had about two hundred of these dolls – two hundred! She even made one of Susie – Mariella sent me a picture of it – and it was a really beautiful, haunted thing, so strange and loving. And no one knew she had created these dolls. At least I didn't. I was really saddened when I heard that. It's all so difficult to explain.

I don't know what I'm saying exactly, except I think we should all be careful with the people we love, because, well, you never know.

*So do you think she just didn't want her work to be seen? Or judged?*

Well, that's interesting, because when we were young Anita was very influenced by a Swiss Dadaist poet and boxer named Arthur Craven, who said something like, 'The best art is never seen.' I didn't agree with that, of course. I'd say to Anita, 'That's just not true. You might think it is, and have some sort of romantic attachment to that idea, but art has its beneficent value and is something that needs to be shared with other people. Others need to experience what you've done. It has something to do with connectivity and, well, duty or service.'

*So, for you, it's a part of the artist's duty, not just to create work but to make sure it goes out into the world and is experienced by others?*

There are obviously a multitude of reasons why people might choose to make art or music, but, as far as I'm concerned, the work I do is entirely relational, actually transactional, and has no real validity unless it is animated by others. It does not exist in its true form unless it moves through the hearts of others as a balm. Otherwise, it is just words and notes and little more.

*So your music is a force for good?*

Well, yes, it is. Music is a spiritual currency unlike any other in its ability to transport people out of their suffering, so I don't take my job lightly. The indisputable goodness of music, the clear benefits it brings — its capacity to enlarge the spirit, provide solace, companionship, healing and, well, *meaning* — is much like religion in a way. I can see why people conflate the two. On stage, I feel the power of the music beamed back at me through the audience, as a sort of refracted and loving sustenance, an in-taking and out-pouring of love. And that power is circular. I've experienced that clear as day with many artists. When we saw Nina Simone perform at the Festival Hall in London, the audience beamed the healing power of her own music straight back at her so that her transformation occurred before our eyes. We returned the music she sent to us, back to her, bright with our love.

*Amazing. Earlier in this conversation, you described your recent concerts as redemptive. Did you mean for you or for the audience? Or both?*

On a personal level, certainly. I think art goes some way to reconciling the artist with the world. I guess that's really what I'm talking about. Music can be a form of active atonement. It can be a way of redressing the balance somehow by explicitly putting good into the world, the best of ourselves. And, of course, that requires the participation of the world.

*So when you talk about music being a way of making amends and redressing the balance, can you elaborate on that a bit more?*

Well, let's just say we all have regrets and most of us know that those regrets, as excruciating as they can be, are the things that help us lead improved lives. Or, rather, there are certain regrets that, as they emerge, can accompany us on the incremental bettering of our lives. Regrets are forever floating to the surface, don't you find?

They require our attention. You have to do something with them. One way is to seek forgiveness by making what might be called living amends, by using whatever gifts you may have in order to help rehabilitate the world.

*Wow, that's a big leap! I assumed that you were talking about making amends with certain individuals, maybe by offering an apology to those you may have wronged in the past.*

Well, there is that, too.

*But you are talking about making living amends through your actions generally, rather than with a specific person?*

The most entrenched regrets we have are generally around those who are no longer with us, right? Or no longer within our sphere of influence. That's why they are so painful, because it feels like there is no recourse. Personally, I have found it is worth something to express whatever contrition we may have towards those no longer with us, in prayer and meditation, and in song. I find that very helpful. And, of course, to live our lives in the best way we can, you know, *in their name*.

*Again, this is very much a religious impulse, the need to make amends, to seek forgiveness and absolution.*

I'm not sure that it is solely a religious impulse; rather, it is a human impulse that religion helps make sense of. I don't mean something prescriptive; it's more about living by example. I feel the work I produce goes some way to redress the balance of the past. At least I hope so. That is certainly one of their intentions. Not the only one but an important one, hence the urgency. The work is perhaps the best we can do, in this respect.

*Is this something to do with getting older, this need to put things right?*

Yes, that's right, entirely – the need to put things right.

*You still have a few years left to do that.*

Have I? I hope so, but, really, who knows?

*That is true. I once asked you if you believed in redemption in the Christian sense, and you replied that you didn't feel you had anything to be redeemed for. But you've obviously changed your mind.*

Yes, I have. I said that in a defensive and cavalier way, because back then I thought we were making a more rock 'n' roll book!

*Really? That was never going to happen.*

That's for sure. Anyway, I think anyone who says they don't have any regrets is simply living an unconsidered life. Not only that, but by doing so they are denying themselves the obvious benefits of self-forgiveness. Though, of course, the hardest thing of all is to forgive oneself.

*From our previous conversation, I'm not sure you've managed to do that yet.*

I think one sure path to self-forgiveness is to arrive at a place where you can see that your day-to-day actions are making the world a measurably better place, rather than a worse place — that is pretty simple stuff, available to all — and to arrive at this place with a certain amount of humility.

*I can't argue with that. And in all of this, I sense that, for you, conversation is very much a way of clarifying, or maybe distilling, your ideas and beliefs.*

Yes. The very fact that I've talked to you about some of these things has been enormously helpful to me. And it's pushed me along the road to wherever I'm going in a way that would not have happened otherwise. For me, conversation, at its best, is a form of advancement and course correction. I don't know about you but I find I have to write my ideas down to really know what I think. And, furthermore, I have to say those ideas out loud, or indeed to sing them out loud, to somebody else, before I know if they are valid or meaningful, or not. It's that relational thing I was talking about.

*Do you feel that the kind of conversation you value is threatened by the increasingly divided nature of our contemporary political and cultural discourse?*

Yes, for sure. I've always enjoyed freewheeling conversations, if only because talking can often reflect back on us the folly of our own ideas. In certain circles there is a notion that by having a dialogue with someone whose views conflict with your own, you might be giving oxygen to bad ideas. What an appalling idea that is. We need to talk about contentious ideas as much as possible, for our own health and the health of society. In any case, I have quite a lot of time for bad ideas. I'm full of them, as you know!

*That has been one of the many surprising aspects of this book! But I guess that, for meaningful conversation to thrive, it's essential that we can agree to disagree: there has to be some kind of mutual respect or understanding.*

We need to be able to exist beyond disagreement. Friendships have to exist beyond that. We need to be able to talk, to make mistakes, to forgive and be forgiven. As far as I can see, forgiveness is an essential component of any good, vibrant friendship – that we extend to each other the great privilege of being allowed to be wrong.

One of the clear benefits of conversation is that your position on things can become more nimble and pliant. For me, conversation is also an antidote to dualistic thinking, simply because we are knocking up against another person's points of view. Something more essential happens between people when they converse. Ultimately, we discover that disagreements frequently aren't life-threatening, they are just differing perspectives, or, more often than that, colliding virtues.

*The religious impulse has been a recurring theme in this book. Has talking about it shed any light on why you feel you need to believe?*

Definitely. I feel more in step with that aspect of my nature, as I've had the opportunity to talk about it in depth. I'm not sure I've arrived anywhere concrete, though.

*Interestingly, the word 'hope' has not featured very much in our conversations, even though it's in the book's title. Is it implicit in everything you do and believe?*

Yes, hope is in every little thing, as far as I can see. Hope is optimism with a broken heart.

*I like that.*

You can have it.

*Thanks. So, listen, you told me once, a long time ago, that until you reached forty or thereabouts you always felt like you were running headlong away from something. That has stayed with me. I think a lot of people, myself included, have experienced something similar without even realising it.*

Well, I suspect I've always said that. And it's not that it isn't true; it's more that you think these things from the point of arrival, but it turns out that the point of arrival is an illusion.

*What do you mean, exactly, by a 'point of arrival'?*

That feeling we all have at times that we have reached a certain level of self-awareness about our place in the world, a feeling that all our travails have led to this point, this destination.

*And you're saying that, with hindsight, those points of arrival are deceptive?*

Yes, because that sense of awareness and certainty often turns out to be just one more mistaken belief in a long line of mistaken – or discarded – beliefs. And when you are engaged in making art, that process by its nature can also continually appear to signal a point of arrival. Like, if I look back at my past work from the certainty and conviction of the present, it appears as if it was a series of collapsing ideas that brought me to my current position. And what's more, the actual point I'm looking back from is no more stable than any of the previous ones – in fact, it's being shed even as we speak. There's a slightly sickening, vertiginous feeling in all of this.

*The sense that the ground is constantly moving beneath your feet?*

Yes, exactly.

*So how do you deal with that?*

Well, I have learned over time that the creation itself, the thing, the *what*, is not the essential component, really, for the artist. The *what* almost always seems on some level insufficient. When I look back at the work itself it mostly feels wanting, you know; it could have been better. This is not false humility but fact, and common to most artists, I suspect. Indeed, it is probably how it should be. What matters most is not so much the 'what' as the 'how' of it all, and I am heartened by the knowledge that, at the very least, I turned up for the job, no matter what was going on at the time. Even if I didn't really understand what the job was. I feel I have committed myself to the work in general, and given my best to each project in particular. There have been no half-measures, and I take a certain amount of pride in that.

*So essentially what you are doing as an artist is constantly stumbling forward.*

Stumbling forward is a beautiful way of putting it, Seán, but I wonder if the notion of forwardness is correct. Perhaps what I mean to say is that although we feel we are moving in a forward direction, in my estimation we are forever moving in a circular way, with all the things we love and remember in tow, and carrying all our needs and yearnings and hurts along with us, and all the people who have poured themselves into us and made us what we are, and all the ghosts who travel with us. It's like we are running towards God, but that God's love is also the wind that is pushing us on, as both the impetus and the destination, and it resides in both the living and the dead. Around and around we go, encountering the same things, again and again, but within this movement things happen that change us, annihilate us, shift our relationship to the world. It is this circular reciprocal motion that grows more essential and affirming and necessary with each turn.

*Do you see this circular motion in your songs, too?*

Yes, I feel as if I am perpetually revisiting or rehearsing the same concerns that have always been there, from childhood to the present day. They just keep coming around, time and time again, like a big wheel, from as far back as I can remember and into the future, but beautifully so, wonderfully so. Does that make sense?

*I'll have to give it some thought.*

I guess what I really mean is that Warren called me last night.

*Oh yeah?*

Yes, he thought it might be time we started working on a new record. He said he was just putting it out there.

# Afterword

~

This book arose out of an uncertain time. In the early, uneasy weeks of the first UK Covid lockdown in March 2020, Nick Cave and I spoke regularly over the phone. I have known Nick for over thirty years, but in that time our paths tended to cross fleetingly, often backstage at his concerts or when I was asked to interview him. The pandemic changed all that. With time on our hands and the world out of kilter, our phone chats turned into extended conversations about all manner of subjects, both esoteric and everyday.

Two conversations, in particular, stayed with me and planted the seed for *Faith, Hope and Carnage*. The first touched on religion and the role that doubt played in Nick's personal theology. Though I have long been intrigued by his use of biblical imagery and language, the conversation suggested an acknowledgement of the divine that went beyond religion as a source of inspiration for his songs.

The second, equally surprising to me, concerned the acute sense of anxiety that he experienced each time he began writing new songs for an impending album. Initially, I felt that both subjects would make for interesting essays in a book about the singular nature and development of his songwriting.

I waited several weeks before tentatively broaching the idea of a book with Nick, by which time I had shifted my thinking towards a series of long-form interviews rather than essays. My touchstone was the *Paris Review*, which, under the aegis of its pioneering editor, George Plimpton, had elevated the in-depth literary interview to an art form. By deftly exploring the impulse to write, the classic *Paris Review* interviews often became revealingly intimate as well as illuminating. There are only a handful of popular songwriters whose work could stand up to that kind of scrutiny, and Nick Cave, I believed, was one of them.

When I tentatively floated the idea to Nick, he said he would think about it – never, in my experience, a good augury. To my surprise, he called back the following day to say he was on board. His touchstone turned out to be more contemporary – the long-form podcast – and his one condition was that the interviews reflect his current preoccupations rather than retreading all too familiar ground.

So it was that, on a Wednesday morning in August 2020, we began conversing on record, a ritual that would last, off and on, until the following summer. Though tentative at first, the conversations soon became more open and illuminating. They usually lasted for a couple of hours, sometimes stretching to twice that length. In between them, I doggedly transcribed and edited the recordings, highlighting passages that I thought needed further elaboration or clarification.

Although I tried to anchor each conversation around a single subject, they often took on a spiralling momentum of their own, with certain themes overlapping and intertwining: creativity, collaboration, belief, doubt, loss, grief, reinvention, tradition, defiance, the endurance of hope and love in the face of death and despair. While imposing some degree of thematic order on each chapter, and rigorously editing the transcripts, I have tried to be faithful to that conversational flow.

Inevitably, Nick's son, Arthur, who died in 2015, is an abiding presence throughout, sometimes explicitly so, always implicitly so. Having followed Nick's Red Hand Files project, I should probably not have been surprised by his honesty and openness about the loss of his son, or the articulate nature of his responses, but I was. Constantly.

Having started off with no real idea of where our conversations might lead, I was also surprised more than once by the turns they took. In all of this, of course, I am immeasurably grateful to Nick for his time, his trust and his incredible commitment to what was, initially, a stumbling journey into the unknown – a leap of faith.

If this is a book that outlines a dramatic creative and personal transformation in the face of great personal catastrophe, it is also shot through with a sense of life's precariousness. Both Nick's mother, Dawn Cave, and his erstwhile partner and close friend, Anita Lane, died during the making of the book. Likewise, his friend, Hal Willner. Since finishing the book, both Mark Lanegan and Chris Bailey (lead singer of Australian punk group, the Saints), who are mentioned in it, have also passed on.

Sadly, as I began writing this afterword, the death was announced of Nick's oldest son, Jethro, in Melbourne.

'We are, each of us, imperilled,' Nick says at one point in *Faith, Hope and Carnage*, 'insofar as anything can turn catastrophic at any time, personally, for each of us. Each life is precarious, and some of us understand it and some don't. But certainly everyone will understand it in time.' The words echo anew.

Seán O'Hagan<br>
May 2022

# Acknowledgements

~

Nick and Seán would like to give special thanks to Susie and Lynette for their love, support and patience.

The authors would also like to thank Jamie Byng and Francis Bickmore at Canongate, Mitzi Angel and Molly Walls at Farrar, Straus & Giroux, Warren Ellis, Elizabeth Sheinkman, Rachel Willis, Brian Message, Tiffany Barton, Bobby Gillespie, Thelma McSherry, Ben Thompson, Jane Ferguson, Ursula Kenny, Alison Rae, Vicki Rutherford, Anna Frame, Jess Neale, Tom Hingston, and all of The Bad Seeds, past and present.

# Index

~

293